Garrie L. Tufford

THREE CENTURIES OF ENGLISH DOMESTIC SILVER

Part of an oil painting by Richard Collins, about 1725, thought to depict John Gay (1685-1732) and his sister, and displaying a silver tea-equipage of the George I period. The silver (*left to right*) shows a covered sugar bowl with moulded foot and cover ring, hexagonal tea-canister with domed lid and sliding top, hot-milk jug, voiding bowl, tea-pot with plain pyriform body and spirit lamp on stand, and, at the front, sugar tongs, the cover of the voiding bowl used as a spoon tray, and spoons.

BERNARD AND THERLE HUGHES

Three Centuries of ENGLISH DOMESTIC SILVER

1500–1820

FREDERICK A. PRAEGER, *Publishers*

NEW YORK · WASHINGTON

BOOKS THAT MATTER

Published in the United States of America in 1968
by Frederick A. Praeger, Inc., Publishers
111 Fourth Avenue, New York, N.Y. 10003
First published in the United States in 1952
by Funk & Wagnalls Co., Inc., New York, N.Y.

Library of Congress Catalog Card Number: 68-21582

Printed in Great Britain

To

HYLDA and WILLIAM HOPLEY

CONTENTS

LIST OF ILLUSTRATIONS

The illustrations on pages 40 and 41 are taken from *The Law and Practice of Hall-Marking Gold and Silver Wares*, by J. Paul de Castro, and are reproduced by courtesy of The Technical Press, Ltd.

1

INTRODUCTION

OF all the antiques that bewitch and bewilder the small collector, domestic silverware is probably the most universally admired and most affectionately treasured. Lacking both the pomp of precious jewels and the fragility of glass and porcelain, it shares with furniture the capacity to grow old gracefully in enduring, everyday service and, in the process, to become intimately associated with all that is best-loved in the English home.

To understand the story of English domestic silver it is necessary to appreciate three main factors, closely interrelated, that affected each trend in its fascinating development. Fundamentally, throughout the collector's period, between 1500 and 1830, there was the general social and economic growth of this country. This resulted in ever-increasing demands for domestic silver plate and attracted Continental silversmiths by the prospect of steady employment, throughout most of the period under review, as well as by the religious tolerance associated with the years around 1685.

Interwoven with this was the ebb and flow of fashion, the vogues for classic, baroque, rococo, oriental, expressed in design or ornament or both. This formed a restless and recurrent theme across the length and breadth of Europe, interpreted by each individual designer and craftsman in his own country's vernacular, whether his medium was architecture or furniture, glass or ceramics or precious metals. Lastly, and often overlooked as an important contributory factor, there were various technical developments—in many of which England led the way and which were directly responsible for manufacturing economies that enabled silver to play an increasingly important role in her domestic life.

In early Tudor England the fabulous magnificence of gold and silver plate was restricted to the wealthy few. Cardinal Wolsey entertained important guests and all their hundreds of gentlemen followers with banquets served entirely on gold and silver dishes to a total of thirty bullock wagon loads. But the will of a small merchant or farmer of the period gives importance to each single silver spoon. Silver plate was the gift of kings and even as late as the reign of Charles I the nobility and members of the royal household presented their king with New Year offerings for which they received in return gifts to half their value in silver plate. A basket of coals in 1640 won the sergeant of the scullery ten ounces of plate, and the gift of a red Turkey carpet was acknowledged with three hundred ounces. Even as a prisoner in September, 1647, Charles I was supplied with "one gilt salt, Tobias; 12 gilt trencher plates, crowned E; 2 knives, one fork gilt; two saucers white; 2 spoons gilt"—the term white being applied to silver lacking the gilt finish.

Records of the fifteenth and sixteenth centuries indicate increasing demands for domestic silver, offsetting the loss of Church patronage at the time of the Reformation. By Elizabethan days the country's prosperity was already an attraction to foreign silversmiths. For the collector, however, comparatively few pieces of silver are available dating earlier than about 1670. Not only was the country less wealthy, but great quantities must have been sacrificed by both parties in the civil war and much more lost in London during the great fire in 1666.

As regards style, silver made before the restoration of the monarchy in 1660 went through the same phases as other domestic craftsmanship. The early Gothic mood was followed in the sixteenth century by the Renaissance emphasis on classic ornament—the grotesque masks, strapwork, acanthus leaves and the like which constituted a recurrent influence in silverwork. Late in the sixteenth century there was a tendency to lighten the ornament and by early in the seventeenth century there appeared in silver as in furniture a more architectural approach to design, with an emphasis on form and outline. Ornament was often restricted to flat engraving or chasing with the same all-over effects then being achieved in low-relief wood carving and in flower embroideries, and displaying a similar tendency towards occasional crudeness and poor workmanship. Dutch influence, largely associated with the later years of the century, was already manifested in the use, for example, of matted grounds—the surfaces given a soft, dull appearance by expertly even punchwork—which went out of favour with the development of the French glitter and sparkle of the 1690s.

As regards production methods, the silver throughout this period and invariably until the 1730s was reduced from the ingot to a workable thickness or gauge with a sledge-hammer. Discs cut from these flat sheets of metal, usually ten to sixteen gauge, were then "raised" into hollow forms such as posset pots merely by hand hammering on the sinking block—shaped with shallow circular depressions to fit various bowl outlines—and on iron or steel stakes, T-shaped or flat. Special hammers were used, avoiding small faces and sharp corners that might cut the metal, and supplemented by mallets tipped with bullock horn. Such hammering had to be interspersed by annealing to keep the metal from becoming springy and unworkable, and final highly skilled hammering planished the silver to an even, lustrous surface. Supplementary parts, such as a hollow foot, would be shaped in the same way and then soldered on, using an alloy of silver and copper or brass with a lower melting point than the silver plate. Early vessels were often filled with the pitch amalgam used by silversmiths and then finished entirely from the outside.

Handles, feet, finials and the like were shaped by casting. They might be made by the *cire perdue* method, the required shape being modelled in wax and enclosed in fire-resistant material: when the wax was melted out in baking the mould the resultant cavity could be filled with molten metal. The more common method was to embed a pattern—of gun-metal, wood or plaster—in a two-part frame filled with an adhesive loam mixture, bake this hard, open the frame and remove the pattern, then fill the cavity with molten silver, finally breaking up the mould to remove the casting. Pieces made in this way showed gritty surfaces requiring considerable smoothing with file and pumice.

Simple ornament might decorate a cast surface, such as scrolls in low relief on a spoon bowl. The opposite effect, in which the ornament was engraved or cut from the surface of the silver with pointed tools, appears on very early work and was much used in the sixteenth century, but is often difficult to distinguish from flat chasing. In flat chasing similar surface ornament was achieved with hammer and punches, showing faintly on the back surface of the metal. A filling of pitch amalgam kept a hollow-ware vessel in shape while being chased, and the silver decorator also used a bowl of warmed pitch in which to anchor his metal at whatever angle he required for working. The engraver, applying less pressure to his work—cutting away fragments of silver instead of hammering it inwards—rested it on a leather-covered pad. Chasing was applied only to the front surface of the silver: when relief effects were required—more common after 1660—it might be combined with embossing, or repoussé work, in which pressure on the silver was applied from the back.

The other form of ornament used in the sixteenth and early seventeenth centuries, but more fully developed later, was known as piercing. The plain silver background to the decorative motifs was cut away leaving them in silhouette. At this period plate silver tended to be considerably thicker than in eighteenth century work, and the holes cut in it correspondingly large. For each section a small hole was first pierced for insertion of a fret-saw, but the steel of this tool lacked the hardening achieved later and required constant sharpening: hence the need to allow space for subsequent filing and smoothing of the cut edges. To compensate for removing so much silver, what remained was strengthened with deeply convex embossing, the whole design being planned to spread the strain evenly.

With the return of Charles II and his court from the Continent in 1660, silversmiths were called upon to produce an immense amount of magnificent plate. Much was needed to make up for what was lost in the war. But in any case those exiled in France and the Netherlands had acquired new tastes in silver as in other furnishings. Silver furniture became a craze with the wealthy and the riot of florid ornament in high relief that characterised furniture carving also appeared on silverware. Design showed a new interest in curves and scrolls, typified in miniature by the change from knopped to trifid spoon (Fig. 38, page 97), and the architectural mood of the period found expression in such details as the pillar candlestick and the wide-spread use of gadrooning (Fig. 1) on light-catching rims and feet. Ornament stressed the classic acanthus leaf motif, and egg-and-tongue borders, together with masks and *amorini* in high relief and caryatid handles (Fig. 2). Much of the work, such as the big, heavily naturalistic flowers, fruits and intermingled animals and birds, typical, for instance, of the period's table baskets, expressed the same Netherlands tendencies in design seen in contemporary wood marquetry.

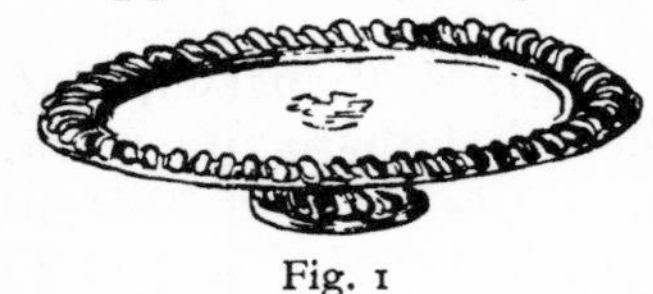

Fig. 1

Fig. 2

The other main influence of the period was oriental, directly influenced by the trade of the East India Company and indirectly through the Netherlands. The same rather naïve scenes and figures which the contemporary rage for "japanning" brought to furniture were frequently engraved on silver of this period. Much of the new tea and coffee equipage design that appeared before the end of the century—in the Netherlands as in England, for the Dutch were early tea enthusiasts—was based on the jugs from which the Chinese poured the water on to the leaves in their cups. Piercing in scale pattern (Fig. 3) was a form of decoration adapted from Chinese porcelain.

Fig. 3

The arrival of William III might be expected to strengthen Netherlands tendencies in design, and more especially in ornament, but the main feature of this period was the immigration of great numbers of French silversmiths—Protestants whose faith was threatened by the revocation of the Edict of Nantes in 1685, and others affected by Louis XIV's decree of 1687 forbidding the manufacture of silver plate.

The Huguenots undoubtedly helped to raise the standard of silverware in England, but their influence has been over-emphasised. The turn of the century was a period of great advance and general social refinement in England. Much of the grace and beauty of the so-called Queen Anne silver design and decoration was the direct result of a more highly developed sense of form. In silver the Queen Anne period is generally dated from the late 1690s to 1730s and was characterised by plain, shapely vessels, often knopped or baluster in outline and round or octagonal—eight-square—on plan (Fig. 4).

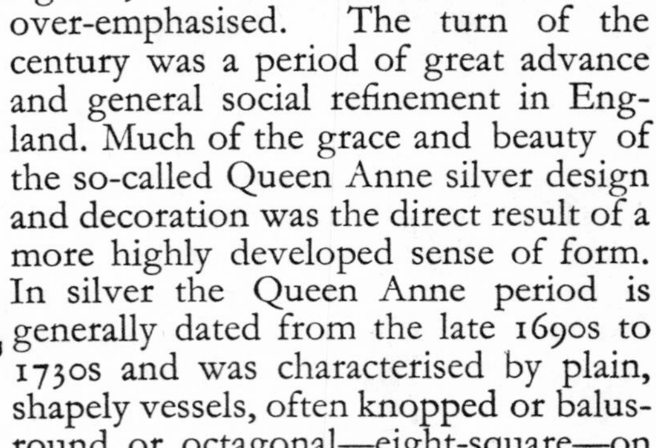

Fig. 4

This was the age that witnessed the wide establishment of professional architects and cabinet-makers, and the mood was expressed in the new brick houses that were replacing the rambling Tudor homes as well as in the smaller domestic furnishings. The tendency to greater formality was but the obvious reaction to the riotous extravagance of Charles II's court; the intermingling of smooth, undecorated surfaces with the gadroons, flutes, and rope edges typical of the period was in harmony with the cabinet-maker's change from heavy carving to smooth veneers and was characterized by the same need to value shape and proportion and discover beauty of line, whether in baluster candlestick or in spherical sugar-bowl.

In the case of silver, however, there was a third, technical influence. The enormous demand for silver plate in the late seventeenth century led silversmiths to clip and melt down coin to obtain their material. In order to stop this abuse an

Act of 1697 differentiated between the quality of silver in the coinage and that required for silver plate. Coin continued to be made of sterling silver, but silver of a higher quality, containing less alloy, was made compulsory for plate until 1720. The distinguishing hall-marks of this "high standard" silver are described in Chapter II.

The other extremely important technical development at this period was an improvement in the production of silver plate from the ingot. Much of the delicacy of the eighteenth century work credited to Huguenot influence might be better attributed to the wholly English invention of the metal rolling machine in about 1697, improved in 1728 when John Cooke added compressing springs to the upper of the two heavy revolving cylinders. An unheated ingot of silver could then be passed repeatedly through a pair of rollers which would gradually flatten the ductile metal into a smooth metal sheet of uniform thickness. One result of this was that for many articles of domestic silver a material was available which was less costly both in weight of metal and in manufacturing-time and labour, so that from the 1730s silverware was made available to many previously unable to afford it.

Fig. 5

As regards ornament early in the Queen Anne period, in addition to such formal details as gadrooning and fluting the silver might be decorated with cut-card work (Fig. 5), attributed to the Huguenot immigrants and dating particularly to the period 1690-1715. The ornament was cut in silhouette from a separate sheet of silver plate and then applied to the plain—frequently curved—surfaces of the vessel requiring decoration. The result was ornament flat in itself but showing in relief against the surface of the vessel.

Whether its surface is plain or decorated the essential characteristic of cut-card work is that it was *applied*: repoussé designs raised with the hammer and ornament cast as an integral part of the body itself are not to be classed as cut-card work. It is sometimes difficult, even with close examination, to distinguish cut-card work from cast decoration, so skilfully has the silversmith achieved his effects; but it is easy to distinguish the cut-card from repoussé as the latter inevitably shows corresponding concavities on the reverse surface.

Cut-card work can be classified into six groups. Early work was plain and narrow, consisting of wide leaf-shape outlines. It encircled the base of hollow-ware, immediately above the foot-ring. The acanthus leaf design was most commonly used until about 1690. During the high standard period cut-card work might decorate the entire lower half of the body, extend almost across the cover, and strengthen the handle-body junction. These simple forms continued side by side with cut-card work of more elaborate style. Plainness of surface itself is no criterion of age. A late development consisted of long, narrow straps in place of the leaf outlines. Each strap might be given a central line or band of ornament.

The second type of cut-card work could be termed card-on-card ornament, and was really a multiplication of the first. It consisted of two or three thin cut-card plates soldered one upon the other, the uppermost being reduced by hand to delicate fret-tracery. The symmetrical grace of such cut-card work, carried out with meticulous skill by the silversmith, gave an effect known at the time as "carving". Sometimes the panels had a spiral curve.

A third type of cut-card work was developed during the last five years of the seventeenth century and became fashionable from about 1700 until the end of the period. In this the plain cut-card work might be surface-ornamented with applied cast motifs, such as mid-ribs of diminishing beading or flower heads on separate ornamental leaves of plate.

The fourth type differed from the third in having its additional decoration chased or engraved in the applied metal instead of being cast and superimposed. A fashionable style had such ornament on every second lobe of the cut-card work around a vessel. Throughout the high standard period leaf-shaped cut-card work might be decorated with engraved mid-ribs, or the entire leaf might be engraved with naturalistic veins.

A fifth type of cut-card work showed a combination of engraved and cast decoration. Thus spatulate gadroons might surmount a series of cut-card panels alternating with shorter leaves of engraved cut-card work. Heavy cast mid-ribs might then be applied as a third layer.

The sixth type of cut-card work was enriched with pierced ornament, this appearing in a wide range of designs. The style was much used to relieve the base line above the foot-ring; on a caster a second circle of it might decorate the body rim, in a different design. Pierced cut-card work was rare before 1685, infrequent until 1700, and restricted to work of the highest quality between then and 1720.

Unquestionably French in its conception was the next phase in silverware. This was the rococo style (Fig. 6) which began to find expression in this country as early as the 1730s, its origin attributed to the Frenchman Meissonier who shook free of the monumental French Regency style by designing restless, asymmetrical forms and decorations with much interplay of C and S scrolls, lighthearted *chinoiseries* and the fantastic rock and shell motifs that first prompted the French nickname *rocaille*. Form and design became subservient to ornament: outlines were determined merely by the juxtaposition of decorative motifs. Embossed, engraved, chased, pierced, cast—the motifs were often of extremely high quality but all too often suffered from exaggeration and contortion that only a great master silversmith could control.

Fig. 6

It was from this over-laboured fantasy that the mood in silver design changed swiftly in the 1760s to a new search for classic elegance and restraint. Here again the change was European rather than English. The name of the architect Robert Adam has been given to the English version

Fig. 7

of this neo-classic movement, his influence on architecture and all forms of domestic furnishing dating from 1758 onwards. But as early as the 1730s the French were deeply stirred by the Greco-Roman discoveries at Herculaneum and these were followed by excavations at Pompeii begun in 1755. As a result, silver forms followed those of classic vases and funerary urns. The emphasis was entirely on design, on structural lines and perfect proportions, on simple curves and unbroken outlines. Decoration was flat or in low relief, the motifs restricted to known classical details, such as paterae (Fig. 7) and elliptical medallions, swags of drapery and the ever-recurrent acanthus leaves, husks, bell-flowers (Fig. 8), and formalized honeysuckle flowers (Fig. 9).

Fig. 8

The mood was universal but here again manufacturing technique affected the English silversmith's response to it. It was in the late 1760s that factory methods began to be applied to domestic silver plate and the factory silversmith was quick to welcome the simplicity of outline and ornament which he sought to reproduce quantitatively and at prices that would make it sell to a yet larger public. The thin, even silver plate made available by the rolling process now proved eminently suitable for stamping, with drop hammers and fly punches, what had previously required shaping by hand. John Pickering of London patented a stamping-machine in 1769, and this was improved by Richard Ford of Birmingham later the same year. Whole sections of an article such as a tea-pot in the new, plain style, straight-sided and with its flat base in the most highly favoured elliptical outline, could be stamped out of the flat metal with dies and assembled by almost invisible soldering.

Fig. 9

Decoration was achieved by stamping the thin silver in low relief between suitably sunk dies, or cutting it in

Fig. 10

innumerable simple open-work patterns determined by varying the punches. Mechanical piercing lacked the boldness and freedom of hand work, but very many more people in this elegant and mannered age were able to grace their tables with salts, sugar-baskets (Fig. 10), and the like, cut in intricate openwork designs that showed against linings of rich blue glass.

In early work the press-stamped piercing formed the background to relief motifs soldered on, but before the end of the century swags, bows and so on were incorporated in the flat, press-cut design. The fly-press contained a small steel tool cut to the shape in which it was required to pierce the silver, and a correspondingly shaped bed into which the tool fitted. By the 1790s a suitable hard steel had been developed so that the tool was capable of enduring long runs without losing its precision of outline, making possible the introduction of more intricate patterns. One successful method of applying the fly-press consisted of stamping small sections from very thin silver with shaped dies and assembling a number of these into various minor articles, such as candlesticks which could be weighted with solid fillings of resin and ashes. By 1770 Matthew Boulton and Henry Fothergill had equipped their Soho, Birmingham, factory for the manufacture of unfinished parts which were sold through Boulton's Birmingham and London merchanting houses to other firms for assembly and finishing.

At the same time, however, the master silversmiths continued the long-proved methods of raising silver by hand and decorating it with delicate engraving and chasing. Even though brilliantly smooth and polished, such a vessel of George III silver will reveal hammer marks on the interior surfaces.

A new type of ornament associated with the late eighteenth century and highly developed in Birmingham was known as bright-cutting. Just as the faceting of stem edges and feet in early Georgian silver was repeated on contemporary table glass, so bright-cutting found corresponding expression in the fine diamond cutting on glass decanters of the 1790s, and also in the inlaid lines of black and white "stringing" and tiny checks found on contemporary furniture. Bright-cutting was at its most popular in the 1790s. It seldom appeared on spoons after 1800 but on tea-services might be introduced as late as 1815, sometimes combined with other decoration. In this form of engraving the tool employed, in various sizes, was a gouge, sharpened chisel-wise, bevelled from corner to adjacent corner and having two cutting points. Edge and point were used as required to produce what was really a kind of chip carving, outlining patterns of flowers, ribbons and so on by cutting narrow channels with variously slanting sides to produce the delicate faceted effect.

The early nineteenth century witnessed yet another approach to classic design and ornament, but this time with a more exact, archeological interest in later, heavier forms. The silver of the dining-room, like the furniture and glass, was praised for its weight and magnificence, and fine workmanship was lavished on plate that to-day appears over-ornate. In this glitter-loving age there was great use of fine fluting and reeding on many comparatively plain pieces which were finished with heavily ornamental handles and feet (Fig. 11), often rather shapeless in their elaboration and making constant, unimaginative use of lion masks in full relief. In the 1830s the creative urge was largely lost, here as on the Continent, and designers resorted not to adaptations of classic themes but to more or less slavish copyings of all the earlier styles, their products offering many pitfalls to the beginner-collector.

Fig. 11

2

HALL-MARKS: LONDON, THE PROVINCES, SCOTLAND AND IRELAND

COLLECTORS of old silver have one great advantage over those who specialize in ceramics or furniture or glass. Somewhere on nearly every specimen will be found one or more tiny marks stamped in relief and often clearly detailed even after centuries of cleaning. Three or four of these marks will tell the initiated not only the quality of a silver object and the area in which it was manufactured, but frequently its date and the name of its maker. Nevertheless, this consideration of hall-marks on domestic silver is deliberately placed after the general survey of design, ornament and technique. The tyro collector cannot be urged too strongly to train himself in the recognition of these salient features rather than to rely upon hall-marks which are occasionally deliberate fakes and, far more often, either incomplete or time-obscured, so that precise interpretation is difficult. Read with discretion, however, hall-marks are of incalculable value, and their study offers fascinating glimpses of the periods that applied them.

In principle, the system of hall-marking is unchanged to-day from its origin in the Middle Ages. When the ancient goldsmiths' guild—the Warden and Commonalty of the Mystery of Goldsmiths of the City of London—was granted a charter in 1327 by Edward III it was already a powerful, highly-organized body, exercising great authority and supervision over the goldsmiths and silversmiths whose shops glittered down Cheapside. It was the Company's responsibility to ensure the soundness of the workmanship and the purity of the gold and silver metals used by its members, and wardens of the Company were chosen to test or assay the quality of the plate. Objects fashioned by any silversmith had to be brought to Goldsmiths' Hall in London, where their silver was tested and, if passed, stamped with a "hall-mark" or device.

In subsequent centuries this law has received only minor modification. It is still a strictly enforced rule that every individual piece of silver, whether coffee-pot or salt, candlestick or salver, must pass through an assay office and there receive its hall-mark, the bare cost of its assay being borne by the silversmith. Silver containing too much alloy to conform to legal requirements is still broken up and returned to its maker unstamped.

Assaying in England dates from as early as 1300 when Edward I ordered that gold should be of the "touch of Paris" and silver to be of "esterling allay", both to be tested on the touchstone. The modern term sterling signifies 925 parts of silver alloyed with 75 parts of copper.

The earliest method of assaying consisted of rubbing the metal on a touchstone, a black, finely-textured basaltic rock or imperfect jasper originally brought from Mount Tonolus in Lydia. Any hard black stone, or even earthenware, is suitable for the purpose: Josiah Wedgwood supplied silversmiths with touchstones of black jasperware, stamped with his factory mark.

A book written in 1667 by W. B., a London goldsmith, described the method of making a touch:

> When your touchstone is very clean, then your silver being filed, rub it steadily and very hard on the stone, not spreading your touch above one-quarter inch long, and no broader than the thickness of a fine shilling piece of silver and so continue rubbing it until the place on the stone whereon you rub be like the metal itself; and when every sort is rubbed on that you intend at that time, wet all the touched places with your tongue, and it will show itself in its own countenance.

This rubbing was compared with rubbings of known sterling silver and the quality assessed according to their respective brightness. The early assayers acquired considerable skill in the use of the touchstone, a practised assayer obtaining results not differing by more than ten parts in a thousand from assays made by modern methods.

The touchstone was replaced by the crucible during the fifteenth century. A scraping taken from a piece of silver was carefully weighed, wrapped in pure lead foil and fused in a shallow porous cup made of bone ash and known as a cupel. Under intense heat any base metal present was oxydised and the resulting slag was absorbed in the bone ash, leaving a pellet of pure silver whose reduced weight showed the percentage of impurities.

Fig. 12*a* (*see over*)

Fig. 12*b*

SPECIMEN HALL-MARKS ON LONDON SILVER
(*continued from previous page*)

First and third columns: so-called leopard's head and lion passant of sterling silver, replaced by Britannia and lion's head erased during the high standard period 1697-1720.
Second column: date letter, the type fount changing each twenty years.
Fourth column: makers' marks, changing from symbols to initials.
Fifth column: sovereign's head duty mark, introduced 1784.

The earliest hall-mark to be introduced on English silver was the device that came to be known as the leopard's head (Fig. 12, column 1), the name being taken from the old heraldic term meaning the head of a lion passant guardant. This has come to be accepted as a mark peculiar to London work, but as early as 1477 an Act refers to the application of "the said touch of London and other places".

In 1423 it was stipulated that as provincial assay offices were set up, in York, Norwich and so on, they should use their own distinctive town marks. At the beginning of the

Fig. 13

Specimen Hall-Marks on Provincial Silver

Typical sets of hall-marks found on English provincial silver, consisting of (left to right): maker's mark; variants of the lion passant guardant with or without the leopard's head, denoting sterling quality; the town's mark; date letter; monarch's head duty mark (after 1784). The Norwich example shows the local use of rose and crown as sterling marks. The Exeter example shows Britannia and the lion's head erased, as applied to all high standard silver.

eighteenth century, however, when a number of these provincial offices were either established or reopened, the leopard's head as a quality or standard mark was included as a matter of course among the punches used by the assay offices of these towns: Exeter continued to use it until 1788, Newcastle until 1813, Chester until 1839 (Fig. 13). Thus, on antique silver, this mark must be regarded largely as an indication of quality, although once the second mark, generally called the lion passant, was introduced in 1545, that became more especially the national proof of sterling quality. London was unquestionably the headquarters of the trade and in the period under review it was left to the provincial centres to introduce subsidiary marks that would distinguish them.

An obvious consequence of such compulsory quality tests was the marking of silver articles by their individual makers who thus accepted responsibility. This became compulsory in 1363. The next requirement, dating to 1378, concerned the provincial silversmith who was then compelled to have his wares marked with the distinctive emblem of the city or borough where the assay was made. Although at this time silversmiths were their own judges of quality, carrying out the assay with a touchstone, they were under the control of the master of the mint, if the town possessed one, or the mayor or some other responsible official. It is therefore possible to distinguish the town in which a piece was assayed. York, Lincoln, Newcastle-upon-Tyne, Bristol, Norwich, Salisbury and Coventry were permitted "divers touches" by an Act of 1423 (Fig. 14).

The system of indicating the date of the assay by letters of the alphabet was introduced in about 1478 (Fig. 12, column 2), to enable the Goldsmiths' Company to identify the year and thence the individual warden or assayer responsible if the hall-marks were found on a faulty piece of work. This became obligatory in provincial assay offices, instead of merely customary, in 1701, each assay office having its own series of letters which could not be interpreted were it not for the accompanying town mark.

The introduction of a date letter was followed in about 1545 by the most immediately recognisable lion mark, that of the whole animal in the heraldic position known as passant guardant—walking to the observer's left and (like the "leopard's head" which it accompanied) with its head

(*Above*) four pomanders of the late sixteenth and early seventeenth centuries, and one (*top right*), of silver and niello, of the fourteenth century. (*Below*) a collection of silver-gilt vinaigrettes, including two by Nathaniel Mills of Birmingham embossed with country houses.

Candlesticks. (*Left*) with vertical columns forming a square and decorated with chasing, and with cut-card work on the flat surface of the base; early Charles II. (*Right*) architectural column with vertical fluting and reeding, and shallow socket containing a short pricket; London 1680.

(*Left*) baluster stem with acorn knop on depressed octagonal base by Pierre Harache London 1683. (*Right*) eight-sided waisted baluster stem and socket; height $6\frac{1}{2}$ inches. Made by Thomas Folkingham London 1714.

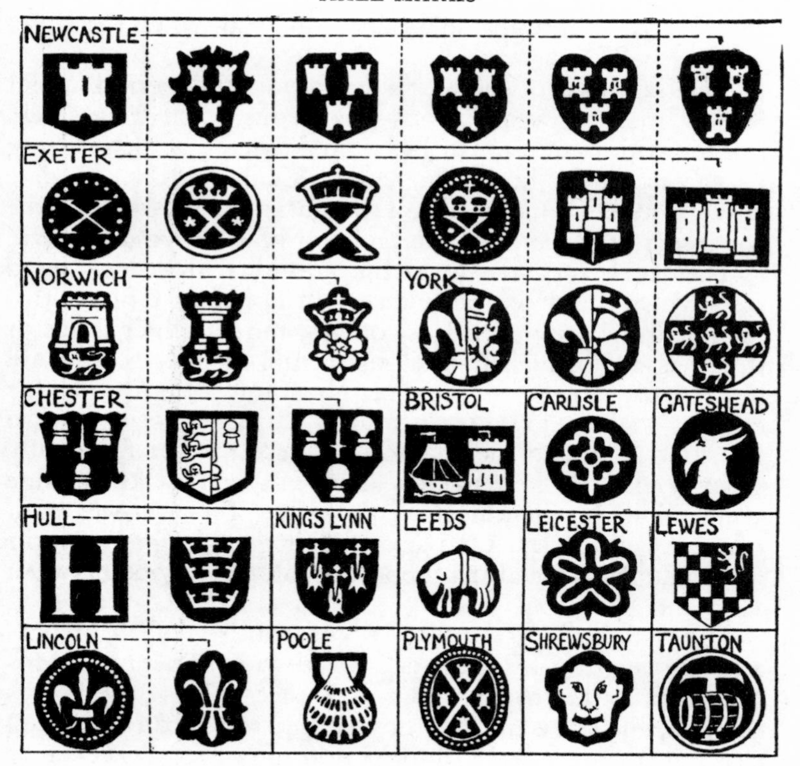

Fig. 14

Examples of the range of punches used by provincial centres to mark their silver. Many were taken from city coats of arms.

turned full face (Fig. 12, column 3). This was described in Elizabethan days as "Her Majesty's lion" and "Her Majesty's touch" and was used by assay offices throughout the country to indicate that the silver passed the test for true sterling even at periods when the silver used for coinage was debased with a greater proportion of alloy.

The last addition to the row of puncheons was the outline of the sovereign's head (Fig. 12*b*, column 5). This was applied to all silver made between 1784 and 1890, with certain exceptions, and indicated that payment had been made of the duty levied on silver plate at this time. The tax was paid through the Goldsmiths' Hall when the silver was assayed.

Thus a piece of silver made during the period under review may show a row of puncheons, each in a shield outline seldom more than $\frac{1}{4}$-inch in diameter, and consisting of the leopard's head, the lion passant guardant, a date letter, a maker's mark (Fig. 12, column 4), the head of the sovereign, and perhaps the emblem of a provincial town.

The date letter and many of the individual marks registered by silversmiths have been recorded either at Goldsmiths' Hall or at the provincial assay offices, and the silver collector thus has an unrivalled basis of factual information to aid him in his survey of the ever-changing delights of this country's silver down the centuries. It is proposed now to consider in greater detail each of these marks: frequently when a piece is incompletely marked specialist knowledge will still make identification possible. First, however, it may be well to clear up a small point regarding two marks not so far mentioned that appear on all plate made between 1697 and 1720.

The standard for sterling silver consists of 11 ounces 2 pennyweights of fine silver alloyed with 18 pennyweights of copper to the troy pound of 12 ounces. This is known as 925 fine, and has remained the required standard for sterling silver ever since 1300. For the period 1697-1720, however, as mentioned in the previous chapter, metal with an even lower alloy content was required for silver plate. This was known as "high standard" silver to differentiate it from the sterling silver which continued to be used for the country's coinage. As the two lion marks represented the sterling standard, new ones had to be introduced for the high standard metal. These took the form of a seated figure of Britannia and a mark known in heraldry as a lion's head erased. The latter consisted of a lion's head side face, "erased" because its neck ended in a wavy line. An Act of 1719, becoming operative in 1720, enabled silversmiths to return to the normal sterling metal, but some work has been produced more recently in the finer metal. For this the same marks have continued to be applicable, so that these marks alone are no assurance of antiquity. Jackson has pointed out that nearly all the London silver plate assayed in 1863-64 was of the finer quality.

The so-called leopard's head, the mark first used by the Goldsmiths' Company and regarded by many as the distinctive mark of London manufacture, was at first known as the king's mark and later referred to in the trade as the "catte's head". It was only in 1854 that provincial silversmiths were allowed to choose where they sent their goods for assaying, so that the leopard's head became a desideratum carrying an implication of a London standard of craftsmanship as well as its official significance regarding the fineness of the silver itself.

Down the years the leopard's head went through distinct and recognizable phases, both in its actual outlines and in the puncheon shields that enclosed them. These changes and their dates have been fully recorded and are of assistance to the collector. Occasionally very early specimens are marked with leopard heads not crowned, but from at least as early as 1478 until 1821 a crown was always included in the design and even this small feature varied considerably, while the face itself frequently lost and regained mane and whiskers. A further guide to the collector is the fact that the outline of the puncheon enclosing the head was altered from time to time.

All these details become important when dating a piece which was made during one of the periods when the style of the alphabet used for the date letter was the same as that for an earlier or later period, such as is found in the London alphabets beginning 1756 and 1836. After disappearing during the high standard period the leopard's head reappeared in 1720, the features and the shape of the shield continuing to vary appreciably until, in 1821, there was a notable change consisting of the removal of the crown.

The second lion mark was introduced in about 1545 as a direct result of coinage debasements in 1542 and 1545 and has remained the mark signifying sterling quality standard to all assay offices. Until 1821 this heraldic lion was passant guardant as described above; after 1821 a lion passant was applied, walking to the left as before with its dexter forepaw raised, but looking straight ahead. Other changes have largely been confined to the outline of its shield or puncheon, which from 1756 to 1896 consisted of a shield with clipped shoulders and a cyma base.

The law of 1363 made it compulsory for every piece of silver to be stamped with its maker's personal mark. The earliest of these mainly consisted of symbols and emblems such as hung outside the old shops, but by the seventeenth century it had become more customary for the smith to use the initials of his Christian name and surname. Even then, however, a small emblem was often included with the initials inside the puncheon outline.

The haphazard use of initials was getting out of hand by the end of the prolific seventeenth century, and the introduction of high standard silver in 1697 was marked by the establishment of the ruling that the maker should use as his mark the first two letters of his surname. This still resulted in some duplication, however, and when silver of sterling standard was permissible after 1720 silversmiths returned to their accustomed initials when using the sterling metal, some merely re-introducing their pre-1697 punches. In 1739 the Goldsmiths' Company acknowledged existing custom by instructing silversmiths to re-register their initials, of Christian name and surname, but in a different type of lettering from that previously used.

Since 1739 a maker's mark has always consisted of his initials in a plain type, with or without an accompanying device within the puncheon outline. From the records of these marks kept at Goldsmiths' Hall and the provincial assay offices many makers can be traced. Occasionally a tiny mark is found beside the maker's puncheon, but this is merely an indication of the individual craftsman who fashioned the piece.

As regards late eighteenth century work, the mark may be that of the firm who sold the silver rather than the individual maker. A wholesaler or retailer, or for that matter any private individual, has the right to register a punch mark at an assay office. The increasing specialization of later work which led to the grouping of a number of individuals within the framework of one firm or factory led to the marking of silverware in the name of the unit which produced or sold it.

Candlesticks. (*Left*) with short octagonal baluster stem rising from depressed octagonal base; by John Pero London 1722. (*Right*) shouldered and knopped stem rising from a depression in a square foot; by Nicholas Clauser, London 1726.

(*Left*) with vase-shaped hexagonal stem and spool-shaped nozzle; by William Townsend 1735; (*right*) baluster stem with fluted mushroom shoulder and loose sconce; by Ebenezer Coker, London, 1763.

Candlesticks of neo-classic design: the first three have urn-shaped sockets and four-sided stems tapering towards high square bases with curved sides, 1770-1780; the fourth has a fluted corinthian column with candle socket and loose sconce within its capital, 1760.

A set of four candlesticks in the Egyptian fashion of the period; by Richard Cook, London 1804.

The invariable use of two letters in the maker's mark obviates any danger of confusion with the date letter in its separate puncheon. Each letter was used for a year and then changed for the next letter of the alphabet. Until 1660 the date of the annual change was May 19; afterwards, in London, St. Dunstan's Day, May 30, was chosen in honour of the goldsmiths' patron saint. The letter indicates the year in which the article was assayed, for its purpose was to make possible the identification of its assayer, while keeping this more or less a trade secret. As subsidiary assay offices became established each had its own list of date letters, or "wardens' marks". Sheffield (from 1844) and Birmingham struck twenty-five or twenty-six consecutive letters, sometimes omitting J because of confusion with I. But for convenience it was more usual to take only twenty letters and repeat them five times during each century in different founts or styles of type. After 1561 identification was made easier by the use of changing heraldic shields to enclose the letters.

As regards the date letters used by the Goldsmiths' Company on London work, these are illustrated in detail on pages 40-41. They began in 1478 with the letter A, each subsequent year being denoted by the next letter in alphabetical sequence, but with the omission of J and of the last five letters of the alphabet. The styles of type used are as follows:

1478-97—Lombardic style with double cusps.

1498-1517—Small early English or black letters (lower case).

1518-37—Lombardic capitals.

1538-57—A mixed alphabet of capital letters.

1558-77—Small black letters (lower case).

From 1561 to 1739 the letters were enclosed in plain, angular, heraldic shields.

1578-1597—Roman capitals.

1598-1617—Lombardic with external cusps.

1618-1637—Lower case script letters.

1638-1657—Court hand.

1658-1677—Black letter capitals.

1678-1696—Black letter lower case.

1696 (March to May)-1715—Court hand.

1716-1735—Roman capitals.

1736-1755—Roman lower case. After the letter **c** the shield became more ornate.

1756-1775—Black letter capitals.

From 1756 to 1835 the shield had a cyma base, and for a few years in the 1756-75 cycle, and consistently thereafter, the shield had clipped shoulders.

1776-1795—Roman lower case.

1796-1815—Roman capitals.

1816-1835—Roman lower case.

1836-1855—Black letter capitals.

After about 1678 the date letter varied in size according to the dimensions of the article being marked. Small pieces were sometimes marked with small editions of the normal marks, but frequently the tiny letter was plainly enclosed in a square with slightly clipped corners.

Even with such a variety of founts it will be seen that there was some repetition: for example in the alphabets beginning in the years 1776, 1816 and 1896. It is essential, therefore, to examine the whole series of marks on a piece of silver in order to fix its date with certainty. In the examples mentioned the alphabet beginning in 1896 is at once distinguishable from the others in the same lower case Roman fount as the base of the shield enclosing the date letter is shaped in a triple curve as distinct from the cyma base of the others. But it is from the other symbols accompanying the date letter that the 1776 and 1816 cycles may be differentiated, and this applies, too, to such other duplications as the Roman capitals used 1578-97 and 1716-35. These symbols, even when smoothed with centuries of wear, will generally indicate, for instance, the shape of the puncheon outline and even the features of the accompanying leopard's head, and similar contributory details which together provide the data necessary for precise dating. Full lists of London and provincial assay letters and their dates are available in booklet form.

Details of the alphabets peculiar to the various provincial assay offices, and on Scottish and Irish work, appear later in this chapter, but as the great majority of work acquired by the collector is likely to bear London marks it may be more helpful to refer briefly first to the other mark common to the English and Scottish silver irrespective of its place of origin. This was the duty mark, found on all silver, with certain exceptions, from December 1, 1784 until 1890, and indicating that a tax on the plate had been paid by the maker. (On Irish silver the metal was marked for tax payment as early as 1730, a figure of Hibernia being used until 1807—not to be confused with the figure of Britannia found on English high standard silver.) It was the responsibility of the assayers to levy the tax and then mark the silver to show that this had been done. The English and Scottish mark—used in Ireland after 1807—consisted of the head of the reigning monarch: here again the full series of marks has been recorded and can be consulted by the collector.

As regards provincial and Scottish silver, however, it must be noted that there was generally a lapse of several years between the accession of a sovereign and the introduction of new punches. Thus silver dating to 1835 may be stamped with a duty mark bearing the head of George IV. It must also be noted that between 1784 and 1890 silver for export—exempted from tax—was stamped with another figure of Britannia instead of the sovereign's head. The accompanying mark of the lion passant should obviate confusion with high standard work when such a piece is found.

Certain articles of silver carry no hall marks. From as early as 1739 it was recognised that some exceptions would have to be made to the general requirement that every piece of silver should be marked. Some work could not be assayed or stamped without seriously detracting from its value, and an Act was passed exempting from assay various small articles such as toothpick cases and the like and also "such other things as by reason of the smallness or thinness thereof are not capable of receiving the marks hereinbefore mentioned, or any of them, and not weighing ten pennyweights of gold or silver each".

Other pieces were exempted because so richly engraved, carved or chased or set with stones "as not to admit of an

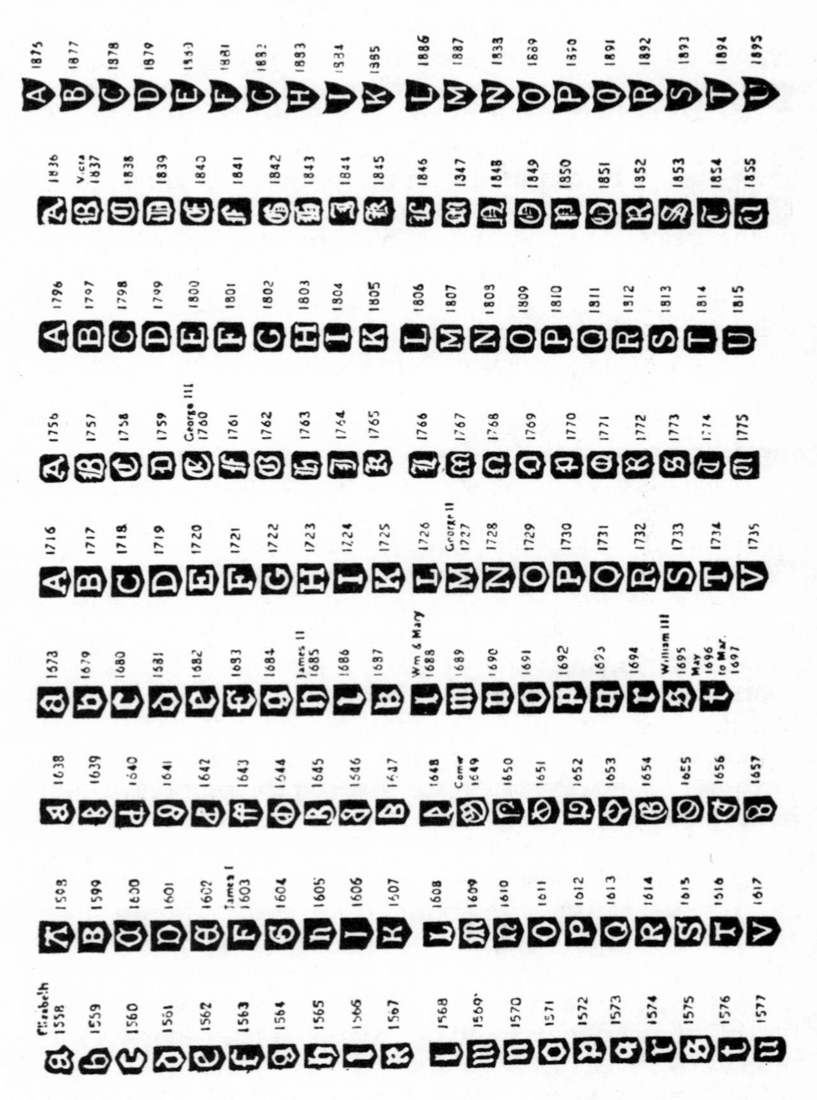

Date letters used by the Goldsmiths'

Company on London work

assay to be taken of, or a mark to be struck thereon without damaging it'. Supplementing these exemptions came a further list in 1790 covering certain articles of any weight and certain others weighing less than ten pennyweights, and also "any wares of silver whatsoever not weighing five pennyweights of silver each", excepting only certain specified pieces, including caddy ladles and bottle tickets, which therefore still had to be assayed (see Chapter 13).

On other pieces, however, the marks are not always found in full. Teaspoons of about 1750 and earlier are often marked with a lion only, though after that date they usually bear the complete set of four or five impressions. The hall-marks may appear in any order, but their position on an article is fixed by arrangement with the Goldsmiths' Company: thus a candlestick is marked on base and nozzle, a coffee-pot below the rim near the handle or else on the base, and so on. In early work the marks were scattered singly over the piece, making it more difficult for the counterfeiter. It is the rule that in a composite piece the largest component part must be stamped in full while other detachable parts need only bear the sterling lion.

Such details tend to minimise the obvious difficulties that were bound to arise in the early days through the dictatorial powers of the Goldsmiths' Company, whose rigorous supervision was largely responsible for the trade's high repute. Indeed, the story of the establishment of the provincial assay offices is largely a story of struggles by makers far from London to avoid the rough handling and dangerous journeys suffered by their handiwork. It was the vigorous protest in Parliament made on behalf of the Birmingham manufacturer Matthew Boulton that brought about a greater consideration for fine ornament damaged by disfiguring punch marks.

Crowns and castles, anchors and ships in full sail—the various devices stamped on English provincial silver have a fascination all their own. So great was the preponderance of London silver manufacture in the past, so chary was the Goldsmiths' Company of decentralising its authority, that there is a tendency to expect the marks on old silver plate to consist only of those applied by Goldsmiths' Hall and to be suspicious of the quality when work is differently marked. The marks on English silver made in the provinces are a study in themselves, however, offering their own commentary on the centuries that produced them.

To-day there are three offices in England where assays or tests of silver are made—London, Birmingham and Sheffield—but in the past offices were operating at many other towns, including York, Exeter, Newcastle-upon-Tyne, and Norwich. It is obvious that the London Goldsmiths' Company could only make spasmodic efforts to control the activities of those early provincial silversmiths, until the change to the high standard deprived provincial assay offices of their powers and for a few years limited the touching of the silver with the new high standard marks to the London Goldsmiths' Hall. This was a period of great difficulty for the provincial silversmith. Local offices were closed and they were compelled to send their plate on the hazardous return journey to London for hall-marking. So inconvenient and costly was this that in 1700 Parliament appointed "Wardens and Assay Masters for assaying Wrought Plate in the Cities of York, Exeter, Bristol, Chester, and Norwich". Mints had recently been erected in these towns for recoining silver money. Newcastle-upon-Tyne, which had been assaying and marking local silver for almost half a century, had to send its goods to York until its assay office was re-established in 1702.

The statutes covering these provincial assay offices decreed among other details that the plate, if exposed for sale, must be marked with the maker's mark, the arms of the city, a variable date letter, and the high-standard marks consisting of the lion's head erased and the figure of Britannia. It is not known how much unmarked plate was made to commission. When the Act of 1719—operative from 1720—permitted the use once more of sterling silver for articles of wrought plate, the provincial offices were not mentioned at all. They interpreted their orders from the clause in the Act that required a maker's mark, a date letter, and "the figure of a lion passant, and the figure of a leopard's head". Hence the continued use of the leopard's head on provincial silver.

In making an individual study of English provincial assay offices it may be well to start with the two that remain to-day—Birmingham and Sheffield.

Birmingham: This assay office, under the management of the Guardians of the Standard of Wrought Plate, Birmingham, was established in 1773 with exclusive jurisdiction over all silver plate within a radius of thirty miles. Its establishment followed seven years of vigorous action on the part of Matthew Boulton. Formerly all Birmingham silver had travelled to Chester for assaying, the dangerous return journey taking nearly two weeks. The assay officials were reported to have repacked the assayed silver so carelessly that "chasing was entirely destroyed; some pieces were broken".

London meetings in connection with the Assay Bills of Birmingham and Sheffield took place at the *Crown and Anchor* in the Strand, and in discussing the Acts setting up the two offices Boulton suggested that they should take the crown and anchor marks, a toss of the coin assigning the anchor to Birmingham, the crown to Sheffield. The anchor might be struck vertically or horizontally and was accompanied by a lion passant guardant, date letter, maker's mark, and, from 1784 to 1890, the duty mark (Fig. 13).

These marks might be placed in any sequence. At a later period a compound punch and fly-press were used for striking. The date letter J was included only in the cycles dated 1798-99 to 1823-24 and 1849-50 to 1874-75. Collectors will find difficulty in distinguishing between the first and second cycles as regards the letters O, S, V, W, X, and Z. The high-standard silver was marked with the figure of Britannia without the lion's head erased.

The duty head for the year 1797-98 was sometimes stamped twice to indicate that the full duty, doubled that year, had been paid. This stamp was usually outlined by an oval shield, but from 1797 to 1812 the punch outline followed the shape of the head, although from 1800 an oval sometimes reappeared. There was delay in changing the duty mark, the head of William IV first being applied in 1834 and Queen Victoria in 1839.

Sheffield: This office, established in 1773, was empowered

Candlesticks with baluster stems and octagonal plinths chased with shells, scale pattern, flaming torches, flowers and foliage by Paul de Lamerie, London 1737. One of a pair of candelabra with branches for four lights by Paul de Lamerie, London 1731.

Two-branch candelabra with central moulded finials which are removable, enabling a third light to be used. (*Left*) circular stem tapering towards the circular base and fluted; by Wakelin and Taylor, London 1786. (*Right*) branches twisting around central finial, London 1810.

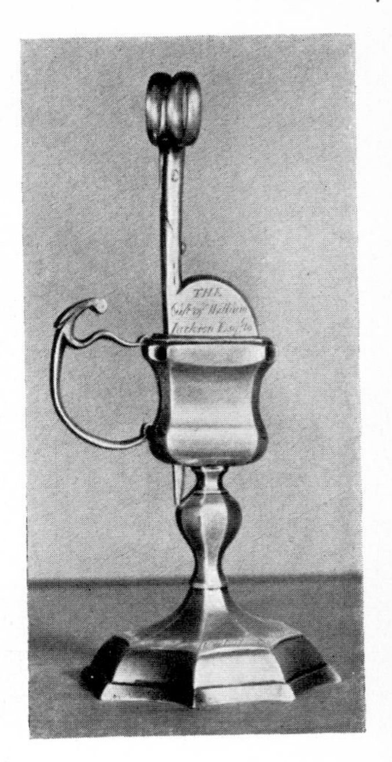

Snuffers and stands. (*Left*) combined snuffer and stand with candlesconce and extinguisher, the short baluster stem with low octagonal base decorated with gadrooning; by John Barnard, London 1697. (*Right*) snuffers with upright stand and vertical socket on baluster stem rising from high octagonal foot; by Matthew Cooper, London 1715.

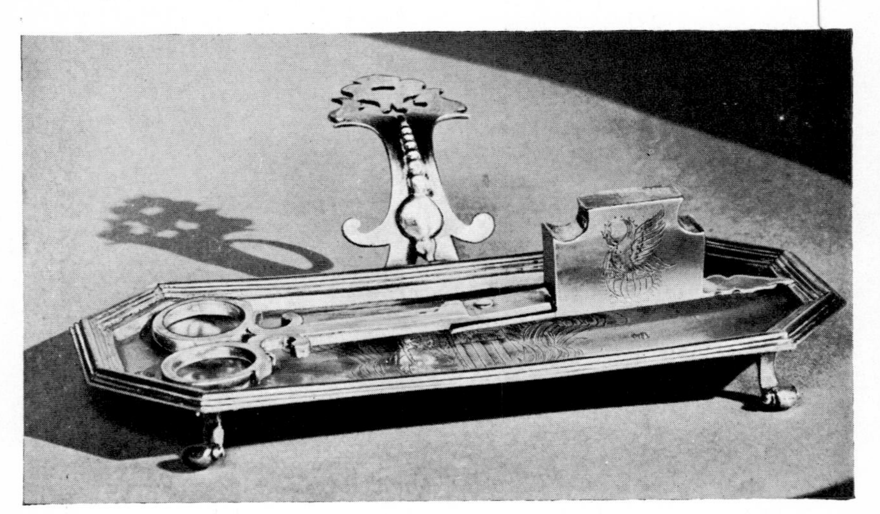

Snuffers and flat octagonal dish with narrow applied moulding, four scroll feet, and a curved pierced lateral handle; London 1677.

to assay and hall-mark silver wares within twenty miles of the city. At the time of its establishment the nearest assay office was at York. The sequence of marks generally observed by Sheffield consisted of the maker's mark, fineness mark, town mark, date letter, duty mark (Fig. 13). On the rare occasions when silver of the high standard was brought for assay during the period under review the fineness mark was Britannia in a square puncheon without the lion's head erased.

Until 1824 the date letters appear to have been selected at random, the first cycle containing type of three founts. On small silverware from 1780 to 1853 the crown and date letter were often combined in a single oval or oblong puncheon, the crown being either above or at the side of the letter. For years 1815 to 1819 the crown is found up-side down. From July, 1797 to April, 1798, the duty mark was struck twice to indicate that the doubled duty had been paid. From 1798 to 1824 the punch followed the outline of the monarch's head. As at other provincial offices, the new monarch's head was not introduced on duty marks until two or three years after his accession.

Chester: The Company of Goldsmiths of the City of Chester was the responsible authority for hall-marking in Chester. The Domesday book referred to Chester as possessing "moneyers" or mint masters, and silver coins were struck there almost continuously until about 1650. Those dated 1645 display the town mark recently struck on silver plate.

There is no record that regular assaying was authorised earlier than the reign of James II, neither town mark nor date letter being used until about 1687. The town mark was "the coat and crest of the city of Chester"—a sword erect between three garbs (wheat sheaves). This continued for a few years, when the word STER/LING impressed in a shield-shaped punch was consistently used, but for no known reason, until the office temporarily closed in 1697.

After the passing of the Provincial Assay Offices Act in 1700 the Chester office was reopened. The town mark was changed to a plain shield enclosing three lions of England dimidiated with three garbs of the Earl of Chester. With the restoration of the sterling standard for silver plate in 1720 Chester adopted the lion passant guardant and leopard's head (Fig. 13). These, with the date letter and the maker's mark, remained in use until 1779 when the earlier town mark of the sword erect between three garbs was revived. This has been used ever since. When the duty mark was added in 1784 silver assayed at Chester bore six marks: town mark, lion passant guardant, leopard's head, date letter, maker's mark, duty mark. Punch marks applied earlier than 1784 were larger than later examples. Several writers have noted that the Chester marks were formerly the same as London with the addition of the city arms, but that since 1839 the leopard's head has been discontinued. De Castro points out their omission to observe that London and Chester date letters were never the same in any one year. To this may be added the point that the punch shapes also varied.

Offices were denoted by statute for assaying silver in other towns, but these have long ceased work. As has been said, an Act of 1423 ordained "that the Cities of York, Newcastle-upon-Tyne, Norwich, Lincoln, Bristol, Salisbury and Coventry shall have divers touches". In addition there were numerous other offices not possessing statutory rights.

Newcastle-upon-Tyne: This was a centre of the silversmiths' craft in the thirteenth century when a mint was established there. Little is known of their early plate, but Jackson considers it probable that each silversmith admitted to the local guild of traders possessed a town mark for his personal use, consisting of a single castle. At first the fineness mark of a lion passant was walking to the right of the observer, and this recurred 1721-27. The single castle was superseded in about 1672 by the town arms of Newcastle—three castles, two placed above one, in a plain heraldic shield: occasionally an elaborately shaped shield was used (Fig. 14). Sometimes the lion or the maker's initials were impressed twice, flanking the town mark (Fig. 13).

In 1702 the Company of Goldsmiths of Newcastle-upon-Tyne was incorporated and an assay master installed. The town mark during the high-standard period was accompanied by the lion's head erased, the figure of Britannia, date letter, and maker's mark. The three-castle mark in variously shaped punches was used until the office closed in 1884. After restoration of the sterling standard for plate the marks of quality consisted of the leopard's head crowned —it did not lose its crown until 1846-47—and a lion passant (not passant guardant) facing to the right. In 1728-29 the lion as generally used became established. These accompanied the town mark, date letter, and maker's initials. Between 1797 and 1799 and from 1803 to 1820 the punch outline of the duty mark followed the silhouette of the monarch's head.

Norwich: Although authorized to assay gold and silver in 1423, no office for the purpose was established until 1565. Jackson considered that in "design and finish much of the Elizabethan Norwich-made plate is equal to that of the best London-made plate of the period".

The town mark was a castle (a castellated tower) over a lion passant guardant, and was often accompanied by a date letter. From 1624 until 1697, when the office was closed, a rose crowned was also included in the hall-mark (Fig. 14). This appears to have been the standard or fineness mark adopted by Norwich instead of the leopard's head crowned, which its outline resembled. Between 1645 and 1687 the rose and crown appeared in separate punches (Fig. 13). Although Norwich was one of the towns named in the Enabling Statute of 1700 no marks of the high standard silver have been noted.

York: An assay office was established at York in 1483 but documentary evidence exists to prove that silversmiths were required, as early as 1411, to mark their own work which "was then brought to the searchers to be touched with the city marks". The city mark until 1560 was described as "the half leopard head and half floure de layce" in one stamp. From 1560 these were augmented by a date letter which was changed annually in alphabetical cycles. The town mark from 1632 to 1698, when the office was closed for three years, was a half rose crowned and a half fleur de lis in a single punch (Fig. 14).

Upon the re-establishment of the York assay office in 1701 the arms of the city, a Greek cross charged with five lions passant guardant, became the town mark. The number of marks now struck was increased from three to five by the addition of the high-standard marks of the lion's head erased and the figure of Britannia. In 1717 the office ceased to mark plate, remaining moribund until 1776. The town mark still remained a cross charged with five lions passant guardant, but enclosed in a square-shouldered shield; from 1787 it was placed within an oval. The old sterling standard having been restored, the lion passant guardant and the leopard's head crowned were struck as fineness marks. From 1812 the leopard's head is usually found with whiskers, but sometimes they are missing. The leopard's head was discontinued from 1848. The monarch's head in the duty mark was enclosed in an oval shield except between 1796 and 1830 when the punch outline followed the shape of the head. The office closed in 1857.

Exeter: There is no evidence that this important assay office had any statutory existence before the Act of 1700, operative from 1701. The city had been celebrated for its fine silversmiths throughout the previous century, and the town mark, the Roman capital letter X, is found on Elizabethan silver. Sometimes the X is crowned, has a pellet on either side and is encircled by a ring of tiny pellets. So numerous are the variations of the punch outline and the actual design of the mark that the conclusion may be drawn that makers struck their own marks (Fig. 14).

Upon the establishment of an assay office at Exeter in 1701 the town mark selected consisted of the arms of the city, the triple-towered castle, called also by collectors the three turreted towers and the three towers. With considerable variations of design this town mark was used until the office was closed in 1882. Until 1720 the town mark was accompanied by the lion's head erased and Britannia, on bolder punches than were used elsewhere, the date letter and the maker's mark. In 1720 the lion's head erased and Britannia were replaced by the lion passant guardant and the leopard's head, the latter on an unusually large shield, but discontinued from 1778. Only four marks

Standish with a bell between the urn-shaped pounce-box and ink-pot; by Thomas England, London 1731.

Standish with moulded rim, cylindrical ink-pot, shot-container and pounce-box; *c.* 1740. Engraved with the coat-of-arms of George II.

Standish with pear-shaped handle. The tray has circular depressions to contain ink-pot and pounce-box, with taperstick between; by George Methuen, London 1751.

Standish with wide gadrooned border: by Robert Innes, London 1752.

Oval standish with reeded and slightly raised rim, on ball and claw feet. The taperstick has a bell base. By Magdaline Feline, London 1758.

Standish with gadrooned rim, shell foliage corners and pierced scroll feet. Fluted vase-shaped containers. By John Parker and Edward Wakelin, London 1771.

then appeared until the introduction of the duty mark in 1784. The change in the monarch's head was always delayed at Exeter, that of William IV not appearing for four years after the death of George IV. The shield was always oval with the exception of the years 1784 to 1786 when it was octagonal, and from 1797 to 1799 when it outlined the head. From 1797 to 1856 the Exeter date letters were the same as London's except that they were one year later and enclosed in shields of different outline.

Salisbury, Coventry, Bristol: Although granted the right to establish assay offices in 1423, there is no record that any of these towns exercised the privilege. Bristol's city arms, a ship issuing from a castle, have been found on a few pieces of silver (Fig. 14).

Silversmiths in certain provincial towns were themselves permitted to apply the town mark in addition to their own and the statutory marks. In accordance with custom the local coat of arms was usually selected as the distinguishing town mark (Fig. 14). Such marks, which are extremely rare, include the following:

Hull: The letter H or the arms of the city, three ducal coronets one above the other in a plain shield. Both marks have been found on a single piece, and date letters occasionally.

Gateshead: A goat's head erased, twice impressed. Late seventeenth century.

King's Lynn: Three dragons' heads each pierced with a cross. Struck during the reign of Charles I.

Leeds: The golden fleece. Struck 1650 to 1702.

Lincoln: A fleur-de-lis, usually within a circle or ellipse of pellets. Examples known from 1560 to 1706.

Poole: An escallop shell.

Shrewsbury: An uncrowned leopard's head. Struck during the sixteenth century.

Taunton: The letter T and a tun. Struck 1640 to 1690.

EDINBURGH 1642 (TYPICAL OF THE PERIOD 1617-1681)	PB		I·F	NO DATE LETTER
1695 (TYPICAL OF THE PERIOD 1681-1759)	AF		B	P
1769-70 (TYPICAL OF THE PERIOD 1759-1784)	PR			P
GLASGOW 1696-7 (TYPICAL OF THE PERIOD 1681-c.1710)	R		R	Q
1731 (TYPICAL OF THE PERIOD c.1730-c.1800)	IB		IB	S
1820-21 (TYPICAL FROM 1819) JD				B
ABERDEEN ABD		BANFF BANF	CANONGATE	DUNDEE
GREENOCK	INVERNESS INS		MONTROSE	PERTH

Fig. 15

HALL-MARKS FOUND ON SCOTTISH SILVER

Rows 1-3: typical series on work assayed at Edinburgh, the first column representing the maker's mark, the second the town mark, the third the quality mark, and the fourth the date letter. The three examples of quality mark show respectively an early deacon's mark, an assay master's monogram, and the subsequent thistle emblem.

Rows 4-6: typical series on work assayed at Glasgow. Rows

Silver plate made in Scotland and Ireland (Figs. 15 and 16) requires separate consideration, the distance involved being too great for the Goldsmiths' Company to administer the law effectively in the early days. In Scotland, the only assay offices were at Edinburgh and, from 1819, at Glasgow. The result was that silver plate made in outlying districts seldom received any mark other than that of the maker, although Scottish law as long ago as 1457 decreed that the fineness of silver plate and its marking should be the responsibility of various deacons selected from among the master silversmiths. Such plate was struck with the personal mark of the deacon-silversmith.

The craft extended to other towns and in 1485 it was enacted that town marks should be struck and that each individual silversmith should mark all his plate with an emblem of identification. Despite such regulations the fraudulent addition of excess alloy continued, and from the middle of the sixteenth century stringent orders decreed that any silversmith discovered selling plate "under just fineness" should be sentenced to death and his property confiscated.

The Silver Standard Act of 1697, which became law before the union of England and Scotland, was not legally binding upon the Scottish silversmiths, who continued using metal of a quality inferior to that required by English law. When the sterling standard was restored in 1720 the law was able to compel Scottish silversmiths to conform by raising the quality of their metal from eleven ounces fine to eleven ounces two pennyweights fine in every twelve ounces of silver. The use of the high standard became an optional alternative.

Edinburgh: In 1585, the Edinburgh goldsmiths had been

---

4 and 5 show the duplication of the maker's mark flanking the town mark before the establishment of an assay office. In row 5 the letter S is believed to stand for sterling quality at a period when no date letter was used. Row 6 shows the full range of nineteenth century marks—maker's, quality, town, duty and date.

Rows 7 and 8: typical town marks used elsewhere in Scotland.

empowered to assay plate made throughout Scotland, a turreted castle becoming the town mark. This was used in varying forms until 1617 when the central tower of a triple-towered castle was raised higher than the others. Until 1681 the maker's mark was struck first, then the town mark, and then the deacon's mark: on some occasions, of course, the first and third marks were identical. A date letter system was adopted in 1681, using a twenty-five letter alphabet, as compared with London's twenty letter cycle.

A royal charter was granted in 1687 and the Edinburgh Goldsmiths' Incorporation was established with former privileges confirmed and extended powers. At this time there were twenty-five silversmiths in Edinburgh, five in Glasgow, and eight elsewhere in Scotland. The deacon's mark was replaced by that of the assay master, his script initials in monogram form being used until 1706 and thereafter separate Roman capitals. This mark was replaced in 1759 by a thistle representing the sterling standard. The monarch's duty mark was struck from 1784. Upon the accession of a new monarch there was usually considerable delay before the head was changed: Queen Victoria was not featured until 1841.

Canongate, now part of Edinburgh, had its own guild of hammermen from 1680 to 1836, this being a combination of master silversmiths, blacksmiths, coppersmiths, and others. Their local mark was a stag's head erased. From about 1790 this was accompanied by an anchor with a cable. No Canongate hall-marks have been noted accompanied by duty marks.

Glasgow silversmiths do not appear to have struck more than their own marks until 1681, although they were already associated with other metal-workers in an incorporation of hammermen. In that year they adopted the town mark, now termed the "fish, tree and bell". This comprised a tree with a bird perched on the top, a hand-bell suspended from the branches, and transversely across or below the trunk a salmon with a ring in its mouth. So many were the minor variations in this mark that it is assumed the town mark was struck by the goldsmiths themselves.

The letter S in various forms is found in addition to the town and makers' marks from 1730 until 1800. This is assumed to indicate that the metal is of sterling quality. Date letters were adopted in 1681 and continued until 1710 when they were abandoned until 1819.

There is no record that an assay office operated in Glasgow earlier than 1819 when the date letter was re-introduced in a full twenty-six letter alphabet and the lion rampant became compulsory as the standard mark. An Act of 1836 (6 & 7 Will. IV *c.* 69) also required the thistle to be stamped on sterling silver, but for some reason this was not brought into use until 1912. Duty marks were struck at Glasgow from 1819 to 1890.

There were some fourteen other Scottish towns with guilds of hammermen. The silversmiths struck their plate with the town mark and their own initials: specimens of such work are rare. Absence of duty marks on such plate during the relevant period indicates that this obligation was avoided, but many examples will be found struck with the local marks and also those of an assay office.

Other Scottish town marks include the following, the dates given here being those determined by Sir Charles Jackson:

Aberdeen (1600-1870): Various combinations of the letters A B D and N. Until about 1780 the letters might be associated with three castles.

Arbroath (1830-40): A portcullis.

Banff (1680-1850): Usually an abbreviation of the town name. Between 1720 and about 1820 a fish was sometimes used.

Dundee (1628-1809): A two-handled vase containing three lilies in various shapes. Some late examples were struck DUN
DEE.

Elgin (1728-1830): The town name in full or the abbreviation ELG or ELN.

Greenock (1758-1830): An anchor, very similar to that of Birmingham. This might be accompanied by a ship in full sail or by a green oak, a rebus representing the town name.

Inverness (1640-1880): The letters INS. Between about

1715 and 1815 a cornucopia might accompany the town mark, this being the borough crest. From 1740 a dromedary, and from 1800 a thistle, might also be struck.

Montrose (1670-1811): Variations of a five-petalled rose.

Perth (1675-1856): A lamb with a flag until 1710, then a double-headed eagle.

Tain and *Wick* struck their town names in full. *Ayr*, *St. Andrews*, and *Stirling* also struck town marks.

Ireland, celebrated for her originality in silversmithing more than a thousand years ago, has within recent centuries followed the styles made fashionable by London and Paris. Unlike England where assay masters were appointed to various provincial towns, the assaying authority in Ireland was vested solely in the Goldsmiths' Company of Dublin. An Act of 1605 ordered silver plate made in Ireland to be assayed and stamped with the lion, harp, castle, and maker's emblem.

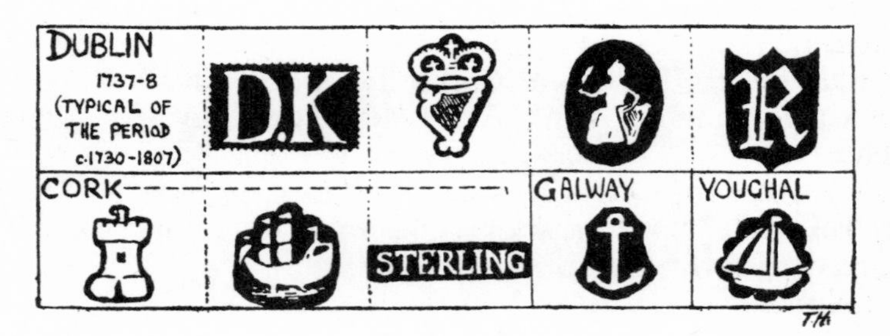

Fig. 16

Specimen Irish Hall-Marks

First row shows a typical range of Dublin marks—maker's mark, quality mark, duty mark, and date letter. Second row shows typical marks used in other Irish centres of the craft.

When the Company received its charter in 1637 it prescribed two marks only: the harp crowned as a standard of fineness, and a maker's mark. Although no provision was made regarding a date letter this also was introduced, becoming established as a twenty-four letter cycle, with J and V omitted, the latter being added in 1841. Not until

1729 were the three marks made a statutory requirement. In the following year a duty of sixpence an ounce was levied on all silver plate made in Ireland, the figure of Hibernia seated and with the right arm outstretched being used by the Dublin assay office when duty was paid. Until 1794 she was in an oval and from then until the Union in a square with clipped corners. Following the Union of 1800 the monarch's head superseded Hibernia as a duty mark. Hibernia then became the town mark of Dublin.

The punch mark enclosing the crowned harp was also changed from time to time. Until 1787 the shape of the stamp followed the outline of the harp; from then until 1794 the punch outline was oval and the harp supplemented by a head and wings. Between 1794 and 1809 it was rectangular with clipped corners. From then until 1820 the harp was in a regular heraldic shield.

Makers' marks from 1637 to about 1850 were usually the initial letters of Christian name and surname, either separate or in monogram. Early in the nineteenth century, the full surname might be struck. Until about 1760 a maker's initials might be crowned or accompanied by an emblem, in the same punch, smaller type being usual in the nineteenth century. The lion marks of English sterling silver are never found on Irish plate and as there was no high-standard ruling in Ireland Britannia and the lion's head erased are also absent.

Silver bearing the Dublin marks is not necessarily of Dublin origin. The law required Irish silversmiths to register their marks with the Goldsmiths' Company of Dublin and send all plate to be assayed there. Many outlying silversmiths failed to comply with these conditions: consequently some Irish silver is found bearing devices indicating that it was not assayed and avoided payment of the duty required from 1730. The principal offenders were the silversmiths of Cork who, from 1656, were members of the Company of the Society of Goldsmiths of the City of Cork, a guild including braziers, saddlers and followers of other trades. Until 1715 the town mark, adapted from the city arms, was a ship in full sail between two castles. These might appear on a single punch, or the ship on one punch might be accompanied by one or two punch marks of the castle. The variety of design indicates that each silversmith was responsible for striking the town mark upon his own plate. Cork silver from 1710 was marked STERLING, sometimes STARLING or STIRLING in Roman capitals. The word DOLLAR was struck upon some Cork silver, indication that the metal was Spanish coinage melted down.

The word STERLING was also struck upon silver made at Galway between 1650 and 1730, the town mark being an anchor. Silversmiths also worked at Limerick, Youghal, Kinsale and other places, but examples of such silver are extremely rare.

While faking of old silver is comparatively rare, it is obviously wise for the tyro collector to learn all he can of the styles and their periods in silver design, and of indications of genuine hand-work in Georgian pieces. Signs of wear can all too easily be added to silver plate and an air of genuineness imparted by the skilful insertion of a small piece of silver bearing perfectly genuine hall-marks of an early date. This may have been taken from an unimportant little silver object, in order to give a much larger new piece a false semblance of antiquity. The edges of the insertion may often be detected with the aid of a glass, however; sulphur fumes will probably expose it, and a blow pipe certainly do so. An article such as a tea-pot may be given a foot-rim complete with a series of hall-marks taken from the stem of a spoon. Not only is the rim the wrong place for the marks, however, but the marks themselves were generally placed to be read with the spoon held vertically, so that the tea-pot has to be held sideways in order to read them—an obvious indication of a fake.

Another fraud to put the collector on his guard is the conversion of a hall-marked piece of genuine but low-priced silver into an expensive article without disturbing the original hall-mark. Many a christening mug, for instance, has received a second handle and become a valuable sugar-basin.

3

POMANDERS AND VINAIGRETTES

FOR many centuries aromatic perfumes were considered essential to the art of gracious living. An important office in any wealthy household was that of the perfumer, employed to keep the rooms sweet-smelling, and, it was hoped, free of disease, in days of perfunctory sanitation.

Shakespeare in *Henry IV* refers to "the perfum'd chambers of the great" and in *Much Ado About Nothing* Borachio refers to himself as "being entertained for a perfumer, as I was smoking a musty room". Every room of consequence in a well-appointed house had its silver or latten perfuming pan (Fig. 17) containing pungent aromatic herbs and spices. Boorde, in his *Dyetary* published 1542, prescribed "a little of some perfume to stand in the middle of the chamber", and in 1564 Bulleyn advised his readers to "Forgette not sweete perfumes of Rose water, cloves, maces, and vinegar in a perfuming pan".

Fig. 17

There were various ways of achieving the required degree of fragrance. The pan, or metal bowl, of pot-pourri was perhaps most widespread, supplemented by the use of elaborately and colourfully embroidered "sweet bags". In his library alone, in 1614, the Earl of Northampton had fourteen of these perfumed bags. More efficacious was the carrying of smouldering herbs from room to room. This led to the practice of burning specially manufactured pastilles in appropriate decorative containers, as continued to be done uninterruptedly until the 1860s. Kenelm Digby, writing in 1644, exclaimed: "Perfumes fill the ayre! We can putt our nose in no part of the roome, when a perfume is burned, but we shall smell it."

There was, too, a passing Carolean vogue for perfuming rooms with liquid scent. These strong-smelling essences might be distributed about the house in shallow circular pans of silver. Such a pan would measure only 1¼ inches in diameter and ¼ inch in depth, being supported upon three tiny ball feet. Its vertical sides were plain and the scent was covered with a finely pierced lid.

Perfume pans and sweet bags freshened the apartments of the well-to-do, but even in mediaeval days the fastidious felt the need of something more personal with which to combat the unappetising odours and lurking pestilence encountered in streets and public buildings. At first, strongly aromatic substances were merely shaped into small balls that could be carried in hand or pocket. Soon, however, for greater convenience, they were encased in small boxes of gold, silver or ivory, such as could be suspended by a chain from the neck or girdle.

Perfumed balls and musk balls are frequently mentioned in inventories from the fourteenth century, when Margaret de Bohun, Countess of Hereford, possessed "a ball of perfume carried in a silver container", enriched with precious stones and pearls. The inventory of Henry V's possessions made after his death in 1422 included several musk balls of gold and silver gilt. The Bury will of 1463 refers to "my musk ball of gold".

Already perfume balls were termed pomanders in France, for in 1411 the Duc de Beri received a new year present of "a beautiful pomander with musk, opening down the middle into two sections and closing with hinges, and hanging on a little chain". The earliest use of the word pomander noticed in England appears in the Privy Purse Expenses of Henry VII for 1492: "To one that brought the King a box with pomandre, ten shillings." As applied to the box containing the perfume ball the word has not been observed in records dating earlier than 1518, when Princess Mary gave a gratuity "to the French queen's servant that brought a pomander of gold". The application of the word to the contents rather than the case itself is found as late as 1683 when the *London Gazette* referred to "a little gold box with a sweet pomander in it".

Henry VIII in 1530 possessed sixteen pomanders, including one inscribed H & K, and another enamelled with ostrich feathers and red roses. The inventory of Mary Tudor mentions "two long girdles of goldsmith's work with pomanders at the end". She also owned a "pomander of golde with a dial in yt". Lady Margaret Long, Countess of Bath, in 1548 wore "a girdle of crown gold set with a great pearl and a pomander". Such a pomander is shown on the portrait of Lady Jane Grey painted shortly before her death in 1554.

Pomanders were more widely popular in Elizabethan days. The subjects of a number of contemporary portraits wear jewelled pomanders hanging by chains from their girdles. In Hereford Cathedral is the alabaster effigy of Anne, wife of Alexander Denton, who died in 1566. She is shown clasping a flat circular pomander patterned with a rosette.

The word pomander is derived from the old French *pomme d'embre*, first mentioned in *Roman à la Rose* dated 1280, and meaning apple or ball of amber, the term *embre* being used for perfume in general. In sixteenth and seventeenth century England it was spelled pomemounder, pomeamber, pommandre, pomannder and other variants. The sweet-scented amber apple or perfume ball contained ambergris, a waxy substance from the spermaceti whale, which when warmed by the heat of the hand softens slightly and emits a fragrant perfume. It is found floating on the surface of the sea in regions frequented by whales. At first the amber apple was a ball of ambergris; more pungent perfume balls were evolved first by the addition of musk, then by blending ambergris with a compound of musk, lavender, nutmeg, mace, and cloves pounded with rose water. In less expensive perfume balls the ambergris was replaced with wax.

Such richly fragrant balls challenged the jewellers and metal workers of their day to devise suitable cases. Exquisitely wrought of gold and silver, and richly jewelled or enamelled, such a case would be worn on a fine chain either round the neck or suspended from the girdle, or attached to the finger by a ring as shown on a portrait of an old man painted in about 1510 by Conrad Faber.

As fashionable articles of jewellery these cases underwent considerable changes in design. At first the usual shape consisted of a spherical open-work frame hinged so as to open across the centre vertically or horizontally for the insertion of the perfume ball. Such a case might be of thinly beaten gold set with jewels, or of delicate filigree work. A ring was fixed at one end for attachment to chain or girdle. The portrait of Nicholas de Stabbourg and his wife painted by Ratgeb in 1504 shows an open-work pomander pendant of gold filigree. By the early sixteenth century the pomander had become a perforated sphere seldom more than one inch in diameter but cut with decorative piercing and enriched with precious stones.

This style continued fashionable until the mid-sixteenth century. A cheaper container for the little apple of scented ambergris was hollowed out of hard wood, decorated with carving and fitted with a wooden lid and a silver rim. The design appears to have lingered on long after the general fashion had passed. Remaining specimens may be dated to as late as the early seventeenth century both by hall-marks and by the style of their simple carvings which might include a rhyming posy or a moral precept.

Meanwhile, even in Tudor days, the pomander experienced competition in high places from the aromatic orange. This, carried in the hand, was believed to be a safeguard against pestilence, more pungent and therefore more efficient than the ball of ambergris. The pulp of the orange was removed and replaced by "a small sponge soaked in vinegar and other confections". Cardinal Wolsey made a practice of carrying such an orange "which he most commonly smelt into when passing among the press".

Aromatic vinegar of the Tudor period was made from the fresh tops of wormwood, rosemary, sage, mint, rue, with lavender flowers and smaller amounts of garlic, calamus, cinnamon, cloves, and nutmegs. These were steeped in vinegar for a fortnight. The liquid was then filtered and added to camphor mixed with brandy or other alcohol.

So great became the belief in aromatic oranges that the spherical jewelled pomander with its solid ball of perfume gave place in the mid-sixteenth century to the jewelled pouncet-box. This was but the jeweller's more decorative alternative to the orange-skin, designed for the same purpose of holding a tiny piece of sponge damped with the popular vinegar. The usual design consisted of a shallow circular box of gold or silver with an elaborately-perforated, highly-domed lid.

Men in high positions had for long carried gold-mounted ebony sticks, as visible symbols of their authority. From about 1530 goldsmiths decorated the heads of these staves with golden pouncet-boxes, finely pierced and fitted with richly wrought ferrules. One of the Hans Holbein portraits of Henry VIII shows the king grasping an ebony staff terminating in a magnificent gold pouncet-box, and the same artist's portrait of the nine-year-old Edward VI illustrates a smaller version. That this was also a feminine fashion is demonstrated by the portrait, painted in about 1540, of Jane Heckington, wife of the Master of the Robes to Henry VIII, who is depicted holding a staff crowned with a richly-worked pouncet-box of gold. A portrait of Sir Nicholas Bacon dated 1579 shows a less elaborate example in gold.

Pouncet-boxes for the pocket or attached to black string were carried by men until after 1610, the practice of inhaling the piquant odour from the box being brought to a fine art. Shakespeare noticed this trait in the contemporary fop and refers to it in King Henry IV part I (1596):

> He was perfumed like a milliner;
> And betwixt his finger and his thumb he held
> A pouncet-box, which ever and anon
> He gave his nose, and took't away again.

Sticks of ebony or malacca terminating in capacious pouncet-boxes which contained sponges of highly-pungent aromatic vinegar were carried by doctors, clergymen and others likely to visit disease-ridden areas in the course of their work. Some examples bear London hall-marks for as late as the 1740s.

Aromatic vinegar made from the Tudor formula proved too potent a perfume for the feminine nose. Early in the reign of Queen Elizabeth pouncet-box and aromatic orange were replaced by the jewelled or enamelled pomander box containing dry perfume in powder form. Such boxes, fashioned as pendants and girdle ornaments, find frequent mention in inventories as pomanders and are illustrated in many paintings. At first the box contained only a single mixture of gums and spices blended by the perfumer or apothecary. By about 1580 the box might be divided into a series of compartments each containing a distinct perfume. Men were not averse to wearing jewelled pomanders. The inventory of the Earl of Northampton taken after his death in 1614, lists "a pomander George with three pendent rubies", and this specimen is shown in a portrait by an unknown painter made soon after 1605.

Early in the seventeenth century pomanders again reverted to the spherical shape. The most fashionable of these opened into several segments, each resembling the section of an orange and containing a different, finely ground perfume or spice (Fig. 18). Such a pomander consisted of a central pillar, hollow and either square or hexagonal, topped with a screw cap and based on a domed foot. Hinged to the base of the pillar so as to open outwards from it were the six or eight segment-shaped perfume compartments, known as loculi, pierced to allow the aromas to escape and fitted with sliding covers which might be incised with the names of the various perfumes they contained, such as lavender, cloves, juniper, myrrh, musk, cinnamon, aniseed. These covers were equipped with tiny knob handles which fitted neatly into corresponding hollows in the central pillar when the pomander segments were closed around the pillar. They then formed a sphere, held in position by the screw cap, which had a loop terminal for carrying. Even the domed

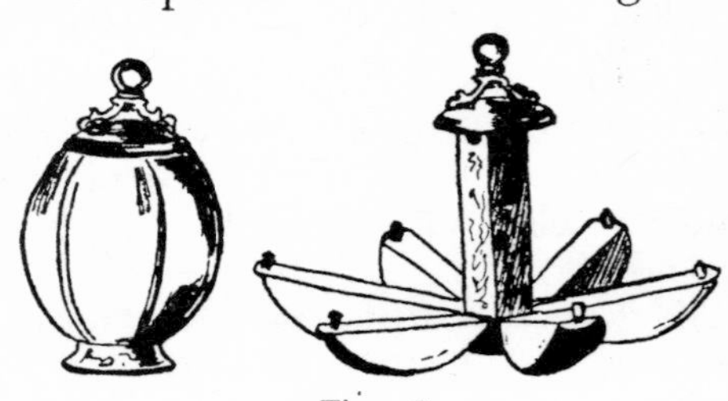

Fig. 18

foot was of service in this design, being based with a perforated plate so that it could contain a sponge of aromatic vinegar.

The decoration engraved on the outer surface of such a pomander was often repeated on the sides of the segments and on the central pillar. More often, however, the interior was plain. Cap and foot might be silver gilt. Pomanders of the seventeenth century varied from $\frac{3}{4}$-inch to two inches in diameter, and silver examples included not only the sphere or apple-shape but also a pear-shape, similarly opening out into segments when these were released from the screw cap at the top.

Fig. 19

At the same time other pomanders were being made in silver in totally different designs, but all with the basic idea of containing a series of sweet perfumes in powder form. These included: the book (Fig. 19); the dice, each of its six sides consisting of a sliding lid to a separate tiny compartment; the skull, opening vertically to reveal several compartments—from two to six or more—when a pin was removed from the cranium; the urn, unscrewing into two or three pieces, the upper cavity invariably intended for musk; or the woman's head and neck, with a vertical central division down the line of the nose and chin and hinged at the base of the neck so that the two halves opened out flat to give access to a series of small compartments or cells of perfume.

Seventeenth century pomanders of all types have been reproduced; those noted have lacked hall-marks and any screws used have shown the British Association thread of Victorian origin.

The pomanders so far described have been elegant trifles for the well-to-do. But even by Tudor days there was a demand for more purely utilitarian and less expensive little perfume balls, to be worn rather than carried and therefore not requiring handsome pomander cases. By the end of

Henry VIII's reign perfumers were threading small balls of pomander paste into necklaces and bracelets. Apothecaries sold such bracelets "made of the elixir" and the *Book of Simples* published in 1562 advocated such "pomanders to be worne against foule stynkyge aire".

A recipe for "Rich Pomander Braseletts" instructed the perfumer to "take two ounces of benjamin [benzoin] and an ounce of storax and beat them very fine in a mortar. Then take twenty grains of ambergris and ten grains of musk and grind them very fine upon a stone. Mix this with the benjamin and storax, and a little gum dragon steeped in orange-flower water until a paste. Then roll in the hands for half an hour; make into beads, run a needle and thread through them, and dry in the sun."

The historian Howes, writing in 1580, records that Queen Elizabeth was "mightily pleased with a fair necklace of pomander which was a series of pomanders strung together and worn around the neck". Fashionable men and women were at this time wearing pomander necklaces concealed beneath their expansive ruffs. Herrick (1591-1674), the son and nephew of jewellers, in *The Pomander Bracelet* confirms that men wore these circlets of perfumed beads:

> To me my Julia lately sent
> A Bracelet richly Redolent:
> The beads I kiss'd, but most lov'd her
> That did perfume the pomander.

Such beads might now be home-made, the basis being "the purest garden mould, cleansed and steeped for seven days in rosewater", to which were added ambergris, musk, benzoin, and other aromatic substances.

An altogether more ambitious concoction which purported to be both pomander and medicament was the goa stone, bringing with it the fascination of eastern lore and remaining in vogue for a century from about 1665. Invented by Gaspar Antonio, a Florentine lay-brother of the Order of Paulistines, who settled in Goa, Portuguese East Indies, goa stones were productive of an annual income of more than 50,000 xerephins by 1698.

Goa stones were composed chiefly of jewel stones—the

Boat-shaped pierced inkstand with cylindrical sockets for silver-mounted cut-glass bottles; London 1780.

Ornate silver-gilt standish by Benjamin Smith, London 1808.

Circular ink-box, the sides chased with oak foliage, and the cover decorated with the figure of Paris from the Strathmore vase. Fitted with silver-mounted ink-pots and quill-holders, the intervening space filled with loose shot; by John Bridge, London 1825.

Standish with elaborately moulded rim and feet. The cut-glass containers, (*left to right*) are shot-holder, wafer-box, its lid consisting of taperstick and extinguisher, and ink-pot. By John Angell, London 1823.

Globe inkstand seen closed and open; London 1788.

chippings, faulty stones and tiny blind pearls for which the jeweller would have no more decorative use but which, none the less, retained the fascination associated with all precious jewels. The formula for their manufacture was: oriental bezoar, white coral, red coral, 2 oz each; hyacinth, topaz, sapphire, ruby, pearls, 1 oz each; emeralds ½ oz; musk and ambergris, ½ oz each; gold leaf as required. The stones were ground to a powder, and mixed with the other ingredients. Rose water was then added, and the resulting paste rolled into balls and dried. These stones were fitted by London goldsmiths into spherical containers of delicately wrought gold, sometimes jewelled. So powerful was the perfume that existing specimens more than 250 years old emit a strong scent of musk and ambergris.

As well as being carried as a protection against disease, goa stones were used as a medicine, a small quantity of dust being scraped from the ball and taken in wine. This supposedly relieved fevers and was an antidote for all poisons, including the bites of mad dogs and venomous serpents. Brooke, writing in 1757, records that he greatly relieved his fevers "by drinking punch into which Goa stone had been plentifully grated".

The popularity of goa stones discouraged the carrying of pomanders which they tended to replace. The sponge-box remained, however. At first this was in the shape of a small vase of gold or silver containing a piece of fine sponge soaked in aromatic vinegar, a tiny loculus beneath the foot containing musk. Sponge-boxes in numerous attractive shapes, resembling contemporary snuff-boxes, were fashionable until about 1780, in gold, silver, painted enamel, porcelain, and gilded pinchbeck. Many were provided with lidded bases for holding musk. Goldsmiths' trade cards of the mid-eighteenth century make frequent mention of "sponge-boxes and smelling-bottles".

The discovery of a more concentrated aromatic vinegar having strong acetic acid as its basis and containing chiefly oils of lavender, cinnamon, cloves and camphor, led to a reduction in the size of sponge-boxes from about 1780. At first known as aromatic vinegar boxes, they were named vinaigrettes from about 1800. These small creations of the silversmith's art were made in vast numbers. Although various designs for smelling-bottles shared their popularity, they continued in fashion until about 1850. The quality of the aromatic vinegar was lasting, for an occasional box is still found containing the original sponge, from which there is an odour, faint and delicate, but unmistakable even after the chances and changes of more than a century.

Vinegar boxes of the early 1780s resembled miniature sponge-boxes. Then a new box container was evolved by the Birmingham silversmiths: a small shallow rectangular box was fitted with a finely-pierced inner lid enclosed by an outer lid, both swinging from a single hinge on the box. When required for use the outer lid was opened and the aromatic perfume inhaled through the grid. These early boxes were solid and heavy in comparison with the later feather-weight variety, and the cases but sparsely decorated with engraving. The inner lid was pierced with circular holes instead of being fretted with elaborate open-work tracery which is one of the charms of the vinaigrette.

By about 1785 vinaigrettes had become quite small, the largest not exceeding 1½ inches in length and 1 inch in width. Some nineteenth century examples are so small that they can be hidden beneath a shilling. Inner lids were now delicately and elaborately pierced and chased in open-work designs of flowers and foliage, birds, scrolls, leaping fish, bowls of fruits (Fig. 20). After 1840 grids were less costly in workmanship, simple patterns of drilled holes being usual. Sometimes such grids are found as replacements in earlier boxes.

Fig. 20

Vinaigrette exteriors were exquisitely engraved and chased, sometimes with the addition of applied decoration. The lid design might incorporate a shield or scroll upon which the owner's coat of arms, monogram, or name could be inscribed.

From about 1830 there was a vogue for decorating vinaigrette lids with engraved or heavily embossed pictures of well-known abbeys, castles, and country seats, such as St. Paul's Cathedral, Windsor Castle, Warwick Castle,

Newstead Abbey. Eventually the embossing became so exaggerated that parts of the picture projected a quarter of an inch above the lid. Some examples were made with open-work lids of elaborate design and without inner grids. Such lids lifted off without hinges. These vinaigrettes were probably used for some scent less volatile than the usual aromatic vinegar. They were made by Thomas Spicer and Nathaniel Mills.

Shapes and designs were numerous: round, oval, rectangular, hexagonal, octagonal. Examples with curved outlines usually bear hall-marks dating them after 1840. The more fanciful designs included representations of hearts, books, purses, escallop shells, travelling-chests, watches. The vinaigrette in the form of a fish with a jointed, flexible body and the sponge receptacle in its head, was made by Lea and Company of Birmingham from about 1815 (Fig. 21).

Fig. 21

More costly and infrequent were vinaigrettes of fine quality gold, hall-marked earlier than about 1820. In *The Early Married Life of Lady Stanley*, reference is made in a letter dated 1801 to "an elegant gold aromatic box" presented by the Duchess of York to Hannah More. Silver vinaigrettes might be gilded, and very frequently grids and interiors were so treated.

Men carried vinaigrettes in their waistcoat pockets, and women in their purses, until the accession of William IV. It then became fashionable to dangle the little article, a man carrying it suspended from the fob and a woman wearing it on a long chain. The vinaigrette might now be fitted with a small swivel ring, or a fine chain attached to the sides.

Hall-marks appear on English silver vinaigrettes, nine out of ten bearing the anchor of Birmingham (Fig. 13, page 31). So carefully were the hall-marks applied that, small as they are, they are still easy to decipher, thus revealing the maker's name and date of manufacture. A full set of marks is normally found on the bottom of the box or around the lip, the standard mark and the maker's mark on the underside of the lid. The grid may be stamped with the standard or the maker's mark, rarely both.

Vinaigrettes were a Birmingham speciality and the makers' marks indicate that Thomas Wilmore, Samuel Pemberton, Nathaniel Mills, John Shaw, Cocks and Bettridge, and Joseph Taylor were prolific in their output. Gervase Wheeler was responsible for vinaigrettes resembling books, and Wardell and Kempson appear to have been the first to make vinaigrettes fitted with loops.

In addition to gold and silver, vinaigrettes of the later period were made of more colourful but less costly materials. From about 1825 the lid might consist of step-cut panels of agate, lapis lazuli, cornelian, or mother-of-pearl, and later the base of the box itself might consist of a matching stone. Uttoxeter paste—a pale blue opalescent "stone"—was sometimes used. A tiny horn mounted in silver with a cairngorm set in the lid in the manner of the Scottish snuff-mull, but with a pierced grid, was a product of the 1820's. From about 1835 large numbers of vinaigrettes were made of gilded pinchbeck, frequently copying designs formerly made in silver.

After the Great Exhibition of 1851 the vinaigrette was displaced by the colourful glass smelling bottle divided centrally into two sections, one to contain one of the numerous newly-invented "artificial essences" or perfumes, the other for aromatic smelling-salts.

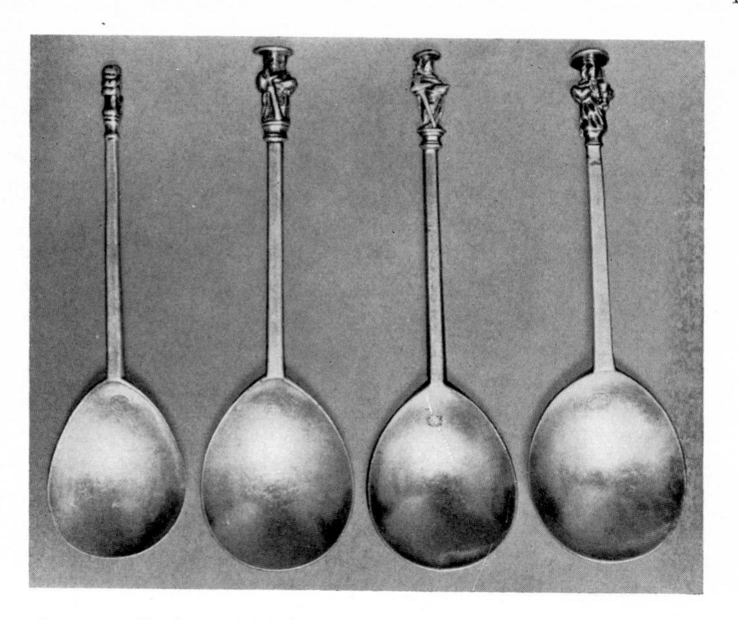

Spoons. (*Left to right*) lion sejant guardant knop by Elston, Exeter 1580; St. Matthew with an axe, Taunton 1660; St. Philip, London 1622; St. John, Exeter 1660.

(*Left to right*) writhen knop, London 1500; lion sejant guardant, by William Bartlett, Exeter 1600; stump top with faceted and tapering stem, maker's mark D enclosing C, London 1635; seal knop, by James Plummer, York, 1615.

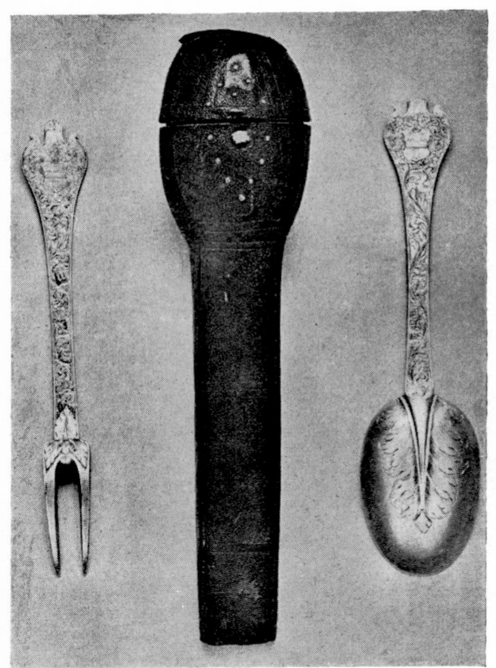

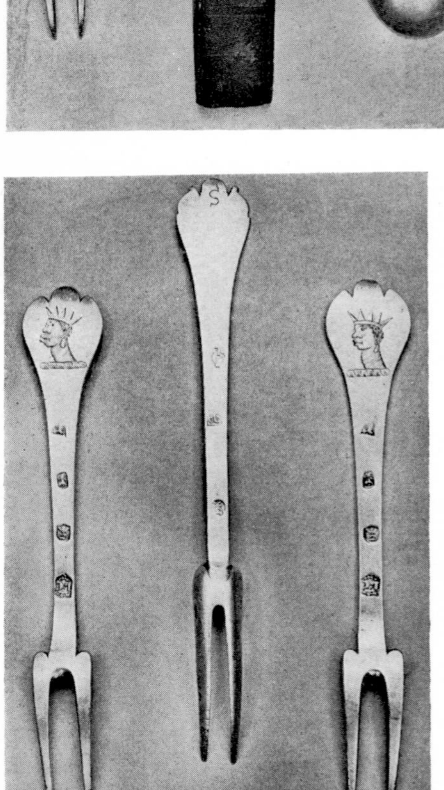

(*Top left*) two-pronged trifid fork with rat-tail trifid spoon engraved *en suite*, in leather case; London 1689.

(*Bottom left*) William III two-pronged trifid forks: the crested pair are by Lawrence Coles, London; centre by David King, Dublin 1699.

(*Above*) four-pronged flat-stemmed fork by John Brooke, London 1698; two-pronged forks, London 1691 and 1707

4

CANDLESTICKS AND TAPERSTICKS

THE rival guilds of tallow-chandlers and wax-chandlers played an important part in the provision of domestic lighting during past centuries. The kitchen of the great house melted down the tallow from each ox and sheep, forming it into huge cakes for conversion into candles by the chandler during his annual visit. But only from the days of George I did candles light the house of even the more prosperous wage-earner: previously open-flame lamps and rush-lights had sufficed.

Silver candlesticks passed through various stages of evolution before reaching eighteenth century perfection. First came the simple pricket with its vicious-looking conical spike which would support any size of candle, contrasting with the more gracious design inspired by the Orient and beloved of Venice, resembling a low bowl with a shaped base turned upside down to support a tubular candleholder. Bringing renewed emphasis to the vertical line came the pillar type that eventually acquired maturity and balance of design with the shapely curves of the baluster, supreme during the early Georgian period.

The frequent references to silver candlesticks in early inventories of household plate indicate that by the fourteenth century they were customary in the homes of the wealthy. No typical examples appear to remain which may be dated earlier than the seventeenth century, however, and few pre-Restoration pieces are known. The state lottery advertisement of 1567 illustrates among the prizes a pair of silver candlesticks with solid sockets, short stems, wide grease pans and spreading bases. This is the earliest instance of socket candlesticks yet noted in domestic silver. Pricket candlesticks continued to be made in silver for a further three-quarters of a century, examples being known bearing hall-marks of the 1640s. Late Elizabethan and James I pictures illustrate socket candlesticks with bases resembling spool-shaped salts of the period.

Fig. 22

The so-called wire candlestick belongs to the first quarter of the seventeenth century (Fig. 22). The heavy moulded and reeded socket was supported by a short baluster above a wide drip pan. But the unusual feature was the lower half of the design. The base consisted of a triangle of wire, each angle supported by a domed foot—an inverted, small version of the socket—and from these, curving inwards to the centre, were three more wires which there bent sharply upwards, together forming the candlestick's stem. More typical was the simple silver candlestick associated with Charles I's reign. This had a small moulded socket and a plain cylindrical stem above the broad drip pan, and below it a plain spool rising from a trumpet-shaped base.

The sumptuous silver designs adopted in England after the restoration of the monarchy in 1660 included more ambitious candlesticks with stems hammered from sheet silver. This was an architecturally-minded age and in early work the stem consisted of a cluster of vertical columns arranged to form a square (Plate 3). These were hammered separately, joined by soldering, and decorated with chasing. A moulded socket fitted down inside the top of the stem so that only the narrow horizontal lip was visible, decorated with further chasing. Instead of a drip pan, a square embossed shelf low on the stem served as a base for the pillar but was of decorative value only, separating the pillar from the flanges of cut-card work that linked the stem with the flat spreading, square foot.

The stem of the fashionable candlestick during the last

quarter of the seventeenth century even more closely resembled an architectural column, decorated with shallow vertical fluting and reeding (Plate 3). A plain abacus at the top separated the stem from a fixed socket inside the column and rising slightly above it, and another, below the column, separated it from the flat spreading square or octagonal base. At first the column was hammered and the base moulded. Towards 1700 the fluted column was cast, and gadrooning was introduced to correlate the spreading rim of the socket, the lower abacus and the flat octagonal foot. Already the fluted column was becoming proportionately shorter and less important as the other features of the design were amplified. In particular a new emphasis was given to the spool-shaped segment joining stem and base which was now chased, the design including a cartouche engraved with the owner's coat of arms. Pillar candlesticks were made throughout the reign of Queen Anne.

Meanwhile, however, the period's love of S-scrolls found expression in the candlestick assembled from castings of these recurving voluted scrolls arranged in a vertical group rising from a base in the shape of four escallop shells. Sturdier, if less ambitious, designs were produced with baluster stems. These appeared in silver towards the end of Charles II's reign, solidly constructed replicas of those found on contemporary standing cups or tall-boys. The dominant central motif was usually more or less acorn-shaped and was of somewhat larger diameter than the swellings above and below (Plate 3). Those above consisted of the socket's moulded rim and rounded shoulder, while below there was a secondary knop, of the same diameter as these, surmounting the uninterrupted outward curve of the base junction. This flowed smoothly into a shallow circular depression in the spreading octagonal base and it was upon this depression that a coat of arms was engraved. At first such engraving was the only ornament on the cast baluster-stemmed candlestick, a form which continued until the end of the century.

By 1690, however, with the baluster as with the pillar candlestick, designers were realising the twinkling charm of candlelight on the patterned surface of gadrooning. At first this simple decoration encircled the socket rim and shoulder, the cup of the acorn, the knop below, and the rim of the octagonal foot which was now deeper than formerly. By 1695 the socket might be vase-shaped and gadrooning might encircle the lower tip of the acorn which might now receive added ornament in the form of three applied lion masks and paws. This gadrooned baluster style continued until about 1700.

The New Silver Standard Act which operated from 1697 to 1720 required silversmiths to use a quality of metal which proved particularly suitable for casting. Queen Anne and early Georgian candlesticks were almost invariably cast in moulds and not hammered out of the metal, as may be seen by the rough unfinished surfaces beneath. It has been suggested that the quality of the metal deterred designers from continuing the sharply moulded gadrooning which would be susceptible to wear, but it is more probable that the general fashion of the period for smooth-faced furniture prompted a return to candlestick designs emphasising grace of outline rather than surface ornament. Just as ornate furniture carving gave place to flat veneers, so gadrooning and applied ornament were replaced by shapely baluster silhouettes.

By 1700 the candlestick with eight-sided stem and socket was well established, harmonising with the many-sided table and chair legs of the period (Plate 4). This had a simple, slender-waisted baluster stem supporting a waisted socket and rising from a shallow circular depression in an octagonal base. Within ten years the octagonal foot had become a high dome rising from a moulded rim and might be engraved with a coat of arms (Fig. 23). The junction of base and stem became more deeply incurved from about 1710 and the facet surfaces of the base were given more clearly defined edges. The vase-shaped socket might be encircled with sixteen counter-ranged triangular facets which would be repeated on the dome of the base. Every possible use was now made of the reflecting surfaces by faceting. In

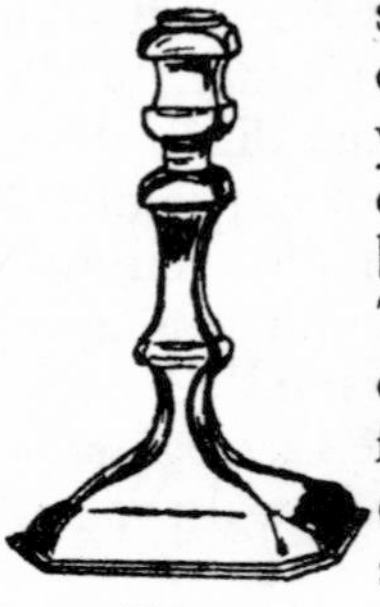

Fig. 23

some George I candlesticks the baluster was square on plan, but with the angles of the stem faceted and the corners clipped on the square base, which might retain the earlier central depression.

The plain octagonal candlestick continued throughout the George I period, the knop between the baluster-shoulder and the foot sometimes being reduced to a narrow collar. In some instances the base was square with the corners set back and rounded, a shape found in contemporary woodwork.

A spreading nozzle to catch the drips of hot wax was rarely fitted to a Georgian candlestick until after 1735. When fitted the nozzle had a wide upcurving rim frequently of similar outline to the base. During the 1730s and 1740s, the shoulder of the baluster was extended into mushroom form and widely fluted. The socket was encircled by one or two centrally-placed ribs and fitted with a loose nozzle. The base was a flattened dome with shaped sides.

Fig. 24

Meanwhile, by the 1720s more ornate styles were also coming into vogue (Fig. 24). The silver showed to great advantage when cast into the sharply defined features then appearing in domestic ornament—the masks, shells, and other vividly naturalistic motifs which in silver design led swiftly on to the full exuberance of the rococo. Heavier than formerly, these candlesticks still retained the basic baluster form and the octagonal foot.

By 1730 such candlesticks were being loaded with ornament. The baluster shoulder might be almost concealed by such motifs as applied masks moulded in full relief, and the lower portion embellished with birds, reptiles, monsters, flaming torches, fruits, foliage, and other finely cast and chased motifs. The socket was elaborately moulded to harmonise.

The candlestick stem in the form of a human figure or demi-figure with arm upraised to support a candle socket resting on its head was a feature of the period, a

Fig. 25

revival of a graceful style introduced from the Continent during the reign of William and Mary (Fig. 25).

The main movement of the 1730s, however, was towards the more fantastic style of form as well as decoration associated with the term rococo then being introduced from France. The more extravagant candlestick designs consisted of restless, meaningless elaborations of scrolls and shells. Simpler designs were chased with the supreme skill of the period's master silversmiths in asymmetrical cartouches, C-scrolls and floral patterns, and such work continued into the 1760s after the more florid shapes had been abandoned.

The plain baluster continued to be produced throughout this period. From the mid-century there was a return to such contemporary furniture motifs as acanthus leaves and gadrooning. The shoulder of the baluster might be decorated thus, and the square foot might have rim ornament to match. By 1760 the stem rose from a swirling dome resting on the upper platform of a two-stepped or three-stepped square foot (Fig. 26). The baluster might be fluted and the shoulder moulded with leaves or other motifs. The vase-shaped socket was fitted with a loose, wide-spreading nozzle. The stem rose from a high incurved dome base of scalloped outline, often striated, matching decoration on the nozzle rim. The sparsely ornamented baluster persisted until after 1770, sometimes with shell ornament decorating a circular base. The inverted baluster is found from about 1710, but is rare.

Fig. 26

By the 1760s the renewal of interest in ancient Grecian and Roman ornament was beginning to find expression in England, sponsored by such leaders as Robert Adam and his brothers. The dignity of the new outlines, emphatically vertical and unencumbered by heavy ornament, well suited candlestick design. Even those makers who continued the traditional baluster shapes seldom failed to introduce some trace of the fashionable low-relief ornament from the limited range of accepted classical motifs.

The so-called Corinthian column dominated candlestick design for a period from about 1760, complete with capital and base, and with a socket inside its capital containing a loose nozzle. Such columns might be fluted or wreathed (Plate 5). The four curved sides of the high base were usually decorated with floral swags in low relief. These candlesticks might be cast until about 1770 when, less expensively, they were made from sheet silver, stamped in parts, joined with solder, and finished with chaser and graver. At first such factory-made candlesticks were weighted with pitch, but later examples of still thinner metal contained lead in base and lower stem.

Neo-classic designs varied in form and treatment. The slender four-sided pedestal tapering towards the foot and bearing a Grecian urn as a candle-socket was the fashionable type of the 1770s (Plate 5). Masks and rams' heads, festoons of flowers or drapery, and every sort of classic motif found a place on such candlesticks, which were mounted on square bases, with triangles and circles as occasional alternatives. The popular stem-shape of the 1780s was circular, tapering towards the circular base and fluted. A parallel change of taste is to be noted in the trend from thermed to turned legs in furniture.

The late eighteenth century styles extended well into the following century. Critics often carp at the poor character of the designs then current, other than the replicas of earlier pieces. By the time of the Regency, candlesticks of finely chased rococo design were again fashionable. It was the florid extravagance of such work that caused rococo to be regarded as synonymous with bad taste.

Silver candlesticks varied from about six inches in height in the days of Charles II to more than a foot during the

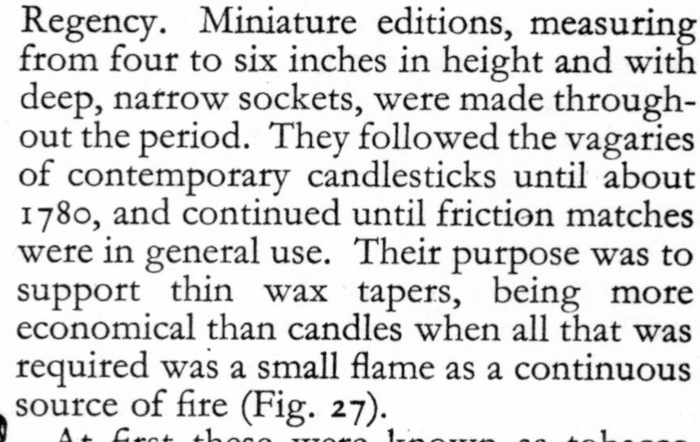

Fig. 27

Regency. Miniature editions, measuring from four to six inches in height and with deep, narrow sockets, were made throughout the period. They followed the vagaries of contemporary candlesticks until about 1780, and continued until friction matches were in general use. Their purpose was to support thin wax tapers, being more economical than candles when all that was required was a small flame as a continuous source of fire (Fig. 27).

At first these were known as tobacco candlesticks and were used by smokers as pipe lighters. Specially refined wax candles costing half a crown each were sold for lighting tobacco in the pipe. This was a custom reserved only for the wealthy, less pretentious people making use of small charcoal braziers placed upon the table. By 1740 tobacco candlesticks were known as tea-candlesticks or tapersticks, being used on tea-table, side-table, and gilt stands placed about the room.

Candles were a considerable item in the expenditure of the more pretentious Georgian household. There might be as many as five hundred wax candles burning for my lady's Assembly, and a few hundred more if my lord invited a dozen friends for faro.

Fig. 28

Branch candlesticks or candelabra of silver were made throughout the Georgian period, but few are known with hall-marks struck earlier than 1730 (Fig. 28 shows an early seventeenth century example). The early eighteenth century style consisted of a stem matching an accompanying set of candlesticks and terminating in a high moulded finial which supported three or four curved branches (Plate 6). Between each candle-socket and branch was fitted an expansive circular drip pan. The branches were removable, enabling the stem

Silver gilt trifid folding spoon and four-pronged fork with engraved stems, William and Mary period.

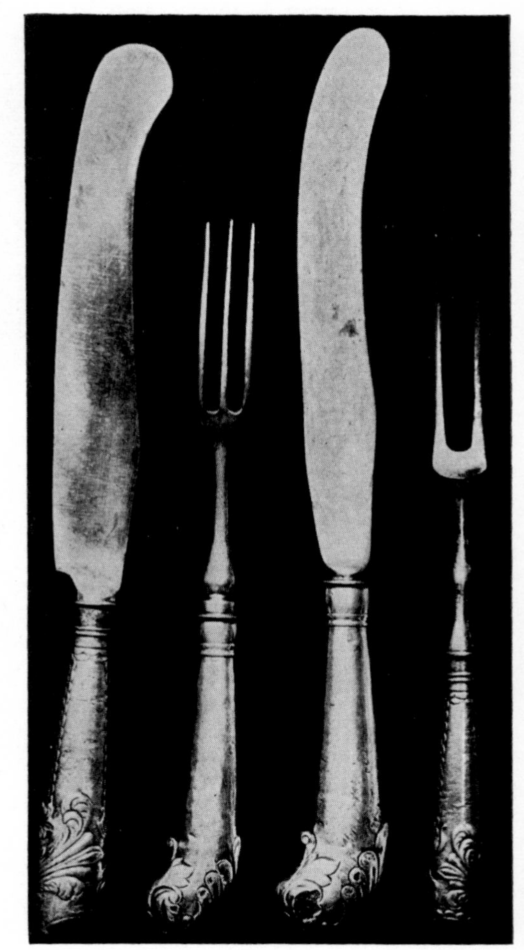

Table knives and forks with matching hafts of stamped silver: (*centre*) pistol-butt hafts; (*left and right*) tapering cylinder hafts. Second quarter of the eighteenth century.

Queen Elizabeth's great salt, surmounted by a knight in armour. The salt-container is a shallow basin fitting into the upper part of the body. The body is enriched with three medallions in low repousse and fine chased work. The three cast feet are in the form of sphinxes' heads with forepaws. The four scrolls supporting the lid are in the form of dolphins with ornamental tails. These are later additions.

Silver-gilt bell salt in three tiers, the top forming a pepper-caster. Engraved with strap-work and floral ornament in outline on matted ground. London hall-mark for 1599.

Standing salt wi steeple cover, t cylindrical body stan ing on three half-b feet held by bir claws; maker's mark branch, London 162

to be used as a candlestick. Twin branches were usual, however, and these might twist around a central finial which now consisted of a candle-socket fitted with an elaborately moulded removable cover. When the decorative cover was removed, three lights could be used. Candlelabra stems and bases repeated candlestick modes of the period. Some George II candlesticks were fitted with three-light branches during later periods. So important a section of the trade was the manufacture of candelabra during the reign of George III that some silversmiths appear to have made little else. Factory examples lack the individualistic beauty of design associated with those from the workshops of master silversmiths (Fig. 29).

Fig. 29

Sconces or wall lights of silver decorated the homes of nobles and merchant princes from the days of Henry VIII. The majority of existing examples, naturally scarce, bear hall-marks of the second-half of the seventeenth century (Fig. 30). The usual style was composed of a thin silver wall plate in the form of a cartouche, lavishly embossed with cherubs, flowers and other motifs of the period, encircling a central reflecting surface sometimes plain but more usually engraved with the owner's coat of arms. One or two moulded branches, each terminating in a drip pan and candle socket, curved gracefully from the lower surface. When mirror glass became available its reflective brilliance at once brought it into use in association with candle sconces, and few sconces wholly of silver may be dated later than the end of the seventeenth century. Mirror glass sconces fitted with silver branches were advertised consistently during the reigns of Queen Anne and George I.

Fig. 30

The hall-marks on an early silver candlestick are usually found on the underside of the base, and the practice of placing them there continued with those made in cast metal at a later period. On the factory-made example in stamped silver the marks were usually struck on the outer edge of the base.

5

SNUFFERS AND THEIR DISHES

THE true charm of candlelight, a steady, unflickering flame, fumeless and odourless, was unknown until early in Queen Victoria's reign when an obscure Lancashire weaver devised the non-guttering candlewick. In the course of burning, the wax or tallow of a candle tends to melt more rapidly than it can be consumed by the wick. The invention caused the wick to burn uniformly short. Smaller and more closely woven than earlier wicks, it included a tight strand woven down one side which curled the charred end of the wick towards the outside of the flame where combustion was most rapid.

Throughout all the previous centuries of candle-burning the thick, loosely-plaited wicks had required constant attention to keep the flame bright and steady. Otherwise, the long, grease-soaked wick would curl over until its hot charred end dipped into the gutter of melted wax on the candle top, causing the flame to flare and reduce the light. This gave rise to the saying "there's a thief in the candle". To avoid this "guttering" the snuff was from time to time removed.

Trimming was done with a "very useful domestick machine" called at first a snuffer, then snuffers, and finally a pair of snuffers. This scissor-like instrument, carrying a small box upon its under-blade, was used for snuffing, that is, cutting off and carrying away the charred end or "snuff" of the wick.

Snuffing was an art. If done properly the candle burned economically and with maximum brilliance; if accomplished awkwardly clothing or furniture might be marred with a greasy streak. Quarles cautioned his readers in 1638 that "too much snuffing makes a wast," and in 1667 Heywood noted that "if you snuffe too deepe, out goes the light."

In large establishments, religious and secular, the candle room, or "chaundlerye", was in the charge of an official who, according to *Household Ordinances*, "setteth nyghtly, after the seasons of the yere, torchys, tortays, candylles of wax, and mortars." The chandler employed one or more servants to patrol the premises snuffing candles and replacing those burnt out. In 1450 Aungier was engaged at Syon solely "to lyghte and quench the tapers and candles and snuffe them".

In the homes of gentry, tradesmen, clergy, farmers, and so on, snuffing was delegated to one of the several servants. Satirically, Dean Swift, in his advice to servants, suggested that they should "snuff the candles at supper as they stand on the table, which is much the surest way, because if the burning snuff falls from the snuffer, you may have a chance that it may fall into a dish of soup, sack posset, rice, milk, or the like, when it will immediately be extinguished with very little stink".

Boyer in his *Dictionary Royal*, 1722, defines a "snuffer" as "he that snuffs the candles at the Playhouse". In 1814 W. Wilson noted that "Betty Gray had been a snuffer of candles at the playhouse". Tavern drawers combined the duties of barman and snuffer and were distinguished by candle-snuffers hanging from the girdle, as seen in Hogarth's painting "Night".

One of the earliest English records of snuffers is found in *The Boke of Curtasye* of 1460, which describes snuffers as "sesours schort and round with a plate upon". Mann's *Housekeeping Expenses* five years later records that "my master bowt a snoffer to snoffe candels with." Previously, in medieval days, the instrument had been known as candleshears, and consisted of a pair of plain scissors with the lower blade flattened and dished to receive the smouldering snuff. Such shears, made in iron, continued in farmhouse use until the end of the seventeenth century: in 1611 a dozen pairs cost thirty shillings. No examples appear to remain in either gold or silver.

Octagonal trencher salt with sloping sides and flat rim surrounding the central depression, London 1635.

Circular trencher salt, sides moulded with ovolos and domed foot enriched with knurled chasing; by Anthony Nelme, London 1697.

Circular trencher salt with highly convex body encircled with strengthening rib; by William Fleming, London 1705.

Octagonal trencher salt with plain incurved sides and oval central depression; by Arthur Dicken, London 1720.

Octagonal trencher salt with incurved sides and oval central depression; London 1726.

Oval trencher salt with plain incurved sides and circular central depression; by Charles Martin, London 1729.

(*Left*) spool trencher salt with gadrooned rim and foot and its body encircled with punched decoration; London 1725. (*Right*) salt-cellar with hemispherical bowl and moulded decoration in the form of mermaids and festoons; London 1745.

(*Above left*) stemmed salt-cellar with hemispherical bowl and reeded lip and round spreading foot; 1800. (*Above, right*) salt-cellar with lion mask feet and festoons of flowers and foliage; by Edward Wakelin, London 1741. (*Below left*) pierced salt with blue-glass liner by R. & D. Hennell, London 1775. (*Below right*) Regency salt-cellar with four moulded feet and applied rim, with salt-spoon; London 1816.

Snuffers fitted with wick-containers were being used in England by the mid-fifteenth century, and were developed in gold, silver, brass, and iron. To each blade was attached a semi-heart-shaped box, the complete heart being formed when the sharp blade closed upon the charred wick. This left the snuff loose and smouldering in the box.

The earliest remaining examples of snuffers in England are those made for Cardinal Bainbridge in 1512 and now in the British Museum. These are of silver gilt, the upper surface of each box being enriched with coloured enamels depicting the arms of Henry VIII, and those of Bainbridge surmounted by a cardinal's hat. The boldly-curved handles, tapering and bevelled-edged, are bent into external loop scrolls, each terminating in a sitting squirrel motif, one of the charges in the cardinal's arms. Christopher Bainbridge became Archbishop of York in 1508 and was created a cardinal in 1511, receiving his cardinal's hat during the following year. These snuffers may have been a gift from the king on that occasion. The cardinal was poisoned two years later by his secretary.

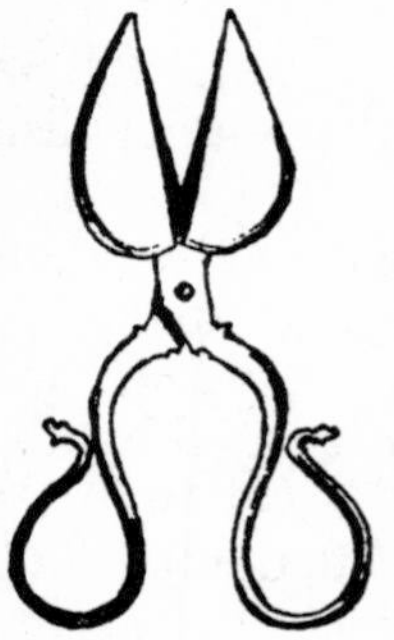

Fig. 31

Throughout the sixteenth century basic construction of gold and silver snuffers remained unaltered (Fig. 31), although handles had become straight by the mid-century, and terminated in circular bows. One of the blades was extended into a spike projecting beyond the pan. Its purpose was for lifting the thief from the melting wax before snuffing. By 1600 the spike had become more extended and flattened, being known as a save-all; in the eighteenth century it was termed a prick-wick.

The pans were extravagantly large during this period to accommodate the thick wicks then in use. These provided surfaces for that elaborate embellishment which craftsmen in metal loved to lavish upon their ware. They might be enriched with deep chased coats of arms or with classic themes, such as the Loves of the Gods, the Labours of Hercules, Medusa's Head, and various myths immortalized by Homer and Virgil.

By about 1600 the airy double pan had been superseded by a single open-sided semi-circular box attached vertically to the under blade. To the upper blade was fixed a flat press-plate fitting snugly into the box. When the snuff was cut from the wick the plate forced it against the inner wall of the box where it was immediately extinguished. The desire for elaborate decoration continued until Cromwellian days.

Silver snuffers from these early days are rare. Comparatively few people could afford them in precious metals fashionably engraved with coats of arms to serve the double purpose of ornament and of identification if stolen.

After the Restoration, silver snuffers became more numerous, with straight, flat, smoothly-plain stems connected to the bows with S-shaped scrolls, and a smaller box, now rectangular, with incurved corners. They were usually equipped with a rectangular dish upon which they lay when not in use. Every woman of fashion displayed a pair of silver candlesticks, snuffers and a snuff-dish upon the table in her bedroom. Pepys in 1667 wrote in his *Diary* that "this night comes home my new silver snuff dish, which I do give myself for my closet." This indicates that silver snuffers and dishes were not necessarily sold *en suite*, although in 1686 the *London Gazette* referred to "a Silver Snuffer-dish and Snuffers chain'd".

The Charles II snuffer dish was usually shallow, flat-bottomed, and rectangular. The rim was décorated with narrow applied moulding or beading, and the vessel was raised upon four scrolled feet. A pierced or bossed handle curved laterally from one of the long sides. By about 1675 a broad moulded rim was usual and the nearly flat, horizontal handle might be pear-shaped, and ornamented with beading or, rather later, might be fitted with a finger ring beneath. Most examples were engraved with coats of arms.

Noteworthy among the trays of this period was the design shaped to follow the silhouette of the snuffers themselves, with a vertical rim. This was raised upon three ball feet and attached to the wider end was a projecting handle in the form of a serrated leaf with a finger-ring beneath it.

The upright snuffer stand, with a vertical socket to receive the snuffer box, was a late Charles II innovation (Plate 7).

The socket was supported by a short baluster stem and a low, broad hexagonal or octagonal base, usually moulded and with gadrooned edging, matching candlesticks of the period. A large scroll handle was attached to a narrow face of the socket, and one of the wider faces was generally equipped with a narrow vertical loop to receive the hook of a cone-shaped extinguisher: the other face might be engraved with a coat of arms. To the remaining narrow face might be soldered an attachment into which fitted a candle socket with a wide drip pan (Plate 7). At first the socket rim was finished merely with narrow beading; from 1690 large gadrooning was usual, matching similar decoration on stems and feet. The shanks of snuffers fitted into these stands tended to be shorter than on snuffers intended to lie on flat dishes, and from 1690 fashionable examples were scrolled.

Snuffers and stands in this style remained in vogue until about 1725. Georgian versions were supported on high hexagonal moulded feet. Sometimes a cast motif decorated the narrow face opposite the handle.

While snuffer-stands were in fashion, the simple snuffer dish continued plain and unoriginal in style. Then, early in the reign of George II, this flat dish was in turn elaborated by the silversmiths. It offered more scope than the upright stand for the rococo ornament coming into fashion, and in consequence rose once more into fashion. The long sides were incurved and the ends might be slightly raised; everted rims were enriched with finely-chased cast rococo work; a scroll handle replaced the plate-and-ring pattern; and from about 1740 four moulded scroll feet were usual.

Snuffers themselves remained plain. The normal box shape continued to be rectangular but other forms became frequent—oval, semi-circular, lozenge and barrel-shaped—and might be fluted and engraved. Until about 1750 the underside of a pair of silver snuffers was flat, like scissors. Then three short feet were provided, one beneath each handle bow and one beneath the box, raising the instrument slightly above the tray surface, making it easier to pick up (Fig. 32).

Fig. 32

An immense amount of ingenuity now began to be lavished upon the ornamentation of snuffer handles, every conceivable device being exploited to enrich handles and bows. Nevertheless, as working instruments, snuffers continued to suffer from the one great defect that the charred end fell from the container as the blades were reopened. After each candle was snuffed the container had to be emptied: as early as 1574 Fellowes noted "a bason of pure gold wherein they bestow the Snuffings" and in the eighteenth century this was still a necessity. Some assistance in conveying the snuff to the receptacle was provided by a patent device of 1749 introduced by Benjamin Cartwright of the Strand, London. This was a spring that controlled the movement of the blades and obviated unintentional opening which might scatter the charred waxy wick. As the patentee explained, it was "contrived for preventing danger by fire as they, by only opening them, cut off the snuff of the candle and retain it so close that it can neither set fire to anything by its scattering: also, by means of these secret springs, immediately discharge themselves without trouble or soiling the fingers".

The pivoting joint of the snuffers was covered by a boss concealing a coiled spring so arranged that it closed, and kept closed, the snuffers after use. These bosses became a field for finely designed and exquisitely worked rosette ornament. The value of Cartwright's invention was quickly realised by silversmiths, for few snuffers bearing hall-marks later than 1755 fail to incorporate the spring. Apart from this development, little change took place in silver snuffer design until about 1810. Mechanical devices to permit the snuffing of several candles without interruption were apparently too elaborate to be successful. Among these was one patented by Christopher Pinchbeck in 1776 in which an automatic slide "securely locked up the discarded wick and put out the spark in a recess beneath the box."

A notable development in the decorative role of the snuffer, indicating the ever-widening market for ornamental but less costly specimens, was the introduction of snuffers in which the cutting blades and box were of burnished or damascened steel while the handles, bows and prick-wick were of silver. The box might be decorated with one or more applied silver mounts. These, made in two qualities, light and heavy, were all of delicate workmanship. Quantities of these mounts and handles were devised and made by Matthew Boulton. The firm of Harwoods, also of Birmingham, were early nineteenth century specialists in such snuffer units, which were finished and assembled by silversmiths. Considerable numbers were made to accompany Sheffield plate snuffer dishes.

Sir Edward Thomason, a Birmingham silversmith, recorded in 1810 that in many instances the steel box and press-plate of such snuffers were close-plated, the whole instrument then resembling silver. This would appear to be only an aid for selling to the uninformed, for close-plating, if held for more than a moment in a flame, quickly loses its silver coating.

Snuffer dish design in the early George III period resembled that of the more important trays and waiters. Rim-beading was a characteristic feature, the gadroon and scroll patterns being especially common. Applied decoration such as rams' heads and garlands, pierced work and chasing, were all used. Snuffer dishes, their upright rims of pierced open-work, and finished with handles and feet, were made by R. Morton and Company from 1775 and copied by others. The elongated oval or canoe-shaped snuffer dish with scroll-ends was a rare design made from about 1785, but snuffer dishes were now made in a tremendous variety of styles in both silver and Sheffield plate. The pattern books of Watson and Bradbury illustrated 165 such designs between 1788 and 1815. In about 1800 appeared the four-lobed snuffer dish made to accommodate a pair of extinguishers in addition to the snuffers.

Fig. 33

A new variety of chamber candlestick appeared late in George I's reign (Fig. 33). This had a slot to hold a pair of snuffers beneath the low sockets rising from the centre of a circular or oblong dish. It was usually accompanied by a cone extinguisher having a ball on its apex.

The prevailing heavy style of ornament appeared on snuffers and their dishes in about 1810. The dishes became larger and for the next twenty-five years tended to be overladen with florid mounts elaborately chased, shellwork and foliage being especially favoured. The silver snuffers themselves had their boxes and wide handles chased in high relief designs of shells and flowers.

Douters or out-quenchers constituted yet another adjunct to candle burning, used to prevent smoke or fumes when the light was extinguished (Fig. 34). There is an early reference to them in Wyclif's Bible of 1382 (Exodus 25) where mention is made of "candle-quenchers whereby the snoffes ben quenched".

Fig. 34

Early specimens were made *en suite* with snuffers. In 1535 Coverdale noted "snuffers and out-quenchers of pure gold". These douters bore a basic resemblance to snuffers but in place of the box and press-plate the arms of the scissors terminated in flat discs between which the wick might be nipped. Douters are rare, and throughout the period followed the fashion in snuffer decoration. Some later snuffers served also as douters, discs being fitted on extensions from box and press plate. A writer in 1645 bitterly complained that douters "extinguished the light with an ill-favoured stench".

6

STANDISHES AND INKSTANDS

A LEATHER-BOUND compendium of practical information "made easy" was published in the 1740s with the title *The Young Man's Companion*. Under the heading "Materials for Writing" this contained the following verse:

> A Pen-Knife Razor-metal, Quills good store;
> Gum-Sandrick Powder to Pounce Paper o'er;
> Ink shining black, Paper more white than snow,
> Round and square Rulers on yourself bestow;
> Small compasses to rule your Double Lines,
> Wax, Sand and Black-lead Pens for your Designs:
> These with a willing Mind and ready Hand,
> Will make this Art your Servant at Command.

The list speaks for itself. Black-lead pens were pencils, their points being of lead in fact as well as name. The verse follows a paragraph of directions for taking "the first, second or third Quill in the Wing of a Goose or Raven" and forming it into a pen by pointing and slitting the lower end of the barrel into two nibs. Nor has the form of pen made to those directions been improved upon. Another page contains a recipe for making ink of oak galls, very little if at all different from that found in the excavated ruins of Pompeii. But about the containers for these tools there is, unfortunately, nothing.

Until the mid-sixteenth century it was not considered dignified for a noble or moneyed aristocrat to pen his own letters. This work was delegated to resident scriveners who kept their writing accessories in pewter or brass receptacles known as standishes. Even when writing became one of the polite arts essential in the education of a gentleman, there was work in plenty for the itinerant scrivener who travelled the country with a case containing quills, ink-horn, sand-box and knife swinging from his girdle. Until as late as 1895 a rent collector in Wolverhampton was to be seen going on his rounds with a goose quill stuck in his hat, and an ink-horn slung by a cord from his button-hole.

With the elevation of the art of writing came a corresponding rise in the status of the standish among a gentleman's personal effects and its appearance in silver. As early as 1474 Swayne mentions "j quartari paupiri & j standisshe viijd". The inventory of Henry VIII's plate, taken in 1520, records a "standysshe with a lyon thereuppon", possibly reference to a hall-mark on silver plate. The standish of this period consisted of a plain square or oblong tray standing flat upon the table and containing "ink-horn, pens, penknife, pin dust and sealing wax". Later four ball feet might be soldered beneath the corners to raise the tray from the table. This type of standish continued into the seventeenth century, when it was termed an ink-holder.

Fig. 35

The Elizabethan standish was more elaborate, the various containers being fitted upon a silver plate which might be rectangular or circular. (Fig. 35 shows a type depicted in a painting of the Elizabethan Court of Ward's and Liveries.) During the first half of the seventeenth century such standishes might be constructed with scalloped or leaf-shaped plates. The accounts of the Earl of Northampton in 1614 refer to a "standish of silver made scalloppwise, with a little inkhorne, sold unto Mr. Binge at v^{s} the ounce conteyning 33 ounces". The only silver standish to survive the vicissitudes of the Civil War is hall-marked 1630. This is shown in Fig. 36. Upon the tray stands an ink-pot, a sand dredger and a small container for the recently introduced sealing wafers.

Fig. 36

Fifty years later Hulme defined the Charles II standish as "a place for ink, sand box, taperstick, and a long box in which to lay wax, pens and knife; all fixt together, yet all but a standish". The sand-box, necessarily movable, fitted into a socket on the tray.

Another type of contemporary standish comprised an oblong box with a hinged lid concealing ink-pot, sand-dredger and wafer-box, a drawer underneath holding quills and other accessories. Late in the seventeenth century appeared the double-lidded box. In this, a pair of flaps operated from a single central hinge down the length of the box which was divided into four compartments, three small rectangular ones at the front for receiving ink-pot, sand-dredger and wafer-box, and a long narrow one behind in which to lay the quills. Such inkstands in silver continued throughout the Georgian era until the time of William IV.

Near the end of the seventeenth century, too, appeared what has come to be regarded as the standard silver standish and was an elaboration of its original form. With minor variations, this continued throughout the eighteenth century. It consisted of an oblong tray raised on four simple bullet feet and used as a platform for the appropriate receptacles to contain ink and pounce, flanking either a bell or a shot container for cleaning pen nibs.

By the beginning of the eighteenth century the typical standish tray, known at the time as a plate, would carry ink-pot and pounce-box fitting into a pair of sockets either depressed below the platform surface or raised by low moulding.

The ink-pots which stood in the early square standish were plainly cylindrical and seldom provided with covers. Interiors were lined with closely fitting horn containers for the thick ink of domestic manufacture, for which the ingredients were supplied by the apothecary. Not until the 1680s was it possible to buy ready-prepared ink powders which were mixed with beer.

By about 1600 the silver ink-pot was fitted with a concave cover centrally pierced with a hole large enough for easy dipping. The mouth and base were encircled with simple moulding matching that strengthened the rim of the tray itself. This was the conventional design until about 1700 when smooth-faced hexagonal ink-pots were fashionable, the lower moulding being twice the width of the upper, which matched that bordering the tray.

The early Georgian ink-pot usually resembled a wide, squat baluster. It fitted into a depression in the tray platform, the base was free of moulding and the upper rim might be gadrooned. This was the standard shape for standish ink-pots throughout the period. From about 1760 urn-shaped ink-pots on short stems with circular feet had a short vogue, the bodies of some examples being fluted.

Following the invention of tough flint-glass in 1676, liners of blown glass were fitted into silver ink-pots in place of horn. But almost a century elapsed before silver-mounted cut-glass bottles began to be used on inkstands. At first these were cylindrical with bodies ground in wide vertical flutes and facet-cut shoulders (Fig. 37). By 1780 shoulders were encircled with deep diamond cutting. Square glass bottles with flat shoulders, used to a lesser extent during this period, became fashionable from about 1790, their faces decorated with shallow diamond cutting. By 1810 they were usually decorated with all-over diamond cutting in deep relief. A series of cut-glass ink-pots from 1820 were urn-shaped with short stems and circular feet.

Fig. 37

The pounce-dredger on a standish always matched its accompanying ink-pot. At first the concave lid was pierced by plainly drilled holes arranged in concentric circles; by 1700 these might be encircled with decorated saw-cut perforations; by 1725 the circular holes had been replaced by saw-cut crosses; from about 1765 curved saw-cut perforations arranged in balanced, all-over designs were fashionable.

So closely did the pounce-box and ink-pot resemble each other that accidents were frequent. Beresford, writing on "The Miseries of Human Life" in 1806, complained of the frequency with which "the ink glass is emptied (by mistake for the sand glass) on a paper which you have written out fairly." He was but repeating Howell's annoyance when, in 1640, he had poured the "ink box" over his writing in mistake for the "sand box".

The terms "pounce-box" and "sand-box" have been used so often interchangeably that it may be well to differentiate between them. Doctor Johnson defines pounce as "the Powder of Gum Sandarach, so called because it is thrown upon paper through a perforated box." According to the 1728 edition of *Chambers's Cyclopaedia* this gum, a finely pulverised resin from the arar-tree of north-west Africa, was sprinkled over writing paper "to make it less apt to imbibe the ink, the writing thus appearing more precise, sharp and determinated". It was usual to prepare parchment for writing by rubbing its oily surface with pounce, and this was equally necessary with some poor quality writing paper. In any case the unglazed paper required pouncing after a mistake had been erased. It must be emphasised that pounce was not intended to dry wet ink. If an error were made in writing, this was erased with a penknife. To write again over the roughened surface it was necessary to "pounce it o'er with sand"—sand being the shortened term for gum sandarac. The powder was then rubbed in with a dog's tooth or an agate to prevent the ink from running. Surplus pounce was poured back into the concave lid of the box by funnelling the paper.

Writing paper until the nineteenth century soaked up the ink so that there was no need to dry the newly written sheet. When glazed writing-paper became general, early in the nineteenth century, the ink was dried by casting white sand over the sheet, but this was superseded some twenty years later by commercially developed blotting-paper. In 1519 Horman recorded that "Blottynge papyr serveth to drye weete wryttynge lest there be made blottis or blurris." Shop inventories of the Elizabethan period indicate blotting paper to have been a usual article of merchandise.

Parchment required different treatment. Its surface was roughened for writing by rubbing with a pad of gum sandarac to prevent the ink from spreading. Wet ink was dried by sprinkling it with fine white sand known as "writing dust".

Such sand was not included in standish equipment which was intended primarily for use with writing paper. There is no association between the "sand" sprinkled on writing paper and the "writing dust" on parchment. When glazed writing paper became generally used, commercial houses continued the tradition of drying wet ink with sand, a process noted in use at the Wolverhampton office of the L.M.S. Railway as late as 1925.

With the advent of glazed note-paper on a commercial scale, the pounce-box became non-essential to the standish. Lamb, writing in 1820 of "South Sea House", remarked that "pounce boxes have gone retrograde". It was replaced on the standish by a wafer-box formerly often the centre-piece to the tray. This might be surmounted by a miniature chamber candlestick or taperstick complete with handle and extinguisher and fitted with a sealing-taper.

The wafer-box was designed *en suite* with ink-pot and pounce-box. The earliest wafer known is fixed to a letter dated 1624. In 1635 Charles I issued a licence for the monopoly of making wafer seals to sell at one hundred for a penny. Such wafers were small adhesive discs, about the size of a shilling, made of flour mixed with gum or gelatine and dyed, usually Chinese red, with non-poisonous colouring matter. Black wafers were applied on occasions of mourning. Envelopes were seldom used, the correspondent taking pride in the skill with which he folded the letter so that no scrap of writing was visible and there would be difficulty in opening and refolding the sheet without detection. This was then sealed with a moistened wafer.

In some circles it was considered vulgar to send a letter sealed with a wafer moistened with the tongue. In Maria Edgworth's *Patronage*, written about 1810, an incident is recorded in which a cabinet minister has sent a letter sealed with a wafer to a duke, upon which "the Duke's face flushed violently, and he flung the note to his secretary, exclaiming, 'Open that if you please sir—I wonder how any man can have the impertinence to send me his spittle'." Sam Weller, on the other hand, made a point of swallowing the wafer which his lady's lips had touched in sealing.

It appears that the majority of later standishes possessed

wafer-receptacles. Sometimes the wafers were kept in the hollow depression of the tray with the pins. There were, of course, separate wafer-boxes just as there were separate ink-pots, quill-holders and so on. These turn up in any material from the agate ware of Whieldon and the colourful enamels of South Staffordshire to silver and the finest porcelain and glass. When the stamped and gummed envelope became general soon after the establishment of the penny post in 1840, the wafer-box became a receptacle for stamps.

Wafers were not proof against the inquisitive. In 1728 Fielding wrote "'Tis but wafer-sealed—I'll open it and read it." Communications of importance were fastened with melted wax upon which was impressed the mark of a personal seal. It was for this reason that standish equipment might include a taperstick in which was fitted a special taper intended for melting the wax.

The well equipped silver standish included a quill-cleaner containing small lead shot by which accumulations of ink sediment might be removed from the nib—a frequent necessity. Ink until the mid-nineteenth century was a thick liquid containing a considerable amount of gum arabic. The early quill-cleaner or shot container was a plain, heavy-based, open-topped cylinder, and this remained a usual form until the early Georgian period. From about 1730 the fashionable quill-cleaner was a short, wide-footed urn with a spreading lip gadrooned to match similar decoration around the lower body.

Before the middle of the eighteenth century the quill-cleaner also performed the duty of quill-holder and was made to match the accompanying ink-pot and pounce-box. The shot was concealed beneath a cover matching that of the ink-pot but pierced with three, four, or five holes. In some instances quill-cleaner and ink-pot were combined in a single receptacle, the ink contained in a glass liner surrounded by shot. In such instances the large central hole in the lid was accompanied by three perforations for quills.

The fashionable silver standish during the reigns of the first two Georges carried ink-pot, pounce-box, and a small hand-bell with a baluster handle. The mouths of early bells were encircled with plain cushion moulding and by 1750 might be more spreading, with gadrooning to match the bases of ink-pot and pounce-box. The bell shoulder might also be decorated with wide concave flutes. In place of the solid silver handle there might be a taper socket. Either the bell or the quill-cleaner might also serve as the cover of a wafer-box sunk into the platform of the standish tray.

The tray of the typical silver standish at the beginning of the eighteenth century was straight-edged, plainly and deeply dished with a simple bullet foot at each corner and no rim decoration. By the second quarter of the century the tray was becoming shallower and its ends might be bowed. Simple reeded rims and plain cushion rims were general. This was the conventional standish tray until about 1745 when elaborate rococo rims became fashionable and feet often resembled those of contemporary furniture, scrolls and volutes being popular. Simple versions of this form continued until about 1760, the most notable variation consisting of a pear-shaped handle extending laterally from one of the long sides. From about 1750 it was usual for the standish tray to be provided with a dished channel running the full length at front or rear, or both. In this trough was placed the penknife, usually with a carved ivory handle, its blade enclosed within a sheath to match. This was used for making and mending the quill pens.

Standish trays from about the 1760s might be fitted with applied pierced sockets to hold silver-mounted cut-glass bottles for ink, pounce, and shot. These became known as inkstands, a term always used at Soho by Matthew Boulton to distinguish such pieces from the old-style standish. The strengthening moulding around the socket rims matched that around the stand to which the sockets were soldered. The four-bottle inkstand made its appearance at this time, but the three-bottle form continued in greater demand. The development of large-scale factory production in the later eighteenth century brought inkstands, like other silver ware, into the homes of a far greater public than had been wont to use silver before. As regards inkstands a contributory factor in cutting the costs of material and labour was the use of bottles made of flint-glass. Factory-made inkstands, always inclined to be flimsy, were now turned out by the gross.

During the 1770s the inkstand might be bordered with a pierced gallery, its design matching that of the bottle sockets. The new style also departed from the conventional rectangle: oval and boat-shaped examples were frequent, sometimes fitted with swing handles. In some of these the border piercing was made low and the sockets three to four times taller than usual. During the 1790s sockets might be unpierced, their reeded rims matching the strengthening moulding that encircled the stand itself. For half a century from about 1770 a series of inexpensive inkstands were issued, built almost entirely from silver wire in varying sections.

The flimsy factory-made inkstand of Birmingham and Sheffield prompted master silversmiths to make standishes of high craftsmanship in a bewildering array of fanciful designs. From about 1820 such standishes tended to be flamboyant. Wide-moulded rims around top and base of the tray were typical, together with plain, highly raised sockets for silver-mounted bottles of cut-glass. Feet were of the lion's paw variety.

Ornate silver-gilt ambassadors' ink-stands were produced during the reigns of George IV and William IV and were widely copied in finely finished bronze and, less expensively, in brass. The standish tray now became the top of a box-structure containing a deep drawer and raised from the desk by four elaborately-moulded feet. Pounce-box, pen-holder and wafer-box were discarded in favour of a pair of handsome covered ink-pots, the central position being occupied by a group of statuary or model of a celebrity.

7

SPOONS

AMONG the most ancient of English crafts was that of the spoon-maker or spooner, working in wood, horn or metal. Spoons of precious metals were wrought by goldsmiths and silversmiths for ecclesiastical purposes, but not until the thirteenth century were silver spoons introduced as articles of domestic table ware. The silver spooner became well established during the following century, but so precious were his products considered by their owners that finely-tooled leather cases were made for them. Silver spoons in their leather cases receive frequent mention in wills of the period.

Until the mid-seventeenth century the silver spoon consisted of a bowl and stem hammered from a single piece of metal and a decorative knop of cast silver soldered into a V-shaped notch in the stem end. The knop was often gilt. The early spoon averaged three-quarters to one and a half ounces in weight, but its length seldom varied more than between six and seven inches. (Fig. 38 shows the various stages in spoon development.)

At first the bowl was shallow and fig-shaped, wide near the rounded end and tapering to merge into the stem. Such a spoon was designed to lift food from a trencher plate rather than to scoop up liquids. Soft foods were termed spoon-meat until the Cromwellian period: as late as in 1639, O. Wood was advising his readers to "Eate neither Milke, Broathe nor spoone meate." Designs better suited for liquids developed early in the seventeenth century, when the bowl tended to be shorter, wider and deeper. By the middle of the century this oval outline was replaced by a

Casters. (*Left*) cylindrical body with vertical sides and cover hammered into alternate convex and concave folds; London 1683. (*Centre*) cylindrical, with domed cover pierced and engraved, by Richard Biggs, London 1701. (*Right*) with pyriform body; by John Sutton, London 1707.

(*Left*) octagonal baluster body, shoulders decorated with cut-card work, cover pierced and engraved; Edinburgh 1703. (*Centre*) octagonal pyriform body, with cover pierced with scroll work; by Edward Vincent, London 1716. (*Right*) with baluster body and dome pierced in vertical panels; by Augustin Courtauld, London 1726.

(*Above*) London made casters. (*Back row*) one by John Deacon, 1764, and one of a pair with octagonal bodies by Edward Jones, 1717. (*Front row*) two of the mid-eighteenth century, by John Deacon, 1764, and Samuel Woods, 1745, and one of a pair with vase-shaped bodies, by William Bateman, 1808.

(*Left*) spice-dredger with octagonal body sloping inward from the base, and expansive foot-ring; the domed cover pierced with formal decorations. By Glover Johnson, London 1718.

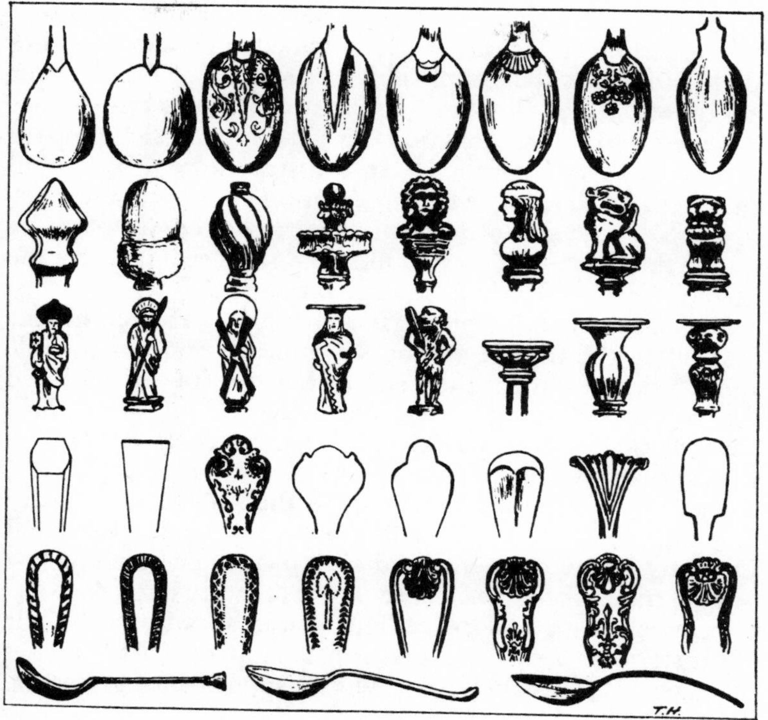

Fig. 38

SPOON DEVELOPMENTS

Top row: bowl shapes showing the plain outlines of fourteenth to sixteenth centuries; late seventeenth century hammered ornament; cast eighteenth century rat-tail; leaf and shell drops of the 1740s-1750s; drop with cast ornament; fiddle shoulders.

Second row: early knop finials—diamond, acorn, writhen, Gothic, two versions of the maidenhead, two versions of the lion sejant.

Third row: other pre-1660 knops—four apostle designs (St. Peter, St. Thomas, St. Andrew, St. Simon Zelotes), the woodwose, and three seals (one of the sixteenth century and two of the early seventeenth century.)

Fourth row: the change to flattened ends—sixteenth century slipped end; mid-seventeenth century Puritan; two post-1660 trifids; wavy end, c.1690; Hanoverian, early eighteenth century; Onslow, mid-eighteenth century; fiddle, later eighteenth century.

Fifth row: later eighteenth century styles—two feathered ends; two bright-cut; thread and shell; king's pattern; queen's pattern; husk.

Bottom row; spoon silhouettes—pre-1660; 1660-1770; post-1750.

true ellipse, the curve no longer related to the stem junction.

The earliest stem was diamond-shaped in section, tapering slightly towards the knop. This was succeeded by a slender hexagonal stem, still tapering towards the knop but slightly flattened at the bowl junction. From about 1550 the upper and lower surfaces of the hexagonal stem were broader and flatter than the sides, which thereupon suggested faceting. In the late sixteenth century these narrower edges might be rounded, until the stem became oblong in section. By the time of Charles II it had become broad and flat.

The knop finials which gave character to silver spoons until after the middle of the seventeenth century include about a dozen standard patterns. Hall-marking has enabled the collector to place these chronologically. Additional ornamental knops were taken from family crests or designed to customers' orders. These are of particular interest to the collector. Typical are the owls on the spoons of Edward Waring, The Lee, Wolverhampton, who formerly lived at Owlbury and who mentioned eleven of them in his will—one of the authors was present when the twelfth was discovered beneath a floor at The Lee in about 1912. The Vintners' Company possessed some knopped with bunches of grapes: in 1545 they sold "vj gylt spones with grapys on the knoppys, weyng ix oz."

One of the earliest spoon knops was the diamond point—a simple pyramid—examples of which are struck with hall-marks dating late into the Henry VIII period. The acorn knop, seldom made after the fifteenth century, is usually found in association with a small bowl. Acorn spoons were mentioned in a will made in 1348 and proved at the Court of Hustings three years later: "John de Holegh bequeathed to Thomas Taillour twelve silver spoons with acorns". Again, in a will of 1361, John Botillir, draper, bequeathed to Isabella, his wife, twelve best spoons with gilt acorns. Such designs as the acorn and contemporary fir-cone prompted more formal patterns. Among these may be mentioned the writhen knop dating from about 1480 to 1550. This consisted of a ball marked with spiral twistings, sometimes elongated and varying in pattern.

While a silver spoon was recognised as a particularly

personal possession—often the only ornamental valuable a man would own, and the recognized gift at a christening—it was to be expected that the decoration would often assume a human form associated with the saints whose stories were woven into the people's everyday lives. These spoons became numerous in the sixteenth century but occasional specimens and references in wills indicate an earlier origin. Perhaps the earliest was the design termed the maidenhead, known in the late fourteenth century and specifically associated with the Virgin Mary as early as the mid-fifteenth century. In early specimens the head forming the knop might wear the horned headdress fashionable in the first half of the fifteenth century. Anne of Bohemia, wife of Richard II, had introduced to England that strange head attire of gold and silver lace draped over a framework of wire in a two-horned outline some six inches above the wearer's head. Various other styles of coiffure followed on maidenhead spoons, the most usual design showing the coiffure and dress of the Tudor period and based on a fleur-de-lis. Obviously many a minor spoon-maker ignored the original intention of the design and also the contemporary term maidenhead, for the elaborately braided hair found on some specimens is a coiffure which the custom of the period restricted to married women. Maidenhead spoons are frequently mentioned in wills and inventories of the yeomanry during the Elizabethan period. For example in 1580 Thomas Middleton of Sherworth in Cumberland bequeathed "half a dosen of spones with the maden heades". In 1548 the Vintners' Company made a record of a dozen spoons with "maydyn heyds on the knoppys, gylt, weying xiij oz.," priced at four shillings and fourpence the ounce.

Only a little later came the apostle spoons, familiar objects in wills and inventories throughout the fifteenth and sixteenth centuries and appearing occasionally still earlier. Typically, the knop consisted of a representation of one of the Apostles, standing on an architectural moulding with a large-rayed nimbus surrounding his head and appropriate emblems, frequently the instruments of his martyrdom, in his hands. Apostle spoons were sold singly, and in sets of thirteen including the master-spoon bearing the figure of Christ in majesty, holding the orb and cross, and raising the right hand in blessing. The bowl of this spoon might be engraved with the sacred monogram in gothic characters.

The usual attributes of the Apostles on spoon finials are: St. Peter, a key; St. John, a chalice; St. Andrew, a saltire cross; St. James the Greater, a staff and other pilgrim equipment; St. James the Less, a fulling bat; St. Philip, a pastoral staff, or sometimes a basket of fish; St. Bartholomew, a butcher's knife; St. Simon Zelotes, a long saw; St. Thomas, a spear; St. Jude, a cross or club; St. Matthias, an axe; St. Matthew, a wallet, sometimes an axe. A representation of St. Paul carrying a sword often replaced St. Jude in a set; St. Mark and St. Luke sometimes replaced St. Simon and St. Matthias. Until as late as the reign of Charles I it was customary for a godfather to give a child at a christening a spoon knopped with the Apostle whose name he was given.

A very different spoon knop figure was the woodwose or wild man, swinging a club or holding it against his shoulder. This was a favourite device with decorative craftsmen and appeared on spoons between about 1450 and 1600. Thus in 1583 Marion Chapman of Newcastle-upon-Tyne possessed "one dozen sylver sponnes of the wylld man, gylte on the endes", valued at £4. 3. 4. The moor's head was another alternative in the sixteenth century.

Heraldry was another obvious source of knop designs. The lion sejant guardant was contemporary with the maidenhead. In 1548 the Vintners' Company had a dozen spoons "with lyons on the knoppys, gylt, weying xv oz.", and priced at four shillings and fourpence the ounce. The inventory of Harrie Strowther taken in 1582 refers to "xj sylver sponnes with lyone knopes, gilt at the endes, wainge xvj ounces and a half 52/-". This seated lion was a squat, big-headed creature: even when its body was placed across the top of the stem its head faced to the front of the spoon.

Seal-top spoons were made until the early years of Charles II, but few examples are known with hall-marks earlier than Elizabeth's reign. In this design the stem

(*Left*) cruet with openwork frame and lateral handle; by Charles Kandler, London 1727. (*Right*) cruet frame of the Warwick type, with a pair of cut-glass bottles and three octagonal baluster-shaped casters; by Edmund Pearce, London 1709.

(*Left*) Warwick cruet frame with three casters and a pair of flint-glass oil and vinegar bottles; by Samuel Woods, London 1750. (*Right*) Warwick cruet frame with casters enriched with rococo embossing; by John Delmester, London 1760.

Table basket pierced to resemble o
wickerwork, with swing arch handle
inserted base; by Pierre Archambo, Lon
1735.

Table basket with sides and foot-rim pierced in a repeat design of scrolls; by Joseph Sanders, London 1738.

Swing-handle table basket ra
from a single piece of silver pl
pierced in a repeat design of scr
and crosses, and mounted on f
scroll feet. Rim enriched with app
rococo moulding; by Edward Fel
London 1747.

terminates in a baluster topped with a flat disc. Very occasionally from about 1600 the seal might be hexagonal. The seal is usually pricked with a monogram, initials, or a date. Identification marks on a knop-stemmed spoon generally consisted of initials and date in pricked work on the back of the bowl. The initials might be surrounded by decorative scrollwork.

What is known as the slipped-in-the-stalk spoon, with the stem ending simply in a slanting cut from the front of the spoon, was principally in fashion during the early Stuart period, although examples are found with hall-marks ranging from the end of the fifteenth century to the early years of Charles II. This style of spoon was made from a single piece of silver, with the stem widening only slightly but thickening considerably towards the top. The earliest were slender-stemmed, but from the end of the sixteenth century they were made longer, stouter and stronger, and a short tongue might strengthen the back of the bowl. The owner's initials were sometimes impressed upon the bowl near to the stem. In a late example initials might be pricked upon the slipped stalk.

From this developed the stump-end spoon of the early Stuart period with a facet-sided stem, hexagonal in section, tapering sharply to a point. By about 1660 the stem had broadened and flattened into the design known as the puritan spoon, oblong in section and cut squarely across the top. This is found only with an egg-shaped, nearly elliptical bowl which the stem joins with a short V-shaped tongue. Ornament in relief sometimes decorates the stem end.

The puritan spoon marked a turning point in spoon design. Thereafter instead of an added knop the stem-end ornament consisted merely of some elaboration of the flat end itself. Immediately after the return of Charles II and his court from the Continent in 1660 the trifid-end spoon appeared, the stem-end being hammered into a semi-circle which was cut vertically with two deep notches near to the sides, dividing the terminal into three sections, two small ones flanking a large central lobe. The stem and bowl junction was strengthened with a short V-shaped tongue, centrally ridged and with a depression at each side. By 1670 the end was shaped into an elliptical form and given a slight upward curve. The notches were cut nearer to the centre, the three resultant lobes being about equal. The hammered stem and bowl were now strengthened by what collectors descriptively term a "single drop". The rib on the bowl was made deeper and longer, extending about two-thirds of the way down the bowl. This was the first of the well-known rat-tail spoons which continued fashionable for about half a century.

From about 1680 the back of the spoon bowl might be ornamented with foliated scroll-work hammered in low relief and known as "lace work", the rat-tail forming the central theme of the design. The end of the stem at the front might be similarly decorated. Within ten years such scroll-work covered the back of the bowl and the length of the stem both back and front. During the early 1680s a series of spoons was made in which the stem terminal was decorated in relief with a portrait of Charles II. This surface ornamentation was produced by hammering and chasing. The varieties of the trifid are numerous, some finely engraved, many gilded.

The expanded stem was no longer notched after about 1690, but terminated in a series of small arcs, the central, larger curve being given an upward curl. This is now known to collectors as the wavy-end spoon. The bowl became narrower in proportion to its length and the ridge of the rat-tail was decorated with a series of diminishing beads.

With the new century the fashionable spoon had a more gracefully waisted stem with a less expansive end consisting merely of an unbroken semi-circle. This developed into a plain arc, but in many a transitional specimen a vestige of the trifid design remained in the outline. The tip of the end was made rather thicker than formerly and was still given a forward curve. From it, nearly half way up the front of the stem, a tapering central ridge was introduced, much resembling the rat-tail on the back of the spoon bowl, which might be similarly ridged and channelled but was tending to become more extensive and less sharply defined. This type of spoon continued fashionable until about 1730.

Early in the reign of George II, however, both the rat-tail and the repetitive stem decoration tended to disappear, replaced by smaller thickenings known as drops. The underside of the bowl was plain except for a small single or double drop at the stem junction, only very slightly shaped into a ridge within its rounded outline and reproducing the shape of the thickened, up-turned stem end, now invariably rounded and with no more than about half an inch of slight ridging up the stem. Such spoons were made until about 1765.

As was to be expected, the all-pervading escallop shell motif of the period might take the place of the rounded drop on the back of the spoon bowl by about 1740 and led to other shell and scroll decoration cast in low relief and soon extending more than half way down the back of the bowl.

The period's love of scrolled and knurled finials found expression in the Onslow pattern with a wide-scrolled turned-down finial. This was made shortly before 1750 at a period when the whole outline of the spoon was becoming more graceful. The waisted stem widened a little at its junction with the bowl, to avoid the sharp angles found in earlier work. The bowl itself was no longer an ellipse but egg-shaped, tapering towards the bowl tip. A plain or leaf drop masked the stem and bowl junction.

The most notable change in spoon design in the mid-eighteenth century, however, affected its general outline. Just as the straight stem gave place to an S-outline in harmony with current fashion trends of the later seventeenth century, so a vogue for plainer curves prompted spoon-makers of the 1760s to design a stem balancing the single curve of the bowl, its end curving backwards instead of forwards so that the tip, still slightly thickened and ridged, rested on the table. This was what is known as the "Old English" pattern, which has remained the standard shape for silver spoons ever since.

During the 1760s decoration down the length of the stem appeared, emphasising its graceful outline. The popular feather edge consisted of a border chased with short oblique lines similar to the barbs of a feather. A stem thus ornamented often terminated in an embossed escutcheon engraved with crest or initials. Alternatives were the threaded edge and an edge composed of tiny beads. Bright-cut engraving decorated spoons in the 1780s, reaching its peak of fashion during the following decade.

Although these edgings were most applicable to plainly tapering stems they also appeared on the shaped stem known as the fiddle pattern which arrived late in the eighteenth century. At first the slender stem was given square shoulders a little above the bowl junction; then these were balanced by similiar square-shouldered widening of the stem into a broad thumb rest. Fiddle designs are found in several varieties, plain, threaded edge, thread and shell, and, later, the florid king's pattern.

On the earliest type of silver spoon the hall-mark appeared inside the bowl near to the stem. A few specimens dating to 1450 or earlier are marked with uncrowned leopards' heads. Provincial assay offices struck the marks of their towns, but few pre-Elizabethan provincial examples are known. After 1363 a maker's emblem was also struck, appearing on the back of the stem close to the bowl junction, together with the date letter. The lion was added to these in 1544, being struck between the date letter and the maker's mark. After about 1660 the marks were spread out further on the back of the stem, the date letter being centrally placed. The town mark remained in the bowl until about 1670 when it was struck on the back of the stem next to the maker's mark.

8

KNIVES, FORKS, AND FISH-SERVERS

THE mediæval knight had little need for a separate knife to assist his fingers at a repast when his sheathed weapon was ready at his side. The dining table was bare of knife, fork and spoon and but sparingly equipped with dishes. Each diner helped himself from a central dish or bowl, and metal goblets held the drink. Individual plates were lacking until the days of Henry VIII and meat might be served direct from the fire on to thick slices of bread. Jean de Garlande in his *Dictionary* of the thirteenth century records that two persons commonly shared a bread *couvert*.

At this period it was only among the rich nobility and high clergy that knives were reserved specifically for table use. Their blades resembled elongated and widened spear-heads, the back edge being thick and heavy, tapering to a finely-ground cutting edge. These blades were fitted to costly and elaborate hafts. Like other adjuncts of eating and drinking, these knives were personal to the owner and greatly prized. The lord of the manor kept his in a gold or silver casket containing also his salt-cellar and his box of precious spices. This casket, known as a cadenas and frequently taking the form of a silver ship complete to the smallest detail of rigging and crew, was placed before him as he sat down to the meal (see chapter 20). Each guest would be expected to bring his own knives, generally a pair, one for cutting meat, the other for bread, in a decorative sheath suspended from the girdle. A special knife with a long, wide blade was supplied to the carver. Later this might be accompanied by a serving-knife with a long, broad blade, square-ended and with a rounded edge for lifting the cut meat from the dish to trencher or plate.

The blades of early English table knives were of fine steel, stamped with the bladesmith's mark, the majority being registered in London or Sheffield. Early specimens had pointed or wedge-shaped ends, but later designs, after about 1660, might be either rounded, curved or spatulate, the latter becoming almost standard throughout the eighteenth century. In this design the end widened out, "to eat fruit juice with" according to a contemporary diary.

One inexpensive form of table knife had blade and handle forged as a single piece of steel, to which wooden plates known as "scales" were riveted to form a grip—a method still to be bettered for kitchen knives. Decoration on the blade itself did not become prominent until the seventeenth century, when an inscription and the name or coat of arms of the owner might be introduced. On the shoulder of the blade, however, it had long been customary to apply engraving or chiselling, two small masks being common until 1650.

The tang head of the early table knife was forged into a decorative shape consisting of a series of knops and a baluster, but in this instance, too, design was affected by new post-Restoration fashions and from 1665 the tang head tended to become shorter. A silver or silver-gilt ferrule was then fitted over the end of the haft, matching a finial on the haft tip. Here again opportunity was found for decoration: some ferrules were chased with floral designs and from 1675 they might be deeply embossed. The majority, however, were severely plain, a style which continued throughout the eighteenth century in both knives and forks.

For centuries the knife, with some assistance from the spoon, met all the diner's needs, the fork being regarded as an eccentric novelty. There are records of forks in mediæval days but they are rare. The inventory of Pierre Gaveston, favourite of Edward I, tells us that he possessed sixty-nine knives but only three forks and these were used for eating pears. Forks first came into general use in Italy during the sixteenth century, being delicately wrought and exquisitely elegant for the dainties of the table.

There are records of forks being sold by the dozen in late Elizabethan days, but the fork as an article of common use at meals became established in England in the early seventeenth century, its acceptance probably influenced by Thomas Coryate who wrote a record of his experience on the Continent in 1611. Describing his journeyings, he "observed a custom in all these Italian cities and towns that is not used in any other country I saw in my travels, neither do I think that any other nation of Christendom use it, but Italy. The Italians, and also most strangers that are comorant in Italy, doe always at their meals use a little forke when they cut the meate. . . . Anyone touching the dish of meate with his fingers, from which all the table do cut, he will give offence unto the company as having transgressed the law of good manners and for his error he shall at least be brow-beaten, if not reprehended in words. This form of feeding I understand is generally used in all places of Italy, their forks for the most part being made of iron or steel, and some of silver. The cause of this curiosity is because the Italian cannot endure to have his dish touched with the fingers, seeing all men's fingers are not clean alike. I myself thought it good to imitate the Italian fashion by this forked cutting of meat, not only while I was in Italy, but also in Germany, oftentimes in England since I came home." The new fashion met with considerable opposition and was the subject of satirical verses. Many thought it coarse and ungraceful to throw food into the mouth "as you would toss hay into a barn with a pitch-fork".

The earliest existing silver fork was made for the Earl of Rutland, receiving the London hall-mark for 1632. By 1652 Heylin, in his *Cosmography*, was referring to the use of silver forks "which is by some of our spruce gallants taken up of late." In 1659 Richard Cromwell, the Lord Protector, paid Edward Backwell £2. 8. 0 for six meat forks. Prince George of Denmark had twelve silver forks made for him in 1686 at a cost of thirty shillings.

Some early forks had two prongs, others three or four. The number of prongs is of no chronological significance as four-pronged silver forks are found with early hall-marks, although the two-pronged variety is more numerous.

From the earliest days of their acceptance in this country forks were principally regarded as the natural companions of table knives and the main consideration of their handle treatment must be in accordance with this ruling. An exception, however, was the table fork of silver, which more usually was associated in style and treatment with its accompanying silver spoon, the steel knife used with these being of some quite different design. As might be expected, therefore, the form of handle on silver forks followed the development seen in silver spoons.

Early examples were thick and straight, either square, round or hexagonal in section. As the silver fork came into more general use in England, the handle was flattened out, a form suited to the beaten metal usually employed. This led to the flat stem design with the wide trifid top which in turn soon developed into a stem which was narrow throughout most of its length and broadened out in a graceful curve to contain the trifid terminal. This terminal still retained its angular notches but by the end of the seventeenth century these had disappeared and the shaping consisted wholly of curves, the central lobe of the trifid projecting beyond the lesser lobes flanking it. In the eighteenth century the prongs grew longer in proportion to handle length, and the trifid shaping to the terminal was lost in a single expansive curve. The last vestige of the earlier shaping was the development of the central lobe into a rib down the front of the handle.

During the reign of Queen Anne some silver handles were fitted to forks of steel and in such work handle design matched that of the accompanying knife. It was more usual, however, to make the fork in solid silver following the style applied contemporaneously to spoons. During this curve-loving era the whole design of the silver fork followed the current fashion. Just as chair-backs changed from straight lines to body-fitting curves, so the silver fork acquired up-curving prongs, arching stem and a balancing upward curve to the rounded handle-end. From 1765 silver handles might be decorated with various engraved designs, such as the feather-edge and the bright-cut. At this time, too, came the

Pierced table basket, its scalloped rim edged with applied moulding. Cast circular foot-ring with motifs in high relief. By G. Herbert and Company, London 1752.

Pierced table basket with sides built from openwork sections, and with a ropework rim; by Charles Aldridge and Henry Green, London 1771.

Oval table basket with sides and swing handle of silver wire; by William Vincent, London 1771.

Silver-gilt table basket and stand in the neo-classic style, with ram's-head handles; by Wakelin and Taylor, London 1780.

Table basket, its body raised from a single plate of silver, and with pierced rim and foot-ring; by Michael Plummer, London 1792.

Dish rings. (*Left*) earliest type, shallower than later, with top and base rims of equal diameter, and showing the pronounced spool shape; pierced and chased with four escutcheons surrounded by flowers, foliage, and scrolls; Dublin 1750. (*Right*) pierced and embossed with festoons of flowers, birds, and squirrels, on a background of trellis work; by Joseph Dixon, Dublin 1772.

Embossed and fret-cut dish rings stamped with Dublin hall-marks of 1770.

(*Left*) neo-classic design, pierced and engraved with husk patterns depending from formal medallions on a background of vertical pales; by Joseph Jackson, Dublin 1777. (*Right*) with press-cut piercing; by Joseph Jackson, Dublin 1788.

well-known fiddle handle with square shoulders, followed by its offsprings, the massive king and queen patterns, the thread, and the thread-and-shell, which mark the early years of the nineteenth century (Fig. 38).

Meanwhile, from their earliest appearance in England, other forks had been given handles in a wide range of materials to match accompanying table knives, many the work of brilliant artist-craftsmen. These handles varied in colour, texture and decoration and might be the work of jeweller, silversmith, ivory-carver or potter, blades and prongs being made by cutler and silversmith. Apprentices at the various crafts involved studied under master craftsmen for as long as eight years before becoming journeymen. Examples which have been preserved reflect the long hours and infinite patience spent in their production.

The wealthy delighted in handles made of costly materials, silver, ivory, amber, enamel, tortoiseshell, mother-of-pearl, and semi-precious stones such as agate and onyx. Some handles were elaborately inlaid with precious metals. But for common use there were knives and forks with plain wooden or bone handles holding tangs of steel.

The provision of knives, forks and spoons by the host, as an essential part of the table equipment, did not become the accepted fashion, even among the elite, until late in the seventeenth century. Complete matching sets of table cutlery were then made and the table laid very much as to-day. Not until well into the eighteenth century did this become general, and until 1750 a traveller rarely left home without a compact set consisting of knife, fork and spoon. Remaining specimens are frequently of solid silver enclosed in cases of tooled leather. Such sets were ingeniously contrived to occupy as little space as possible. The fork might become a handle for the spoon, the prongs fitting into silver loops fixed on the back of the bowl. As an additional convenience a tooth-pick might fit into the handle of the fork, unscrewed by an ornamental finial.

Few examples of English table knives and forks remain which may be dated earlier than about 1600. Some of the finest hafts made during the next century-and-a-half consisted of figures exquisitely carved in ivory. At first these were slender, full-length robed figures reminiscent of the stone sculptures in cathedrals. This style appears to have been fashionable until about 1670 when their place was taken by carved figures in contemporary dress, more in keeping with the spirit of their period. Such handles were made until about 1750 and again in the mid-nineteenth century.

Similarly to be associated with other contemporary fashions, many knife and fork handles after 1660 reflected the new vogue for smooth, colourful surfaces expressed in marquetry furniture. These tapering cylindrical ivory hafts were decorated with floral designs carried out in silver wire, coloured composition, and—like marquetry—with small pieces of green-stained ivory. Such hafts terminated in deep, straight-sided caps of silver and were fitted with ferrules to match. As with marquetry, however, the vogue soon passed. By 1720 elaborate decoration was abandoned and the ivory stained green. Shape remained unaltered although the silver terminal cap was considerably shortened. The green stain was an attempt to imitate the vivid green of the more costly malachite, which it effectually superseded. When the ivory was carefully stained and polished the resemblance was perfect. The green-stained ivory haft with its end curved like a pistol butt dates from about 1750. As a rule such handles are rather lighter in weight than their predecessors. Stag horn was also used throughout the eighteenth century and it, too, might be stained green.

Hafts of polished agate, attractively mottled in red, pink, or grey, were fashionable from Elizabethan days until about 1730. Early Stuart hafts in this medium were octagonal and slightly tapering; after the Restoration the tapering cylindrical form was in vogue until the end of the century. In the eighteenth century the tapering cylinder might be cut with sixteen facets. Some early Georgian handles of agate were fluted, the inner side of the grip being cut with notches.

Contemporary with agate hafts were those of red and yellow amber. They followed the plainly tapering cylindrical form, but sometimes the terminal was carved into a classical head. Some early examples are known in which a beautifully carved ivory face has been inserted into the head. Hexagonal hafts were sometimes constructed from plates of yellow amber cut so thin as to be almost transparent, and mounted on metal foil painted in colourful designs. All these materials were associated with silver fork-prongs and silver mounts linking handles and blades.

Reference has already been made to the pairing of silver forks and spoons. Not until the eighteenth century, apparently, was there much attempt to make matching knives and forks of silver. Most seventeenth century knife handles of solid silver appear to have been imported, for very few have been found bearing English hall-marks. These followed the general forms of fashionable hafts and might be embossed, engraved, or inlaid with niello—a black composition of silver, lead, copper, and sulphur. From about 1665 English silversmiths made plain, tapering cylindrical knife hafts, which were sometimes gilded. By the century end these tapering shafts were plain-surfaced hexagons and octagons, with terminals carved in elaborate designs. Early in the Georgian period these were superseded by the pistol-butt haft which had made its appearance during the 1690s.

By the beginning of the Georgian era matching knives and forks with silver hafts were coming into vogue, but the solid silver was uncomfortably heavy and the shape of the knife blade was clumsy. The hafts assumed a variety of patterns, the most usual being reeded, plain with a shell embossed on the finial, and in the pistol-butt curve. By about 1760 they tended to become less weighty owing to the increasing cost of silver, and from 1775 prices were lowered considerably by stamping the hafts from thinly rolled silver. Such knives and forks were made at Sheffield in tens of thousands. Very thin sterling silver was used and the two halves of the haft were struck from dies and then soldered together. The central hollow was filled with shellac poured in while liquid. The tang of the blade or fork was then secured and cemented inside the handle before the shellac set hard. Cost of manufacture was thus reduced to nearly one-thirtieth of its former figure, and the metal reduced to less than half its former weight. Early in the stamped period London silversmiths made hafts shaped partly by means of cast dies and partly by hand.

The Act of George III, 1791, altered the law regarding hall-marks. Only a very few specified articles among small pieces weighing less than five pennyweights were now necessarily hall-marked. Knife and fork hafts were not specified and were therefore optionally exempt. The weight of silver in such handles varied from 15 to 20 dwt. per dozen. Silver handled cutlery made towards the end of the eighteenth century and lacking a hall-mark is often marked STER LING, the only other device being the maker's mark. Such handles were usually made in Sheffield.

When it became customary for the host to supply guests at table with knife, fork and spoon, it was not long before additional table accessories were introduced. Among these was the gold dessert or fruit-knife with a solid haft of the same metal. These avoided the unpleasant results of fruit juice upon steel, but were necessarily rare. During the reign of William and Mary, however, fruit-knives of silver were made with solid hafts. At first these were of the same size and shape as the ordinary steel-bladed knife, but by 1720 they began to be made slightly shorter and were accompanied by matching forks. By 1740 both knife and fork had become considerably shorter, this feature being referred to in 1770 when silver dessert knives were patented by Dru Drury, a London goldsmith.

During the remainder of the century dessert knives with accompanying forks were used as a matter of course by the gentry. In 1820 Sir Edward Thomason of Birmingham patented a method by which a steel edge could be given to the blade of a gold or silver dessert knife. At this period, too, blades were elaborately engraved. From about 1840 the hafts might be plated, and by 1850 ivory hafts were usual, plain or ornamented with deep silver ferrules.

It is doubtful if pierced fish-slices were made earlier than the reign of George III: only very occasionally is a specimen found struck with a hall-mark earlier than 1770. Fish-slices at first were broad bladed, resembling a builders' mortar trowel, triangular or diamond-shaped, and ornamented with openwork foliated scrolls in a wide variety of designs. This

(*Left*) tea-canister with sliding top and domed lid; by Thomas Parr, London 1713.

(*Right*) plain triangular tea-canister by Anthony Nelme, London 1716.

(*Left*) tea-canister with high-stepped lid, sliding base, and pewter lining; London 1725.

(*Right*) oval tea-canister with elaborate lid-ornament; by William Vincent, London 1769.

(*Left*) ogee tea-canister with engraved decorations; by Louis Guichard, London 1754.

(*Right*) oval tea-canister with embossed decoration by G. and H., Birmingham.

A COLLECTION OF EIGHTEENTH-CENTURY TEA-CANISTERS

(*Top row*) a set of vase-shaped tea and sugar canisters in ogee silhouette, embossed and chased; by George Smith, London 1758.

(*Second row*) a pair of rectangular canisters with stepped lids, by Pezé Pilleau, London 1749, and a set of three square-sided *bombé* canisters by William Cripps, London 1755.

(*Third row*) a pair of plain rectangular canisters with domed lids; by Andrew Raven, London 1703. A set of three square canisters with bright-cut engraving; by T. Phipps and E. Robinson, London 1793.

(*Bottom row*) a set of rectangular *bombé* canisters with embossed decoration and moulded feet; by Phillips Garden, London 1759.

decoration was achieved by cutting away the background, leaving the pattern in solid silver. The purpose of this was to allow the server to strain the liquid from the fish. Such decoration might be augmented with engraving. Some of the more ambitiously-worked blades are so lavishly and delicately pierced that little metal remains and to the casual observer the ornamental designs might appear to lack strength; so cleverly arranged are points of contact, however, that the scrolls reinforce each other. The solid silver handles of these fish-slices matched those of contemporary feather-edged forks with escallop shells at terminal and ferrule.

From 1780 the broad blades of fish-slices began to assume somewhat the outline of a fish, but they were pierced with the conventional neo-classic patterns found alike on table baskets, sugar-bowls and salt-cellars. Simple decorations composed only of vertical and horizontal pales were very frequent. A series of fish-slices was made during the 1790s in which a rectangular blade, rounded at the end, was pierced with a wide border enclosed in one or two engraved lines, similar lines edging the blade.

By about 1800 the pierced design might resemble the backbone and ribs of a fish (Fig. 39). In some examples at this time the blade was made more exactly in the outline of a fish, but with foliated scrolls in the open-work.

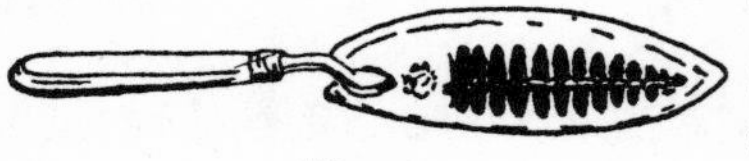

Fig. 39

Some highly effective piercing was achieved by repeating such simple motifs as a series of lunettes within a narrow engraved band encircling the blade edge. The pierced outlines might be brought into relief by the addition of small dots and simple classic ornament bordering the curves. A more elaborate style was an intricate adaptation of the Greek honeysuckle ornament, a series of running scrolls terminating at each end of the pattern in an individual scrolled foliated motif. An unpierced area of the blade near the handle was decorated with the coat of arms, crest, or cipher of the owner.

The blade was always symmetrical until about 1800 when it changed to the form perpetuated in modern fish knives,

Fig. 40

a shape used for knife blades from Anglo-Saxon times (Fig. 40). On some fish-slices of this type the "cutting edge" was decorated with a border of foliage and flowers in bright-cut engraving. The back edge was plainly engraved with a single or double line running the entire length of the blade. In a favourite London-made pattern the blade was engraved with a fish, or with a pair of fish crossed, against a cut-away foliated background (Fig. 40). From about 1820, these designs might be accompanied by matching forks.

Until about 1850 the silver-ferruled handles of fish-slices might match those of the forks and spoons in a set. The majority, however, until about 1800, were fitted with ivory handles stained a rich green, and either plainly turned, or turned and carved. The spiral handle was an exclusive design.

Fish-knives as distinct from fish-slices were a much later addition to fashionable table appointments. The earliest known to the authors—reduced copies of the contemporary fish-slice—bear on their blades the London hall-mark for 1821. The earliest literary reference to fish-knives appears to be in T. Cosnett's *Footman's Directory* published in 1825.

The fish-server was also made from about 1800 (Fig. 41). Basically this consisted of a fish-slice, but over the blade

Fig. 41

was fitted a second smaller one controlled by a spring. Pressure on a lever above the handle raised the small blade so that flat fish could be held securely between the blades for serving. The same design was used for asparagus servers. Decoration was alike on the two blades, largely consisting of the conventional pierced lunettes and horizontal pales which then constituted the stock-in-trade of the unambitious manufacturer of table silver.

9

SALTS

THE richly-worked standing salts of past centuries are symbols of a vanished social system in which ceremonial and colour reigned supreme. Of silver, given sunshine radiance with a double coating of gold, these salts belong to the age when the lord of the manor, whatever his rank, dined in state at the head of the tables that were ranged down the sides of his hall, with his family, personal retainers, and passing guests sharing his meal. This entailed formal observances in which the standing salt played a prominent part.

In the fifteenth and sixteenth centuries the preparation of the dining-tables was governed by rigid rules, so definite that they were set out in detail in the period's various books of etiquette and manners. The butler entered the hall carrying over his left shoulder folded cloths for cup-board and tables, towels and napkins. First he covered the cup-board with a diaper cloth, then the lower tables, the high table, raised on a low dais, being covered last.

Returning to the pantry the butler draped a towel evenly about his neck and another over his left arm. Upon this he placed four or five "pared loaves" covering them with the lord's napkin. Eight loaves to eat and three or four trencher loaves were placed on this, until trenchers of wood gradually came into general use. In his left hand he carried the principal standing salt, his right hand holding brightly-polished knives for carving and serving.

Bread at this period was baked in the form of thick flat discs. Only to the lord of the manor and guests of high rank was fresh bread served, the remainder receiving it one day old. Members of the household were supplied with three-day bread, and square trenchers were cut from bread four days old.

The standing salt was placed on the high table slightly to the right of the lord's seat. Three or four bread-trenchers were set to the left of the salt, the two knives being laid pointing to the salt, their blades beneath the trenchers. Beside them, folded in a napkin, lay a silver spoon. These were all concealed beneath another napkin. A second, less magnificent, standing salt and two trenchers were set at the end of the same table.

The butler then distributed down the lower tables trencher salts less than one-inch high. These were already filled with salt "sutille, whyte, fayre, and drye", its surface having been smoothed with a salt-planer of ivory, measuring three inches long by two inches broad. The butler then arranged on the cup-board the household silver plate including a drinking-cup, a two-eared basin and a spoon for each diner. The ewery board was set with basins and ewers filled with rose water, hot and cold.

The lord of the manor took his place, and as he began to say grace the butler removed the napkin covering the principal salt. The person of highest rank then washed his hands with the aid of two servants, one to hold the bowl with a towel beneath, the other to pour water. The remainder of the company then washed in order of precedence. Meanwhile servants handed cushions, and the pantry boy distributed napkins and trenchers.

The meal then proceeded, with little variation in ceremony from one generation to another. Salt was taken from the trencher salt with the knife end and placed on the bread trencher, hence the term "trencher salt". After each course servants cleared the tables, leaving only the salts, whole bread, and drinking cups. After the final course of wafers and sweet wine everything was removed from the tables with the exception of the principal salt which remained until after grace had been said, when the butler carried it away. The diners then again washed their hands.

The extent to which salts were used may be gauged from

the plate inventory of Edward III taken in 1329 and listing 589 salts of various types. Great salts according to examples specified in wills and inventories were commonly of silver double gilt, occasionally of gold. In early days they were designed with fantastic elaboration, often in the form of animals, such as the elephant salt belonging to the Company of Cutlers. The body of this example is studded with gems and carries a golden tower-howdah terminating in the receptacle for salt. In the British Museum is a salt with a shell container resting on a whale and surmounted by the half-length figure of a mermaid. Such standing salts were succeeded late in the fifteenth century by the hour-glass pattern of gothic design, usually sexfoil in form and fitted with covers (Fig. 42.)

By 1530 Renaissance art had completely changed the form of English standing salts (Figs. 42 and 43 indicate the change from Gothic to Renaissance design). The new design might be either cylindrical or square, and heavily and elaborately embossed with strapwork and other contemporary designs. It was fitted with an equally elaborate cover which in many cases was surmounted by a cast figure in full relief.

Fig. 42 Fig. 43

Only during the Elizabethan era did silver plate enter the homes of the well-to-do clergy, gentry, tradesmen, farmers, and others. Provincial wills and inventories of the 1580s show that double-gilt standing salts were widespread in such establishments, as many as half-a-dozen sometimes being mentioned. The will of Isabel Rood of Durham who died in 1582 refers to "my beste sylver salte", described in the inventory as a double-gilt salt with cover, and valued at £3. 0. 6; her "leaste sylver salte", covered and parcel-gilt, was valued at £2. 2. 6. In the same year the inventory of John Sotherne, Newcastle-upon-Tyne, mentions "one salt with coveringe, doble gilt, weainge vj ounces and three quarters, at 5/- an ounce, 33/9." Another silver salt with cover, ungilt, is valued at 4/8 an ounce. The weight of silver salts usually exceeded ten ounces, such as Richard Marshall's "salte, with a cover, double gilte, xviij unces", valued at £6 in 1588.

Towards the end of the sixteenth century less elaborate, less expansive standing salts were being made, thus widening the scope of the silversmiths' work. These were the bell salts dating from about 1580 and continuing until 1620 (Plate 15). None has been found hall-marked before 1590, but that they were in use at least a decade earlier is evidenced by the will of Roger Radcliffe, Mulgrave Castle, Cleveland. Made in 1583 and proved six years later, this will refers to "my greatest gilte salte; one gilte salte called the bell salte; and my great white salte". The bell salt was shaped like an elongated bell about ten inches high and was made in three sections. Two salt cellars fitted one above the other while the topmost section served as a pepper caster, its hollow ball finial being pierced for this purpose (Fig. 44). The whole was supported on three ball feet or more rarely ball-and-claw feet. As a single entity it was used as a ceremonial salt before which grace was said. It was then divided into its three parts as a pair of salt cellars and a pepper caster for use during the meal.

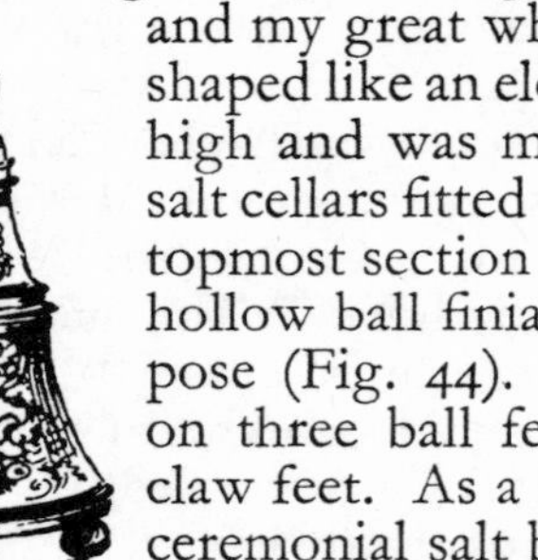

Fig. 44

Bell salts, usually double gilt, were covered with chased ornament sometimes on a matted ground. Patterns might be in the form of foliage and arabesques, or strapwork enclosing flowers engraved in outline. The dome of the upper section was chased or engraved with acanthus leaves, the pierced ball finial being left plain. A shield on the lower section was engraved with a coat of arms, crest, or cipher.

A bell salt of single section and less than six inches tall was a less expensive form of standing salt before which grace might be said. The domed cover was surmounted by a ring with which it was easily removed. This design was mounted upon a moulded foot-rim.

Contemporary with the bell salt from 1590 was the 18-inch high steeple salt (Plate 15). This ceremonial salt had

Fig. 45

a cylindrical body, plain, engraved or embossed, with a cover in the form of a small reversed bowl rising from a loose rim that fitted snugly over the mouth of the container. Rising from the cover was a tall, steeple-like, four-sided pyramid, which might be finely fretted, ending in a knop finial. The steeple salt was supported upon three feet, which might be ball, ball and claw, or half-ball and claw (Fig. 45).

The Puritan dislike of display was responsible for the virtual disappearance of the domestic ceremonial salt from 1650. Bodies of standing salts became cylinders or cubes, smoothly plain or slightly engraved. Remaining specimens are rarely found equipped with lids. To the rim are soldered three or four C-shaped brackets—occasionally double-scrolls are found—and these terminate in scrolls or other finials resembling those supporting the earlier steeple covers. These would be sufficient alone to support the open napkin which covered the salt until grace was begun, but they suggest no more than a vestige of the dignity and honour formerly pertaining to the standing salt.

By the second half of the seventeenth century the custom by which the senior members of the household dined together in the common hall had long been superseded by the use of a private dining apartment for those who formerly occupied the high table. The standing salt still found its place on the lord's table, but the elaborate ceremony of earlier periods never returned.

Domestic standing salts of Charles II's reign possessed little of their former magnificence. The fashionable salt resembled the slender hour-glass style of the early sixteenth century, but was broader in proportion to its height. Usually termed the spool-shaped salt and about eight inches high, it was raised from two pieces of silver with a convex band concealing the join around the centre of the body.

The surface might be left plain, but many were engraved. Others were decorated with repoussé work and chasing, in which case the narrow waist was raised to a position about two-thirds up the salt. In some instances the body was shaped from a single plate, with a single invisible join. In the square and rectangular variants of the spool, the body was less expensively built from flat pieces of plate. Brackets for supporting the napkin curved upward from the rim and sometimes an inner series of brackets would support a cover.

With the building of new houses in which architects separated the family dining-parlour from the servants' quarters, the ceremony of the salt was discontinued. Even in earlier days, however, the taking of salt from the great standing salts had been restricted to ceremonial requirements. Diners helped themselves from the trencher salts. These were short cylindrical containers, about one inch high and three or four inches in diameter, with applied moulding encircling rim and base. A shallow salt-container with a wide flange was set within the vertical-sided carcase, resting upon its rim. Undecorated except for coats of arms or similar devices, silver trencher salts were double gilt to match the ceremonial salt. Inventories indicate that they were not numerous, trencher salts of pewter being placed upon the lower tables.

Trencher salts in the early seventeenth century (Plate 16) might be circular, square, or triangular or octagonal, their sides vertical, sloping or concave. The Restoration brought nothing more spectacular, the fashionable trencher salt (Fig. 46) being circular with inward sloping sides matching the spool-shaped salt. It was nearly three inches high, its rim and foot enriched with wide, highly-convex gadrooning, its body remaining plain or encircled with a border of simple punched decoration. Later in the century the body might be decorated with spiral fluting, a wide everted rim and an expanded base. Salts of this type are found with hall-marks as late as George I. Plain circular trencher salts raised from single discs of plate are found with hall-marks dating from 1670.

Fig. 46

The reign of William and Mary witnessed changes to the trencher salt which might be half an inch deeper than formerly. The round body became highly convex and was enriched with fluting or ovolo decoration (Plate 16). This was supported by a spreading foot rim highly domed and ornamented with knurled chasing, or consisting of narrow moulding.

Fig. 47

With Queen Anne came the fashion for eight- or twelve-sided trencher salts with swelling or incurved sides (Fig. 47 and Plate 16). In this design a shallow oval or circular depression formed the salt container. By 1715 the flat base might spread more widely than formerly (Plate 16).

A type of trencher salt derived from the spool-shape appeared early in the reign of George I and continued for about twenty years (Plate 17). This consisted of a plain circular bowl, with a gadrooned rim and set upon a widely spreading foot. Embossed ornament was usual, applied card-work or leaf-work decorating the lower part of the bowl in more elaborate examples.

Trencher salts were quickly superseded by new designs after about 1730, when silversmiths were beginning to exploit the plate prepared by the newly invented spring-rolling machine. The new style of salt was a small hemispherical bowl with an everted gadrooned rim, and raised upon three scroll feet foliated at the bowl junction. These bowls, like the majority of salt-cellars made during the next century, were in sets of at least four, the number always being even. Seldom are sets exceeding four found with early Georgian hall-marks. At first the surfaces of such salt cellars remained plainly smooth, a style which has continued uninterruptedly until to-day. Decoration might occasionally be added to the bowl in the form of sparse chasing in floral and other patterns.

Before the middle of the eighteenth century hoof feet had become fashionable on salt-cellars, curving gracefully to the bowl, the joints being decorated with lion, ram, cherub, mermaid (Plate 17) or other masks interspersed around the bowl by embossed floral or drapery festoons (Fig. 48). Alternatively the feet might also be in the form of escallop

Fig. 48

shells with matching decoration at the bowl junction.

Open-work salt cellars became fashionable from about 1760 and continued throughout the Georgian period (Fig. 49). These were fitted with blue glass liners for holding the salt and incidentally accentuating the beauty of the silver design. Glass-makers vied with each other in the production of blue liners in exquisite tints. Bristol soon acquired the reputation for its flint-glass liners in a glistening blue. At first the liner was held in place with a detachable pierced rim, but this was shortly abandoned and examples are scarce.

Fig. 49

Great skill and artistry were displayed by the silversmiths responsible for hand-wrought open-work designs cut with a fret-saw. By 1770 the fly-press had been brought into use in the production of formal piercings such as geometrical pales and conventionalized scrolling. Although the result was monotonous compared with saw piercing, the commercial advantages are obvious. Matthew Boulton of Birmingham was responsible for many of the pierced galleries and bowls used in salt cellars of this period, bought and assembled by other factories.

Salt cellars raised upon spreading domed feet had become fashionable by 1760, bowl and foot being decorated with piercing in matching designs. Another, more popular, style consisted of a finely-pierced oval body without a base. The liner rested upon an interior projecting shelf encircling the lower rim of the gallery. Usually such a salt-cellar was given four feet, ball and claw in a variety of patterns being standard. In early examples the rim was undulating, the upper edge of the liner being cut to follow the same outline.

Canoe-shaped salt cellars were made in a wide range of patterns from 1775 to about 1825. In this design the body was supported by a short stem rising from an oval spreading foot (Fig. 50). The rim was either reeded or, more often, gadrooned, and a swing handle of twisted wire might be fitted. At first the ends of the body terminated

Fig. 50

in volutes, sometimes with loose rings swinging from them. From 1780 the volute might be extended into a handle reaching beneath the body towards the stem. Pierced salt cellars in these styles continued until the accession of William IV, although the circular bowl on three legs remained equally fashionable.

10

CASTERS AND CRUETS

MODERN pepper and salt-containers are so generally expected to appear as a matching pair upon the dinner-table that it is surprising to note their development as almost entirely disassociated pieces of silverware. While the ceremonial standing salt was an integral part of the English mediaeval dining ritual, the pepper-caster remained unimportant. The earliest was the diminutive vase-shaped pounce-salt of gold, which was in use to a limited extent when silver-gilt salts became popular in the reign of Henry VIII. In late Elizabethan times the upper section of the bell salt was designed to serve as a tiny pepper-caster, its hollow ball finial being pierced for the purpose (Fig. 44). Such dual-purpose pieces were less rare than is generally realised, many a farmhouse inventory recording possession of such an article in silver. Occasionally one finds reference to separate pepper casters: for instance in 1569 two cost 2s. 6d.

In every large establishment from the fourteenth to the seventeenth century there was a culinary department known as the saucery. *The Survey of Nonesuch* in 1650 recorded "One little Timber building called the Saucery House, conteyning foure little roomes used by the yeoman of the sauces". Here, under the supervision of the yeoman, were prepared piquant table sauces to give zest to foods in days when much had to be salted or dried to preserve it, and when even fresh meats might be the better for masking.

The discovery of America brought spices to Europe more pungent than those of India and Malaya. In 1493 Columbus himself recorded that he brought home a "new pepper more fiery than the black pepper from beyond the Caucasus". This was capsicum from which paprika is produced. The fashion for highly spiced foods was adopted during the early Elizabethan period by all who could afford the indulgence. Pepper was sold in vast quantities at prices varying from two shillings to half-a-crown a pound. But the typical inventory of James Backhouse, a small-town general dealer in Yorkshire, made in 1578, shows him to have carried considerable stocks of more expensive spices including cinnamon at 5/8 a pound, nutmegs 11s., cloves 13/4, large mace 15s., as well as dry pepper at 2/3.

It was the restoration of the monarchy in 1660, however, with the resultant introduction of foreign customs and table manners, together with experienced foreign craftsmen, that witnessed the eclipse of the standing salt and the rise of the silver caster. For the first time the service of meals acquired some of the graces continued to this day. Small family groups, gathered round shapely gate-leg tables, expected elegance rather than the mere quantitative magnificence of the previous century. Typical of the new individual daintiness of the meal were the pepper casters that now began to be fashionable in silver, pewter, brass, and copper. These vessels suggested a suitable field for the newly acquired skill of the period's silversmiths in delicately fret-cutting their thinly beaten metal. Tall, shapely silver tubes topped with decoratively pierced covers thereupon came into use on the dining table for both pepper and sugar. An advertisement in the *London Gazette*, 1676, offered a reward for the recovery of some stolen silver including "Six Salts, a Sugar Caster, a Pepper Caster, and a Mustard Pot". The same journal in 1681 referred to "One Sett of Silver Casters".

Hall-marks of the period show casters to have been made in sets of three, one large for sugar, and two small for Jamaican and cayenne peppers. Single pepper casters were also made: these usually had low, bun-shaped covers pierced with small circular holes (Fig. 51 is a later example of this style), but with the sets intended for different contents the piercing of the covers in matching designs required special consideration.

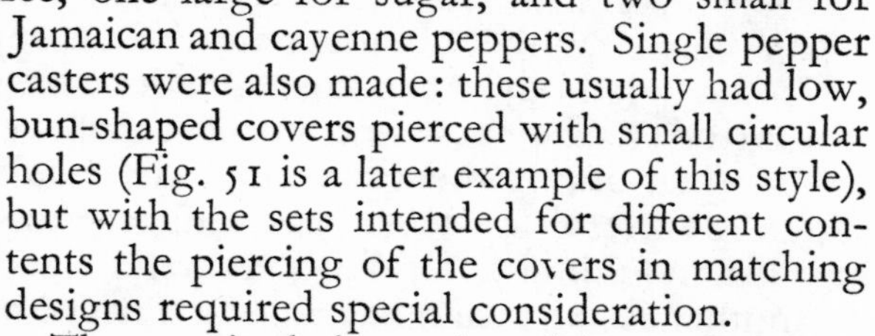

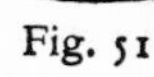

Fig. 51

The seemingly large size of the perforations in the pepper-caster cover has led to the assumption that pepper of the period was very coarsely ground. There is no reason for believing that hand-operated mills failed to produce pepper as finely ground as flour. The flow of the powder from the caster was limited, however, by a silver lining drilled with tiny holes and fitted inside the cover. In some examples the perforation of the lining was restricted to the upper quarter of the cover, so that the pepper was sprinkled only through the fret-cutting at the top. The linings of casters intended for pungent cayenne were more sparsely pierced than those for Jamaican pepper. This method preserved harmony of design in the fret-cutting on matching sets. In many instances the lining has been removed at some later period when the caster has been put to another purpose.

Casters of the Charles II period were cylindrical with vertical sides. The short plain body was a trifle deeper than the high, pierced cover, the rims of both being strengthened with narrow moulding. The sides of the cylindrical cover were simply fret-cut with quatre-foils, stars, fleurs-de-lis, hearts, diamonds and other perforations arranged in artless designs. The slightly raised top was decorated with a cast knop finial, usually vase-shaped. The body was encircled centrally with a narrow band of moulding, and a spreading moulded foot rim lifted the flat base above the table-top. Apart from an engraved coat-of-arms, the body of a caster made before about 1680 was undecorated.

Body and cover were secured with a bayonet fastener which enabled the caster to be shaken with safety (Fig. 52).

Fig. 52

In this, two lugs were soldered diametrically opposite to each other to project below the cover rim. Corresponding notches were cut in the moulding around the upper rim of the body. The lugs fitted into the notches when the cover was put on, and were so shaped to the contours of the grooved body moulding that the slightest twist of the cover was sufficient to make the lugs grip the moulding and hold it securely.

Another caster design had a pull-off cover with a tapering extension sliding snugly into the body. The junction was masked by the moulded strengthening rims of cover and container, these being designed as a single entity.

Silver casters of the late Charles II period might have their cylindrical bodies hammered into alternate convex and concave flutes or folds with the same strengthening effect as the linen-fold panelling in wood, which it much resembled. The edges of the concave flutes were rounded and grooves separated them from the convex swellings. The fluting was continued on the pierced covers which carried vase-shaped finials. Casters of this type were raised upon circular moulded feet, sometimes pierced and chased.

The cylindrical body remained fashionable until the early years of the William and Mary period. It was then given a rounded dome cover slightly smaller in diameter than the body, the fret-cutting more elaborately designed and more skilfully executed than in earlier work. A spherical or vase-shaped finial rose from acanthus leaves in relief on top of the dome. The cover rim and the base moulding might be encircled with matching cable moulding or gadrooning.

A new style of cover decoration became fashionable from about 1705 when the dome was encircled mid-way with applied moulding. The upper part of the cover was fret-cut in geometrical patterns, the lower section in scrolls.

Meanwhile in conformity with the general trend in design during the last years of the seventeenth century, the body shape of casters was undergoing radical alteration. It was at this period that the pyriform caster appeared. This had an elongated pear-shaped outline, circular on plan, and was fitted with a moulded foot, being copied from the oriental porcelain vases then highly fashionable. The lower part of the body was almost hemispherical, the upper part concave and narrowing towards the top, the curved outline continuing in the pierced cover which narrowed to a diameter little more than half that of the lower body. The tall domed cover was finely pierced with formal ornament and finished with a cast finial rising from acanthus leaves in relief. The pyriform caster was usually entirely plain except for a horizontal band of moulding encircling the body at its greatest diameter. A low, circular moulded foot was applied, sometimes with a gadrooned rim. From about 1715 the concave curve of the upper body was more acute. This type of caster was made continuously until about 1750. Simple pull-off covers were usual, but examples are known in which the pierced dome has a cylindrical extension overlapping the upper part of the body (Fig. 53).

Fig. 53

By the end of the seventeenth century pyriform casters began to be elaborated, the lower part of the body being fluted, with narrow bands of formal leaves or other conventional designs above. The largest knop on the cover finial was fluted to match a similar decoration encircling the foot rim. A series of casters made during the first quarter of the eighteenth century dispensed with the central line of moulding on the body and was enriched with applied radiating cut-card work, sometimes chased with panels and intersecting bands. The decoration ornamented upper and lower parts of the body, one design being inverted.

As a natural complement to the pyriform came the other typical outline of the period—the Queen Anne baluster caster. In this the body outline was reversed, the greatest width coming near the top, from which it curved smoothly inwards down to a widely flaring foot. The central break in the curve of the body was dispensed with, but often a stronger outline was obtained by making the narrow body octagonal, mounted on a high-moulded octagonal foot. The octagonal domed cover, encircled with a raised band, was pierced with formal decoration, radiating straps in relief supporting the baluster-shaped finial. By George I's reign the pyriform caster might be made octagonal on plan with the curves of the lower part of the body tending to sag. The octagonal cover was fret-cut with alternating designs in vertical sections. Pepper-casters now tended to diminish in size. The largest examples made late in the eighteenth century are no more capacious than those regarded as small early in the century.

From about 1750 the hemispherical lower section of the pyriform body was replaced by the ogee outline. This was still undecorated, but narrow bands of gadrooning might encircle the cover rim, the shoulder of the body and the foot. The fret-cutting on the high-domed cover was

(*Above*) tea-pot, its pyriform body decorated with cut-card work. This has a gadrooned foot-rim and moulded spout. By David Willaume, London 1706.

(*Below*) bullet tea-pot with moulded foot-rim and ivory handle; by Thomas Tearle, London 1727.

(*Above*) tea-pot with foot, its ogee body decorated with chasing; by James Walsh, the assay master's mark being that of Hugh Gordon, Edinburgh 1757.

(*Below*) engraved tea-pot with cylindrical body, straight spout, and ivory handle; by William Vincent, London 1776.

designed in narrow diagonal panels, geometric and curved patterns alternating. Some covers tapered in wavy outlines.

At this period a pyriform caster might be lavishly embossed in swirling designs culminating in an elaborate cartouche on the upper body. Less expensively, the lower part of the body was embossed with swags. The cover was embossed and chased with a spiral pattern, the fret-cutting this enclosed being less extensive than formerly.

Cylindrical casters with dome covers and bayonet fasteners were again fashionable during the reign of George III, the covers being finely fret-cut in the neo-classic style. Small casters were now made in sets of six or more. A long series of small cylindrical casters made during the late eighteenth century had pierced sides and were fitted with blue glass liners. Early examples were pierced with pales and arches interspersed with festooned drapery and chased with borders of lace-work. Later the pierced sides were ornamented with applied festoons or similar classic designs. The pierced caster usually had a narrow band of strengthening moulding around the body a little below the middle, and a plain moulded base.

From 1790 until 1820 vase-shaped casters were made by the London, Birmingham, and Sheffield silversmiths in considerable numbers. A hemispherical body was supported on a short stem rising from a circular or square foot. The neck was concave and the high-domed cover, fret-cut or plainly pierced, terminated in a simple knop. Contemporaneous were casters with short, plainly cylindrical bodies fitted with elaborately designed covers. The early forms of caster were also made throughout the eighteenth and early nineteenth centuries.

Handled casters resembling miniature flour dredgers were made by English silversmiths for nearly half a century from about 1690. These have come to be known to silver collectors as kitchen pepper pots. Yet it is highly improbable that such solid silver vessels were ever intended for kitchen use—and improbable, even, that the majority were intended for common pepper. Their heyday was the period when the Englishman delighted in many pungent spices, and no longer depended on the yeoman sauce-maker to mete out his flavourings, preferring to sprinkle cinnamon and the like over his food at table.

The William and Mary spice dredger was about four inches high, cylindrical of body and plain-surfaced, with a spreading base rim simply moulded or gadrooned, and a flat S-handle with a short tail. The body was not raised from the solid plate but shaped from metal rolled flat and almost invisibly joined in a vertical seam, the circular base being inserted and soldered into position. The low-domed pull-off lid, pierced with circular holes, had a cylindrical extension overlapping the upper part of the body which it perfectly fitted. The body-lid junction was masked by a moulded rib encircling the body and a strengthening rim around the lid. These might be designed as a single entity matching the foot. When a dredger of this pattern had been in use for a time the cover was liable to spring off and release the entire spicy contents over the food.

The Queen Anne spice dredger had a low-domed cover attached to a cylindrical body by a bayonet fastening (Fig. 52). The peak of the dome might be drilled with several circular perforations surrounded by fret-cutting in curved designs extending to the rim. Others were fret-cut all over.

George I spice dredgers were frequently octagonal, sloping inward from base to mouth. The S-handle might be given a curved tail, and the deep, expansive foot rim was built from sections of plain moulding. The octagonal domed cover, encircled by a raised band, was pierced with formal decoration and supported a vase-shaped finial of cast silver. In early examples, with vertical octagonal bodies, narrow moulding encircled the base, matched by moulded ribs below and above the lid junction. This design, too, included a knop finial. The upper curve of the handle might be plain, reeded or notched.

Spice dredgers from 1730 reverted to the cylindrical body, usually plain-surfaced, but occasionally enriched with rococo ornament. The bun lid, with circular perforations and the peak culminating in a low button finial, might be of the pull-off variety, have a bayonet fastener, or be screwed into position upon a corresponding thread worked into the body rim.

Towards the end of the eighteenth century when it became customary to sprinkle cinnamon on hot buttered muffins, small casters were used, of spice dredger size but without handles. These were known as muffineers. The majority were vase-shaped, never more than four inches high, with low-domed sprinklers drilled with fine circular holes. The bodies of eighteenth century examples might be embossed or engraved: later they were seldom ornamented. Another series of muffineers had their bodies fret-cut in the neo-classic style and contained liners of blue glass. These usually had narrow bands of strengthening moulding encircling their bodies a little below the middle, and plain moulded bases.

Oil and vinegar were tabled in silver and glass for at least two centuries before their containers were directly associated with the silver casters of pepper and sugar. As sets of casters were developed, however, silversmiths seized upon the opportunity for achieving decorative effect with immensely handsome combinations of these various condiment-containers fitted into elaborate frames.

Gold and silver cruets are recorded among domestic plate from early in the fifteenth century, generally in a matching pair and without a stand. The household plate of Sir Thomas Ramsey, Lord Mayor of London in 1577, included "2 gilt crewettes with covers" weighing twenty-seven ounces avoirdupois. A cruet was defined by Cotgrave in 1611 as "a Violl wherein Oyle or Vinegar, is served to the Table." These must not be confused with the pre-reformation flagon-like containers also known as cruets and made in matching pairs to contain holy water for ecclesiastical purposes.

Oil and vinegar cruets of gold, silver-gilt, and silver continued fashionable for a quarter of a century after George Ravenscroft invented flint-glass during 1676. In the following year he was advertising "diamond cruets" of one pint capacity at two shillings each. These were long-necked, mallet-shaped bottles with the body surface pressed into raised diamond patterns. Many of these were sold in the shops accompanied by plain, loosely fitting caps of silver, topped with moulded finials and engraved with the owners' crests. Silver-mounted glass cruets are referred to in glass-sellers' announcements throughout the eighteenth century.

During the William and Mary period silversmiths seized upon the opportunity for achieving decorative effects by fitting pairs of silver-mounted crystal-clear cruets for oil and vinegar into elaborate silver frames. The frame design consisted of a flat, solid base, without feet, supporting a pair of openwork guard rings of thick moulded wire. Two small rings projecting horizontally from the guard rings held the silver caps while the cruet bottles were in use, and from the centre of the base extended a pear-shaped lateral handle, similar to those on contemporary standishes and snuffer trays. From about 1710 the cruet stand was raised on four short moulded feet and the lateral handle might be replaced by a moulded vertical ring.

The two-bottle cruet frame might be elaborated after about 1720, consisting of two circular or hexagonal sections joined together. Guard rails were replaced by pierced galleries which extended from wide moulding encircling the platform to a little below the shoulders of the bottles, and were strengthened by further wide moulding around their rims. The floor of each section might be pierced in a design matching that of the galleries. A strong vertical ring handle projected laterally from between the two sections, to both of which it was soldered.

The silver cap to each bottle, now a finely worked example of the silversmith's craft, might be fitted with a spout, while a highly domed, hinged lid gave access to the interior of the bottle. The spouted cap was cemented permanently to the glass neck of the bottle, and from the cap's neck a double-scroll handle curved expansively downward towards the bottle shoulder.

Silver stands and bottle-mountings in these two basic patterns continued throughout the century, but few remain owing to the breakage of the glass. Between about 1735 and 1760 a shield engraved with the owner's coat of arms might

(*Above*) oblong tea-pot made from rolled sheet silver, encircled with a wide strengthening rib and decorated with bright-cut engraving; by Gabriel Godbehere, Edward Wigan and J. Bult, London 1805.

(*Below*) tea-pot with body shaped in wide convex flutes, and with the handle, lid-knop, spout, and foot-ring elaborately moulded; by Benjamin Smith, London 1825.

Chocolate-pots with removable finials. (*Above*) with plain bulbous body and swan-neck spout; by Benjamin Pyne, London 1695.

(*Above*) decorated with strap-work and fluting, and with hinged cover to spout; by John Elston, Exeter 1707.

(*Below left*) with tapering hexagonal body, and domed lid, on stand and lamp; by Thomas Bolton, Dublin 1708. (*Below right*) with plain, tapered, cylindrical body, faceted swan-neck spout and scroll handle and bun lid; by W. Parry, Exeter 1744.

link the two sections, concealing the join. From about 1780 the neck of the silver mount might be extended into a curved spout wholly covered by a lid. This lid was fitted with a vertical thumb-piece by which it was lifted when the oil or vinegar was poured. Some were designed with self-opening lids.

The fashionable two-bottle cruet stand from about 1770 was a boat-shaped tray with pointed ends curled into scrolls. On the tray were soldered a pair of pierced or wire guards, and scroll feet lifted it above the table top. The tray brought with it a centrally placed vertical column rising above the bottles and terminating in an oval loop handle. The loop at first was plain; by the nineteenth century it was lavishly ornamented.

Throughout the eighteenth century such a stand might be matched by a similar one designed to contain three silver casters, two for Jamaican and cayenne pepper and a larger one for sugar. More usually, however, bottle stands and caster stands were combined into handsome frames to house the various condiment containers. The *London Gazette* of 1705 mentions "a sett of casters with 2 Vinegar Cruets in a Frame," and Cripps refers to an example bearing the London hall-mark for 1706.

The cruet frame was basically the two-bottle stand enlarged by the addition of three small circular platforms, making a single five-lobe entity, each lobe supporting a circular guard ring of moulded wire. A vertical ring handle was fitted laterally, placed between the glass bottles. From about 1710 this handle was abandoned in favour of the more convenient vertical column rising from the centre of the platform and terminating in a large oval loop handle, the decorative loop being soldered to the top of the upright. In some instances the loop was made to hinge upon the upright. Vertical scrolls from the guard rings were extended downward beyond the platform, terminating in escallop shells to form spreading feet.

Collectors refer to these as Warwick frames, and until the middle of the eighteenth century there was little deviation. From about 1735, on the guard ring and concealing the lower part of the large caster and the platform of the frame, was soldered a shield-shaped plate displaying the owner's coat of arms, his crest being engraved on each caster and bottle mount.

The cruet frame was greatly elaborated from the middle of the eighteenth century, at first by gadrooning the guard rings and the loop handle in harmony with rococo embossing on some casters. The coat of arms shield was enclosed in a moulded cartouche and the loop handle might be shaped to match. The piercing on caster covers was now designed in narrow diagonal panels, geometric and curved patterns alternating. Some covers tapered in a wavy silhouette. Large Warwick cruet frames were made occasionally from about 1750. Guard rings were fitted to contain six cylindrical and lidded mustard pots of silver, in addition to the other containers, and the number of silver mounted glass bottles was increased to three, the extra one intended for sauce.

The platform of the cruet frame from about 1760 tended to be circular and was enclosed with a deep rim, embossed, or chased or pierced. The frame was now supported on four ball-and-claw feet or, more frequently, on four spreading escallop shell feet. The result rather resembled a giant wine coaster with a central standing handle.

From about 1765 there was a short vogue for silver casters and clear glass oil and vinegar bottles to be replaced by containers—usually pyriform—of the new white enamel glass enriched with designs in colourful enamels. Each was fitted with the silver mounting appropriate to its duty on the table and each might be labelled. An example in the Trapnell collection has its set of five bottles labelled pepper, vinegar, oil, sugar, and mustard.

The success of the white enamel glass in cruet frames, together with contemporary improvements in the quality of clear flint-glass and its capacity to take deep cutting, prompted the silversmiths of Birmingham and Sheffield to produce less costly cruet sets by replacing all-silver casters with silver-mounted glass containers.

Cruet frames and their silver bottle mountings from 1790 to 1825 might be either lavishly decorated or severely simple. It

Fig. 54

has been calculated that one firm of manufacturing silversmiths designed and produced more than five hundred cruet frame patterns between 1788 and 1815. The glass bottles might stand upon an oval, square, rectangular, or canoe-shaped (Fig. 54) platform, four-footed and with a central looped pillar or with a handle at each end. Silver mounted mustard pots became included as standard fitments for the cruet set during this period. Oil and vinegar bottles might be fitted with cut-glass stoppers. The shapes of all containers now matched.

Magnificent conceptions of the cruet set continued to be made by the master silversmiths, ornately decorated and fitted with superbly cut bottles of flint-glass. These ceased to be made after about 1820.

After the Regency the cruet frame platform was usually circular or oval with scroll feet and a high, richly pierced gallery, and a tall central pillar with a loop handle. This design was sometimes catalogued as "Elizabethan" for no apparent reason as it bore no resemblance to the silversmith's work of that period. The caster mounting was now shaped as a small dome pierced with round holes and topped with a vase-shaped finial. Less expensive cruet sets consisted merely of platforms with rococo borders and feet, four matching supports rising from the plate to the guard rings. During the 1840s and later two-bottle and three-bottle soy frames were made basically resembling cruet frames but with lateral scroll handles.

Collectors require silver cruet frames to contain their original bottles of flint-glass. These display a chronological development from which there was little deviation although shapes and styles of decoration naturally overlapped, as they did in the silver itself. The quality of the glass used permits collectors to recognise at least six groups of flint-glass containers.

The early mallet-shaped bottles emit little prismatic light

and the heavy dark material, full of lead, shows striations and small bubbles. By 1750 flint-glass contained less lead and in consequence became considerably whiter and lighter in weight. But prismatic fire was still lacking. This did not become prominent until after 1800, when new methods of annealing had made possible a tougher glass capable of being deeply cut with fine prismatic diamonds.

The early flint-glass cruet bottle was mallet-shaped and the body might be smoothly round or tooled into vertical ridges. The base was raised inside with a slight kick to prevent the rough pontil mark from scratching the silver platform of the cruet frame. During the 1730s the neck might be crudely cut with very shallow flutes and the body in some simple geometrical design such as a group of stars. In the late 1740s the whole surface of the bottle might be cut with large shallow concave diamonds, and the base made without a kick, the rough pontil mark being ground away leaving the surface perfectly smooth. A general feature of the cruet bottle is a row of facets encircling the lower edge of the body and slightly undercutting the sides. This prevents sharp edges from scarring the silver.

By the middle of the century the mallet-shaped bottle gave way to the pyriform outline of the accompanying silver casters. The surface was cut with shallow diamonds and flutes above the waist. A flat circular foot, alternately cut and undercut, was joined to the body with narrow moulding, sometimes enlivened with groups of air beads. This form of cruet-bottle with fashionable variations in cutting was still popular a century later. From 1770 to about 1800 the foot might be scalloped or solidly square.

11

TABLE BASKETS

THE feast in England was for many centuries the conventional background against which a host could parade his wealth by a magnificent display of gold and silver plate upon the buffet. The late Elizabethan and Stuart régimes introduced new foods with new methods of serving them, however, and by the time of Charles I the plate had been transferred to the dining-table.

Among the appointments to grace early seventeenth century dining tables were circular "table basketts and fruit basketts" made from heavy silver plate. These have a special appeal to the collector, for their simple basic design has made these baskets demonstrate, with singular clarity, past changes of decorative mood, assisted and often made possible by developments in basic technique. In a small way they reflected, too, the manners of the times that used them, coming into being with the fashion for more formal table preparation and serving their purpose then as substantial, handle-less centre pieces, but acquiring a new mobility in the following century when the vogue for serving informal tea prompted the "handing" of dainties in silver baskets swinging from arching handles.

In early work, the outer surface of the basket was chased with designs such as fruit and foliage, and arabesque scrolls terminating in eagles' heads, with cherubs' heads and wings at intervals. When this decoration had been worked the plain background about the ornament was removed by cutting completely through the thickness of the metal. The Earl of Northampton's inventory of plate taken in 1614 items a silver table basket weighing 157 ounces, another of 134 ounces, and a fruit basket of 40 ounces.

The rim of the early table basket was shaped in harmony with the body ornament and a plainly moulded foot-rim lifted the flat, inserted base above the table-top. By 1640 a basket might be fitted with a foot-rim having a concave spread in which half of the silver was cut away by vertical piercings, leaving a series of parallel ribs. The junction of the foot-rim and basket-body was masked with cable wire, similar to the decoration edging the rims.

This early piercing was inevitably large, with vigorous curves enabling the cut edge to be trimmed and smoothed. When designs were well-planned, convex embossing tended to strengthen the sides of such baskets which might otherwise be weakened by the removal of so much metal. Few pre-Restoration open-work baskets have survived the melting pot.

After about 1665 the rim of the table basket was slightly everted, and embossing of flower, leaf, and animal motifs more extensive. The centre of the flat solid base might be enriched with a narrow floral wreath raised in very low relief.

Apart from the all-over scale pattern introduced during the 1690s, form, design and method of piercing continued almost unchanged until shortly after the accession of George II in 1727. A bread basket made by Thomas Folkingham, bearing the London hall-mark 1711-12, is in the collection of domestic silver at the Victoria and Albert Museum. This tall, vertical-sided example of scale-pattern piercing, with an inserted pierced base built from soldered sections, lacks the more advanced technique and finish practised by the Huguenot silversmiths then becoming recognised in London as leaders of craftsmanship and design.

The delicate piercing and fine embossing for which the London Huguenot silversmiths have received credit was made possible by an improvement in the metal-rolling machine described in Chapter I. As a result, Georgian silversmiths could achieve richer, more delicate effects in plate designed for the table. Pierced cake and fruit baskets, rectangular and oval as well as circular, quickly developed into an important branch of their craft. By 1730 the body of a fashionable table basket was finely pierced with designs composed of diamonds and circles. Appliqué decoration enriched the rim, which might be edged with beading. The inserted base was flat and chased with an elaborate pattern forming a central reserve upon which the owner's coat of arms was engraved. The base was inserted at the same level as an applied ribbon masking the junction of the body and the plain narrow foot-rim below. A foot-rim was essential to ensure stability upon the table, for the flat base might become warped by careless usage. Two horizontal D-loop handles were attached to the ends of the body beneath the rim.

Paul de Lamerie (1688-1751), a popular but not the most gifted silversmith of the period, made pierced table baskets from 1730 resembling open wicker-work baskets, the sides consisting of geometrical interlacing with matching everted rims. A narrow reeded wire concealed the join between rim and sides. The flat base might be chased to represent wicker-work with a framed oval reserve for the coat of arms. The D-loop handles were twisted in a matching cable form. This attractive pattern was adapted by John Jacob and other silversmiths and fitted with a swing handle (Fig. 55).

Fig. 55

The arch handle is found on table baskets of the early 1730s. At first it was fixed upright, and this style continued infrequently until the 1740s, but by then the usual design was an arch hinged on each side so that the basket swung freely. These handles resembled those on contemporary silver kettles, and in the case of a complete service matching handles were fitted. The arch handle on an early George II basket might be composed of two intertwined silver wires or ribbons worked into the design known as the guilloche. This style is found in varying forms throughout the Georgian period. The same pattern sometimes pierced the applied foot-rim. The pierced swinging arched handle continued in varying designs until after 1825.

Silversmiths began raising the complete basket from a

single sheet of metal in the late 1730s, sides remaining straight but with a more graceful outward flare. The sides were finely pierced and enriched with ornamental chasing, the base remaining solid and usually centrally engraved with a coat of arms. Everted rims became more expansive and were decorated with symmetrically applied foliated scrolls, masks, insects, vine leaves and grapes, wheat ears and other motifs in cast silver enlivened with chasing.

The basket might now be supported on four short legs of cast silver. Volute, ball-and-claw, and scroll feet were fashionable, the body junction being concealed beneath a mask or some other motif harmonising with the main decorative feature of the rim. From about 1740 the feet might be joined with aprons of shell and leaf ornaments, the entire combination of feet, masks and aprons soon being converted into a single elaborate cast ring with motifs in high relief matching those encircling the rim (Plate 22). Into this was fitted the base of the pierced basket.

Silversmiths made great progress in the design of domestic table-ware during the 1740s and pierced baskets developed into truly magnificent pieces of plate for cake, sweetmeats, bread, and fruit. The rim of the cake basket was expanded in such a way as to display as much as possible of the inner surface of the sides which became a field for elaborate decoration (Plate 21). The rim itself was shaped in a curved outline and decorated with cast and chased appliqué work in the form of rococo scrolls. Sometimes a cherub's head or other mask in high relief decorated each end of an oval rim. De Lamerie and other London silversmiths of French extraction such as Crespin and Chaube applied masks in the form of feminine faces, trophies of the hunt, lions, amorini, and flowers.

The finest piercing, however, was the work of native silversmiths who decorated the bodies of their table baskets with repetitive all-over patterns composed of scrolls, circles, crescents, and diamonds in several sizes. This style was superseded by small crosses arranged diagonally in panels, each panel alternating with another designed with pierced scrolls. On a fine quality basket a London silversmith would incorporate French motifs in the swing handle which was

(*Left*) chocolate-pot, the base of its body decorated with cut strap-work, boxwood D-handle; by Thomas Corbet, London 1703. (*Right*) coffee-pot with plain tapered and cylindrical body, and re-curved scroll handle; by Charles Martin, London 1735.

Coffee-pots. (*Left*) with plain bulbous body and ogee lid; by William Cripps, London 1760. (*Right*) tapered cylindrical body embossed and chased, with ivory handle; by Ayme Videau, London 1748.

Tea-kettles with minaret lids, swing-handled stands and lamps. (*Left*) bun-shaped body with moulded swan-necked spout; by Benjamin Pyne, London 1706. (*Right*) with twelve-sided body; by Samuel Margas, London 1715.

Tea-kettles with lids following the body curve, tripod stands and lamps. (*Left*) with globular body; by John le Sage, London 1740. (*Right*) with richly-chased ornament; by Paul de Lamerie, London 1736.

now cast in the form of a pair of recurving foliated scrolls, or a pair of terminal figures supporting a wide bow-shaped arch, its upper surface enriched with flowers and scrolls in relief. In the majority of examples, however, the arch was plain-surfaced or slightly chased. The pin of the hinge was sometimes concealed beneath a circular boss, often shaped as a shell.

Piercing in numerous combinations of patterns began to decorate the basket and its rim to the exclusion of appliqué work from about 1750. The supporting foot-rim was made rather taller and less overburdened with detail, adding immeasurably to the grace of the piece. The base of the basket remained solid, and was embellished with exquisite chasing and a central coat of arms.

In the provinces, as with other contemporary crafts, the older tradition prevailed for two or three decades after it had become outmoded in London. Well into the reign of George III, pierced table baskets were still being made by the old Stuart method of embossing the design and cutting away the background. This was accomplished in a less rough and perfunctory way than formerly, the ornament being enriched with excellent chasing and engraving. This never regained fashion's high regard, however, because the concave surface of the motifs on the basket sides did not receive a fine natural finish equal to that of the interior surface. Some silversmiths combined this embossing with Georgian pierced work, such examples being noteworthy for their beauty.

The London silversmiths developed particularly intricate and involved piercing which reached its zenith during the early years of George III. Shaped panels of silver, finely pierced with geometrical motifs such as quatrefoils, diapers, rows of ellipses, crosses, and circles in various sizes, might alternate with other panels pierced with small foliated scrolls. Such panels, a dozen of which might constitute the sides of a single basket, were pierced by means of light fly-presses capable of punching small work with extreme delicacy, although the majority of designs were considerably less ambitious than the hand-cut variety.

These pierced panels were made singly and soldered into

the form of an oval basket with the aid of beaded ribbon, also produced mechanically by William Bell's patent of 1779. This decorative ribbon outlined the gracefully-curving lines of the panel and served to conceal exterior and interior joins between panels, and also between the panels and the solid shallow oval base. Cost was considerably reduced by these methods which eliminated laboriously deep hand-raising. Sometimes the intersecting ribbons were hand-embossed with small beads increasing in size as they approached the basket edge.

Piercing eventually became a specialised factory trade, the silversmith buying his pierced panels ready-made from the merchant. In some instances each panel in a basket might differ in both shape and design, to a number sometimes approaching thirty. The panels composing each half of a basket might match. Rococo castings and presswork might be skilfully combined with other styles, and when used in conjunction with pierced panels resulted in some extremely elaborate cake-baskets. At first such baskets stood upon graceful foot-rings of cast silver; from about 1770 pierced foot-rims, deeper than formerly, were used because less costly in metal.

The swing handle might be cast and chased, with a light open-work arch between two heavier terminals. Later the handle was slender and of simple cable twist with a length of scroll and leaf work at each end connecting it with the hinges.

Table baskets built almost entirely of silver wire made their appearance in about 1760 and continued without interruption until about 1825. The wire framework with its widely expansive rim might be overlaid with ornamental hammered and chased motifs of trailed floral work. Sprays of wheat, alternating with roses, grapes and vine leaves were highly popular. The concave elliptical base was at first solid silver, with wires radiating from its circumference, and a typical handle consisted of a double strand of wire twisted. Before 1770 the base might be ornamented with piercing, a central reserve of solid silver being left for an engraved coat of arms or other inscription. Early examples of this type were so fragile that few remain.

The mid-George III silversmiths revived the basket of the 1730s with two fixed handles, its body now raised from sheet silver, delicately pierced to resemble wicker and lattice work, and finely chased. The widely-everted rim was embossed with small blossoms and leaves springing from a running tendril. This design of table basket was shallower than the swing handle variety and stood upon a narrow foot-rim pierced to match. Noteworthy are the examples with ram's head handles at the ends.

During the 1780s and 1790s there was a vogue for two-handled hand-wrought silver table baskets with sides pierced to give an openwork ribbon effect, such as a series of overlapping flat rings, or loops with overlapping ends forming a trellis. Exterior surfaces were chased to resemble woven wickerwork, and enriched with deep bands of elaborate appliqué and with decoration around their rims. Such baskets had flat solid bases raised slightly by plain foot-rims.

Another style of table basket fashionable during the 1770s and 1780s was raised from a single piece of fairly heavy silver, the rim embossed with "classical" festoons of acanthus leaves, husks or other swags hanging from small oval medallions. Piercing on such pieces included vitruvian foliated scroll-work and other designs from Greco-Roman sources. Applied foot-rims were pierced to match.

Silver table baskets of the less expensive factory type were becoming shallow and of lighter construction by 1780, as Boulton's pioneer steam-operated rolling-mills were producing a thinner plate. Factory piercing became coarser and consisted mainly of rows of long narrow vertical and horizontal ellipses. These might be arranged to form trellis work and intersecting arches. The introduction of a harder steel for punches enabled these plain motifs to be pierced with speedy precision. Little additional ornament was used apart from intervening rows of small beads. At this time appeared the central spreading pedestal foot.

A series of cake and sweet baskets made from about 1775 had solid, unpierced bodies, either fluted or lobed like escallop shells and ornamented with chased bands of foliage. Later the smaller sizes were shaped basically with a press tool, hand-finishing being carried out by the silversmith. Early in the nineteenth century such baskets were decorated with shell and gadroon mounts, some magnificent examples being the work of Sir Edward Thomason of Birmingham.

kettle with stand, lamp, and wind-
d. Globular body with raised gadrooned
matching the foot-rim; by Edward
Wakelin, London 1757.

Tea-kettle, lamp, and tripod stand fitted with silver guard pegs and chains. Globular body shaped with wide flutes. By Pierre Archambo, London 1734.

milk jug, oval on plan, by Edward Pearce; London 1724.

Hot milk jug in neo-classic style by Nicholas Dumee; London 1777.

Tea-urns with classical vase-shaped bodies on stemmed feet. (*Left*) with moulded handles and applied festoons, London 1770. (*Right*) with wide neck and lion-head handles, Sheffield 1790.

Tea-urns with hemispherical bodies. (*Left*) raised on square platform; by Paul Storr, London 1809. (*Right*) urn supported by four flat columns resting on a flat plinth; by John Crouch, London 1807.

12

DISH RINGS

IRISH silversmiths of the eighteenth century followed the lead of English designers. Yet throughout the decorative phases of baroque and rococo, oriental and classical, there may be discerned an interpretation and elaboration of design that give character and individuality to high quality Irish work. Particular opportunities for displaying the silversmiths' skill are offered by a piece in which embossed and chased motifs are arranged in silhouette or are set off by a background which is itself pierced in an elaborate design.

On the dining table of the well-to-do, superlative decoration of this nature was displayed in that Irish speciality, the silver dish ring. Like the silver table basket in England, this ornate eighteenth century piece often took the place of importance formerly held by the silver salt, even retaining in its outline a suggestion of the earlier piece.

The dish ring, as its name suggests, was no more than a broad ring of silver three to four inches high and seven to eight inches in diameter, like a giant spool-shaped napkin ring. Between the circular rims of solid silver the vertical body of the ring offered considerable scope for imaginative decoration, enhanced by the deeply incurved shaping that gave the piece a pronounced waist.

In view of their variety, both of design and of purpose, it may be well to keep strictly to the usual contemporary name for these rings. Invariably, when assayed, they were entered as dish rings in the books of the Dublin Goldsmiths' Company. *Falkiners Dublin Journal* described them in 1762 as "dish stands" and in 1780 as "Rings for the centre of the Table". In 1777 the London Assay Office used the term "dish stands". Sheffield plate catalogues of about 1800 refer to them as "dish rims".

It is obvious that such a ring of silver could be made to serve several purposes. Some were fitted with linings—bowls of blue glass with cut rims that formed the perfect background to the open-work silver decoration. Others were given delicately pierced silver covers chased and embossed with matching designs, but none of these has been noted with an English hall-mark. Silver dish rings of English origin are rare, and when found are usually oval, although circular examples were made in Sheffield plate.

In Ireland silver-rimmed bowls of bog oak were in daily use long after wooden vessels had vanished from the well-to-do English table. Most authorities suggest, therefore, that the main purpose of these elaborately pierced dish rings was to support such bowls containing hot food, thus avoiding the danger of disfiguring the polished dining-table. It is suggested that bowls of soup, vegetables, dessert and hot punch might be placed successively upon the dish ring during a meal. Undoubtedly some dish rings were put to this use. Their shape indicates probable evolution from the spool-shaped salt with scroll arms rising from the rim, and these arms, according to the Victoria and Albert Museum publication, *Charles II Domestic Silver* (1949), were intended for supporting a dish.

Other dish rings with matching perforated lids may have had their blue glass liners filled with potpourri or other scented material, thus taking their place among the various vessels employed in perfuming eighteenth century rooms. Nevertheless, there is considerable argument in favour of the popular name "potato-rings" for these delightful pieces of Irish silver. This name has lately been somewhat discredited because it has been assumed that the silversmiths' term "dish ring" necessarily implied that the ring supported the dish. Equally well, however, it might indicate a ring to stand on a dish, and thus transform it into a bowl with perforated sides. Extremely interesting corroboration of this is to be found among specimens of pottery in the Earle Collection at Hull Museum. This consists of two pieces of Whieldon pottery, designed and decorated to form a single unit, the one piece a pierced ring and the other a circular dish with a depression fitting the lower diameter of the ring, so that the ring rests upon the dish. Whieldon work may be dated 1740-80, and obviously this specimen suggests a typical example of a potter seeking to reproduce a design then in vogue in a more valuable material.

Those to whom potatoes are invariably served as a moist mash have overlooked the fact that the right variety of potato, baked in its jacket, the white "flour" frothing through cracks in the crisp skin, is an epicure's delight. Such potatoes have their own recognised manner of serving. They are as easily spoiled by a closed container as a slice of toast: instead they must be piled on a snowy napkin and merely held in position by the perforated ring of silver. Indeed it was found that no more than a skeleton shape of silver wire was required to support the folded napkin.

The earliest reference to a dish ring yet noted appeared in the *London Gazette*, 1697, in which "2 Rings for a Table" were advertised. One dish ring of this period is known, hall-marked 1704 and made by Andrew Raven, London. This is a plain spool of solid silver embossed with a large shield for a coat of arms. After this, there is a forty-year lapse before they are heard of again, this time with Irish hall-marks. Irish dish rings remained fashionable in silver until the end of the eighteenth century when there was a short vogue for similar pieces in less expensive Sheffield plate.

Features characteristic of dish rings during this period enable them to be placed in four well-defined groups. In each case the body of the dish ring was formed from a sheet of silver about twenty inches long and five inches wide. This was rolled into a cylinder and hammered into spool-shape on a wooden block. The ends were hard-soldered in a straight joint difficult to discover, although usually visible on the strengthening rings of silver wire which rimmed the piece at top and bottom. Decoration was then carried out by hand.

The earliest type, in which the spool was more deeply incurved than later, was less than three inches deep, upper and lower rims being of equal diameter. It was encircled by a band of ornament in low relief, the usual motifs consisting of scrolls and conventional flowers and foliage, either plain or enriched with chasing. A scroll-framed cartouche might bear an engraved coat of arms. The background was cut away, leaving the pattern in silhouette, but the ornamented area was narrower than those in the later groups, and was bordered top and bottom by wide, undecorated margins. These were strengthened around their edges with square wire. Such rings are rare.

Early dish rings were smaller than those of the second and third groups, yet they seldom contained less weight of metal. One reason was that at first comparatively little metal was cut away from the background. Also the silver plate was still produced by the old sledge hammer process and reduced manually to the required gauge. But the silversmith's constant aim was towards a more economical use of his metal, without sacrifice of effective design, and the wholly press-stamped specimens of the fourth group were even lighter than the smaller early pieces.

Dish rings of the second group were numerous from about 1760 to 1780. The sides were less concave than in the earlier design, and the base rim was made with a slightly greater diameter than the upper rim, achieving a tapering effect. In height this type varied from 3½ inches to 4 inches with base diameters of from 7¾ inches to 8½ inches. The plain upper and lower margins became narrower as the decoration became taller, and their inner edges might be finished with a chased wavy or escalloped border. The outer edges were fitted with rings of square-section strengthening wire.

The ornate decoration of this period is unequalled in the annals of Irish silversmithing. The entire sides of dish rings were delightfully worked in low relief repoussé, chiefly characterised by widely open-cut designs of figures, birds, fruits, flowers and scrolls. Decoration was often fitted into four panels linked by medallions surrounded with formal leaf motifs, each panel depicting a scene of pastoral life, including shepherds and shepherdesses, women gathering fruit, farm houses, cottages, windmills, and animals.

Other designers worked continuous panoramic scenes in which tiny people danced around the ring with real Irish abandon, or followed the chase on horse or foot with hounds in full cry. Some decorations illustrated legendary stories.

Late in this period the oriental influence appeared in dish ring decoration. In these a western interpretation of Chinese architecture and men with large cone-shaped hats was associated with sportsmen in English costume against backgrounds of disproportionate trees and equally disproportionate birds flying wildly across the scene. These flying birds dominated dish ring design at the end of this period, and continued into the third, in association with floral festoons, squirrels, fruit, vineleaves and grapes.

Dish rings of the third period showed much the same general outline as those of the second, but there was a general tendency for the lower rim to end in a pronounced outward flare. The square-section strengthening rings that edged these pieces were slightly lighter than on earlier work, but it was in the general style of their decoration that the third group broke away from the somewhat heavy Dutch naturalism of the preceding style in favour of an airier grace, but a more limited range of ornament.

The change was one of manufacturing technique, and, like the decoration, reflected changes that had taken place earlier in England. The background was no longer cut away by hand to leave the ornament in silhouette: instead an ever-increasing amount of embossed and chased ornament was made separately, by hand or with the aid of a fly press, and mounted on the ring over a complex open-work trellis. In transitional designs the flying birds, squirrels and other similar naturalistic motifs of the earlier groups were applied in this way, over vertical pales with cusped ends or other geometrical designs such as crosses, circles, and squares, the aim of the silversmith being to use the fly press in order to reduce the metal to a delicate tracery.

Soon, however, the full tide of neo-classical ornament swept away the more naturalistic motifs, and during the 1780s and 1790s dish rings were made in which the press-pierced backgrounds supported applied festoons of husks and drapery and similar motifs from the limited current classical range. The meandering shaping to the inner edges of the rims continued on the more expensive dish rings of this group, but was less frequent than on those in the rococo style.

Dish rings of the fourth period, dating approximately between 1785 and 1810, were but the obvious development from the previous style. Weight of metal and cost of manufacture were further reduced by incorporating the main ornamental features, such as classic swags, in the openwork silhouette cut by the fly press. Only the surface detail then required hand finishing. In some examples the waist was encircled with a band of decorated bright-cut design, with rows of vertical pales above and below. Body and rim consisted of a single piece of metal: instead of the attached strengthening-wires the outer edges of the metal were bent vertically to form a thin plain band around top and bottom. Rarely, the upper rim was expanded horizontally and finished with a curved wire edge.

Dish rings have been noted with Irish hall-marks dating from 1745 to 1795, the majority being made between 1760 and 1780. Dublin was the only assay office in Ireland and all authentic examples therefore bear the Dublin hall-mark (see Chapter 2).

Dish rings are nearly always marked on the exterior of the lower rim. The standard mark and the town mark are invariably found, but the date mark is often missing. Because of the difficulties encountered in sending work to Dublin for assaying, many Irish silversmiths illegally issued unassayed silver plate. The result is that dish rings stamped only with the maker's mark are sometimes found. This has proved an excellent opportunity for the fakers who have produced many dish rings lacking hall-marks. A large number of reproduction dish rings were made early in this century. Some of these rings are decorated with ornament from the Book of Kells. Genuine Georgian silver work, however, ante-dated the finding of this source of Celtic design. Unmarked dish rings, or those stamped with indecipherable marks, are therefore considered to lack authenticity and rarely fetch high prices.

Some fakers have worked up a ring of standard pattern and cut the marks from an old Dublin spoon, inserting them in the bottom rim. As in the case of the tea-pot, however, it is impossible for the faker to place such marks in their correct position to be read along the rim of the piece. The marks were usually stamped on the spoon one below the other, and when applied to the rim of a dish ring they can only be read when the ring is turned on its side.

13

TEA-CANISTERS, CADDY-LADLES, AND MOTE-SKIMMERS

FORTUNATE indeed is the collector who can illustrate all the changing moods of eighteenth century silver by assembling a complete chronological sequence of silver tea-canisters. Such an array would tell in fascinating detail of the earliest plain little Chinese bottle shapes, of their more skilfully proportioned, plinth-based successors dating to later Queen Anne and early Georgian days, and of the emergence of curved outlines in inverted pyriform vases and in the cabinet-maker designs like tiny *bombé* commodes around the mid-century. They would display the irrepressible, irresponsible ornament that dominated the rococo style (Fig. 56), paralleling the more sober work of the 1740s and 1750s, and showing how an early adaptation of simple oriental form became, in the rococo mood, an animated fantasy of supposedly oriental decoration. They would demonstrate the swing of taste to the extremes of cold neo-classicism in the later 1760s, with urn and vase canisters (Fig. 57), and the straight-sided boxes, elliptical on plan, which were more cheaply produced in the late eighteenth century factories (Fig. 58). And they would include the yet plainer rectangles dictated by the need for sets of more capacious canisters to fit into the caskets or tea-chests which form a study of their own throughout the period.

Fig. 56

Fig. 57

Fig. 58

Whatever the designs, however, there would appear to be little justification for calling any of these treasures a tea-caddy. In 1711 the *London Gazette* referred to a "silver canister for tea", and that term seems to have been used consistently for metal specimens until the later nineteenth century. Caddy was applied in the nineteenth century to examples in ivory, tortoiseshell and other materials, but the earliest use of the name so far noticed dates to 1790, unless one can include a reference in a letter to Fanny Burney dated 1771 regarding a "tea cadet".

Throughout the period under review many of these canisters were designed as individual pieces. Others harmonised in outline with contemporary silver tea-pots. But by the 1730s fashion was demanding a set of three canisters and a handsome box to contain them. This box, of ornamental wood or of wood covered with some other valuable material such as shagreen or mother-of-pearl, and richly mounted with decorative key-plate, handle and feet of silver, was known at first as a tea-trunk. For those of the second half of the century—when instead of three canisters it became the fashion for the box to be fitted with two canisters and a wide-mouthed sugar box—the general term was tea-chest.

Silver may have been suggested as a material for tea-canisters by the arrival of the leaves from the Orient in canisters of the whitish alloy tutenag, referred to by Lovell in 1687 as being "often taken for silver". Such a canister was sometimes divided into several compartments, and was equipped with a flattish-bowled, short-handled spoon of tutenag or ivory—features which were only developed in England later in the eighteenth century. The early English canister design was taken from the oriental stoppered jar of porcelain, the plain, flat sides rising from a rectangular base and curving sharply in at the shoulders to terminate in a narrow cylindrical neck fitted with a highly-domed cover.

This cover, topped with a knop finial, was detachable, so that the hostess making tea could use it as a measure for transferring the leaves to the tea-pot: a Hogarth painting of the Walpole family, believed to date to the late 1730s, shows Lady Walpole doing this, while a servant stands ready with a silver kettle of boiling water. On the floor is seen the shagreen-covered tea-chest from which the silver canister has been taken and which contains the second of the pair. Such canisters, made in pairs, contained only four to six ounces of tea each—indication of the high price of the luxury drink.

Before the end of Queen Anne's reign the sense of form that typified the period was resulting in more ambitious versions of this design. The corners were chamfered, resulting in two broad faces at the sides and three narrow ones at each end. Flat-faced moulding was introduced as a base-rim, balanced by moulding at the shoulders which now curved steeply up to a flat platform below the cylindrical neck. This neck was topped by a domed and knop-handled cover, but in some examples the entire upper section from the shoulders also constituted a tight-fitting lid, permitting the insertion of a pewter or tutenag liner. By 1710 the top section, complete with dome-capped neck, might slide instead of lifting off, running in grooves under the raised shoulder-rim which replaced the border moulding, of which one section was necessarily mounted on the sliding lid itself. An alternative design had a sliding base, the pedimented foot-rim now becoming an important feature.

The dome-and-neck canister continued to be made until about 1760, the dome becoming shorter and the ends of the box often rounded, after 1735, simplifying the manufacture of the sides from a single sheet of thinly rolled metal. But even by about 1715 other designs were superseding it. The most obvious development was the change to a stepped lid, on a plainly rectangular box, to harmonise with, and very occasionally to match, the deep applied foot-rim built in tiers of plain convex or square moulding. Occasionally moulding to match the foot-rim was also applied half way up the body.

From 1720 the lid might be hinged, which allowed for

the introduction of lock and key. It became taller, flat instead of rounded on top, and surmounted by a heavy knop. This and the lid and rim mouldings might be cast, but more often the mouldings were built from strips of hand-worked silver. With the improvements in the production of rolled plate from 1730, the whole finish became finer. The lid lost its high-stepped design in favour of flatter, ovolo moulding, the flat top sometimes lacking a finial and perhaps engraved. The cabinet maker's technique was also suggested in the occasional introduction of ovolo-moulded bracket feet.

All these designs remained basically alike in their plain rectangular outlines and, in all, the use of ornament was largely restricted to engraved coats of arms. By about 1715, however, narrow borders of engraved scrollwork sometimes appeared below the shoulder rim and above the foot-rim, or around each face on a rectangular example. By the 1720s such borders, although still comparatively uncommon, had developed into wide fields of engraved decoration, supplemented by engraving on the chamfered corners and the dome of the cap. In the 1740s the decoration might be chased in bold relief over the upper part of the body, but many canisters retained the uninterrupted outlines of earlier work. In the 1750s, when such furniture-designers as Chippendale were displaying tea-chests in the current *bombé* outlines of contemporary commodes, it was only to be expected that the silver canister itself would show similar ogee outlines, rounded out at the shoulders, in at the waist, and out again to the moulded base-rim. Some examples were mounted on applied cast feet such as scrolled volutes or beaded acanthus leaves. Alternatively a shaped apron might link outward-flaring foot extensions of the canister body, comparable with the "French feet" equally associated with the period's furniture. The lid was slightly domed and topped with a cast finial such as a shell or a pineapple.

On examples in the rococo style much of the most fantastic ornament was supposedly oriental, and in such work the finial might be a Chinaman shaped in full relief. The background to the imagined scenes of Chinese tea-growing and tea-drinking consisted of the scrolls and shells, asymmetrical cartouches and fantastic rockwork for which the period was renowned. These were embossed in high relief on canisters which basically followed the rectangular outlines of much mid-century furniture in the same "Chinese taste".

Outlines suggested by oriental vases appeared in the late 1730s and were naturally associated with the rhythmic flower designs and swirling flutes and scrolls worked in repoussé on much contemporary tea-table silver. The most usual silhouette in the 1750s consisted of a domed cover topped with a full relief flower or bird finial, supported on a more or less vertical neck above the swelling shoulders of a body in inverted pear outline, which tapered to a circular, applied foot. Lid, shoulders, body, and foot were similarly embossed.

The concurrent changes in design and technique dating to the later 1760s, the emergence of neo-classic styles and the development of silversmithing by factory methods, were associated with a more general popularity for the still expensive but less prohibitively costly drink. Canisters of this period were more than twice as capacious as those of Queen Anne's day, and the range of quality, down to the highly competitive factory product, resulted in a corresponding variety in design. The canister in the shape of a classic vase or urn was a handsome product of the period. Its tapering body was embossed in low relief with classic ornament, flowers, or radiating convex flutes around the base, above a narrow stem and high concave foot, sometimes terminating in a square plinth on ball feet. The incurving shoulders rose to a domed cover—soon this too was in a dished, concave outline—topped with a formalistic finial. The design might also include a pair of horizontal loop handles, a feature that was continued on some canisters throughout the first quarter of the nineteenth century. Tall arching handles date more especially to the period of 1775-95.

By about 1785 the foot and plinth were becoming sturdier. Fluting might rise more than half way up the body, and the smooth area below the shoulder might be enriched with applied festoons, perhaps supported by a pair of rams' heads shaped in relief. A popular design included four loop handles placed equidistantly to achieve an undulating effect.

Rich-looking combinations of fluting and reeding were popular in many designs, and also appeared on some of the silver tea-chests made at this period. Jackson describes one dated 1765 with vertically undulating sides and hinged lid to a rectangular body. This decoration was widely used on the single box canisters of the period which were designed to match tea-pots similarly straight-sided and elliptical on plan. On an early canister of this shape there might be considerable use of embossed decoration around the lower half of the body, which was supported on a foot-rim, and on the domed, ring-handled lid. But the Birmingham silversmiths quickly introduced less expensive designs on which the ornament was bright-cut. The lid was entirely flat except for the cast knob: from about 1780 this was frequently a pineapple, such as Matthew Boulton manufactured in twelve sizes. The lid was hinged so that the canister could be fitted with lock and key.

Other single, straight-sided canisters were square, rectangular, or hexagonal on plan, their sides decorated with chasing, engraving, or bright-cutting, or with no more than applied rims of gadrooning. Similar canisters, in pairs or threes, were fitted into plain chests of richly coloured wood. A design appeared in about 1800 consisting of two separate, lidded compartments, with an additional lid covering both. The return to more flamboyant styles in the 1820s was reflected in canisters, square or oblong, on which the decoration took the form of chasing and deep relief castings. These were often handsome pieces, but they lacked the light-hearted grace associated with the master silversmiths whose imaginations were first caught by the charming ritual of the eighteenth century English tea-table.

The domed lid of the early tea-canister was used to measure the dry leaves into the pot. When this type of canister was superseded by designs with hinged lids, stemmed ladles were used to spoon the tea into the pot. At first the ladle consisted of a deep, shell-shaped bowl, from the rim of which a stem rose almost vertically. Attached to the back of the stem might be a small hook fitting an appropriate hanger in the tea-chest. The bowl of such a ladle was usually hand raised, but cast examples have been noted. Rarely the handle might be of ebony or black-stained boxwood.

As the use of wide-lidded tea-canisters became more universal, tea-scoops with very short stems became fashionable. These were kept in the canisters with the tea. Few were made before 1770, and these were hand raised from thin silver plate. By the end of the decade Birmingham silversmiths were turning out silver ladles in considerable quantities, a manufacture which continued profitable for nearly seventy years.

The ladle bowl might be die struck and the handle pressed, the two sections being joined and finished by hand. Others were stamped, bowl and handle in a single piece. These factory-made spoons averaged three inches in length and a weight of about one-quarter ounce. They were never exempt from hall-marking. The Act of 1790 exempting many small articles weighing less than five pennyweights, specifically excluded "caddy ladles" from this concession. The majority of examples seen by the authors bear the anchor of Birmingham: many others were made in London, Sheffield, and Dublin.

Many a caddy spoon was a little masterpiece of the silversmith's craft. It might be embossed, fluted, engraved, chased or left severely plain. Some were gilt. So fragile were some of the eighteenth century examples that they were liable to break at the bowl-stem junction, but such fractures can be invisibly repaired. From 1820 ornate examples were cast. Silver caddy-spoons were greatly in demand as inexpensive presents, and their variety of design is astonishing, all apparently intended to be as distinctively different as possible from the conventional spoon.

Collectors are always eager to acquire the rare eagle spoon produced during the 1790s by Joseph Taylor of Birmingham. This was made from a single piece of silver in the outline of an eagle, the neck forming the handle terminating in the bird's head, with a burnished eye. The bowl was delicately embossed to suggest plumage. An example, fully hall-marked, was sold by auction in 1930 for £20. A second series, poorly finished and from inferior tools, was made during the 1850s.

The jockey cap (Fig. 59), another early design, is also rare. The cap itself, with a tiny bow of silver wire at the back, serves as the tea scoop, the visor as its handle. This pattern has been widely copied. On genuine examples the hall-marks include a duty mark and are struck on the visor; on reproductions the marks may appear at the back of the cap. Some jockey caps were made in silver filigree: these usually belong to the William IV period. Associated is the stirrup design (Fig. 60). The half-closed hand design is also scarce. The handle consists of a flat wrist engraved with a suggestion of a lace cuff. This design, and the eagle, the jockey cap, and some escallop shells, have bowls larger than is usual in caddy-spoons.

Fig. 59

Fig. 60

A remarkable series of spoons in which the shell-shaped bowls were delicately embossed with floral sprays was made by Joseph Taylor during the 1780s and 1790s. Caddy spoons in the form of fish and engraved with arcs to suggest scales are also collectors' pieces.

War trophies incorporating a standard, pennon, cannon and ramming irons, drum and fife, bayonet and sword, were embossed on a series of caddy-spoon bowls made in Birmingham from about 1805 until 1815. The stem was sometimes engraved with the name of a victory and occasionally with a date.

A popular design for the caddy-spoon bowl was a vine leaf with a bunch of grapes embossed in the centre and the handle formed of a vine tendril in silver wire. Another shape represented a tea leaf with finely chased veins and a stalk handle of twisted wire (Fig. 61). The escallop

Fig. 61

shell in several designs and sizes came from many silversmiths in Birmingham and London, the majority being of eighteenth century origin with handles decorated with bright-cut engraving.

Eighteenth century handles were usually of flat silver decorated with more bright-cut engraving. If the bowl was plain the engraving was carried down into it: the centre of such a bowl might form a field for the owner's crest or cipher. The fiddle-shaped handle belongs to the nineteenth century from about 1805.

The Georgian tea-equipage usually included a tea-strainer or mote-skimmer, mote being the old English word for a minute particle of foreign matter in food or drink. This dainty little tool was like a long-handled spoon. The barb or point on its slender stem was used for clearing the perforations at the base of the tea-pot spout, and the bowl, patterned with perforations, for skimming the infusion in the cup (Fig. 62).

The *London Gazette* for 1697 refers to "long or strainer tea-spoons with narrow pointed handles". They were known as "long tea spoons" throughout Queen Anne's reign. The bowl had rat-tail strengthening and circular perforations. Saw-pierced bowls lacking the rat-tail were of Georgian origin. Early examples were sold *en suite* with tea-spoons.

Fig. 62

It has been suggested that the contemporary tea-pot spout was usually too boldly curved for the spear-topped stem to be thrust down it. This suggestion overlooks the fact that the juncture of spout and body was protected by a perforated tea-leaf strainer. At that period, according to John Worlidge and other contemporary writers, the tea leaves were dried whole. After two or three minutes infusion in the pot "the leaves spread out to their former breadth and shape" and were liable to block up the perforations, obstructing the flow of tea into the spout. The

(*Above left*) shell-shaped sugar-box, London 1616—formerly the property of Samuel Pepys. (*Above right*) sugar-bowl with fluted body encircled with punched decoration, cover and foot-ring gadrooned; by J. Leach, London 1699.

(*Upper left*) plain sugar-bowl and cover, with moulded foot and cover-ring; by G. Jones, London 1729. (*Lower left*) boat-shaped bowl with pierced decoration; by John Lane 1787. (*Right*) vase-shaped sugar-bowl with blue flint-glass liner; by Samuel Taylor, London 1760.

Milk-jugs. (*Left*) with moulded foot and spout, and broad double scroll handle; by John White, London 1728. (*Right*) with wide spout and three legs on hoof feet; London 1739.

(*Left*) with helmet-shaped body on spreading moulded foot; London *c.* 1740. (*Right*) with embossed ovoid body and handle with recurved scroll and ornament; by Christian Hillan, London 1740.

spear-knop of the mote-skimmer was used to remove these from inside the perforations.

Another widespread misapprehension concerns the perforations in the bowl of the mote-skimmer. Some collectors consider these too large to collect tea dust. In this connection it must be remembered that Georgian tea contained all the foreign matter now extracted by mechanical means. Such as floated on the cup of tea could be removed in the skimmer bowl. The skimming was sometimes done by the "tea-blender", usually the most presentable house-maid or parlour-maid, who had charge of the tea-table equipage, preparing the tea and handing a cup to each guest and member of the family. On less formal occasions, however, mote-skimming was each individual's own concern. Giant specimens usually bear George III hall-marks and were designed for use with contemporary tea-urns.

Some collectors of "strainer spoons" express their belief that they were used in France as snail-spoons, shell-fish-spoons and absinthe-spoons. While somewhat resembling the mote-skimmer, such spoons show certain dissimilarities of design in keeping with their different purposes.

14

TEA-POTS, COFFEE-POTS, AND CHOCOLATE-POTS

THE tea-table silver of Georgian England, and in particular the pots for tea, coffee, and chocolate then given pride of place on so many formal and informal social occasions, makes an exceptionally interesting collectors' study. On such pieces the smiths lavished much of their finest craftsmanship in domestic silver, producing beautiful and surprisingly original designs. In this chapter only the shapes that were generally fashionable will be described: the independence of designers resulted in numerous minor variations (Fig. 63 indicates the general changes in tea-pot outlines).

The earliest known silver tea-pot, now in the Victoria and Albert Museum, is unrelievedly plain. It has a tall tapering cylinder body, and its short, straight tubular spout projects from considerably above half height. The high conical lid is hinged to the handle socket and surmounted by a plainly turned silver finial. The leather-covered D-handle, riveted into silver sockets, is placed at right angles to the spout. This silver tea-pot would now be classed as a coffee-pot were it not for the engraved inscription: "This silver tea-Pott was presented to ye Com^tte^ of ye East India Cumpany by ye Hon^oue^ George Lord Berkeley of Berkeley Castle A member of that Honourable and worthy Society and A true Hearty Lover of them 1670". Lord Berkeley was on the committee of the Company from 1660 until 1697, and married the daughter of John Massingberd, the Company's treasurer.

Few silver tea-pots appear to have been made in England before the reign of Queen Anne. By about 1680 tall angular shapes had been abandoned in favour of shorter tea-pots,

Fig. 63

TEA-POTS

Top row: rare late Carolean; Queen Anne, Oriental style with lidded spout, and octagonal version.
Second row: bullet and Scottish bullet; inverted pyriform, George II period.
Third row: late eighteenth century neo-classic; serpentine design; example raised on footed stand.
Fourth row: early nineteenth century, on a tray (this has the popular peaked top, and a bone handle); less balanced design on ball feet; fantastic revived rococo.

their gracefully-curved bodies resembling those of the Chinese porcelain jars then being imported. A curved spout emerged from low on the incurved body, directly opposite the handle. The high-domed lid continued the curves of the body. In the later examples a plain shallow foot rim was added.

Queen Anne tea-pots might have either melon-shaped or pyriform bodies. The former, derived from the earlier Chinese form, was a squat affair of small capacity with a simple curving contour, somewhat ribbed to resemble the fruit, and sometimes a flat base without a foot-rim. Pyriform or pear-shaped bodies, which might be either round or polygonal on plan, are usually found with deeply moulded foot-rims.

At first the tea-pot was severely plain, but by the turn of the century silversmiths were adding exquisite chasing or engraving. The lower part of the body might be enlivened with applied cut-card work, sometimes chased with foliage. The early spout was a slender tube with a single graceful curve, the lines of the lower end now designed to combine harmoniously with the curves of the body. In about 1705 the moulded swan-neck spout arrived, the opening usually fitted with a small hinged flap to minimise loss of heat.

For the handle, leather-covered wood was usual but required frequent renewal when cracked by the changing temperatures. Ebony or blackened boxwood were often used for the replacement. Early handles were of the plain D-shape, but by 1710 the recurving scroll handle had arrived, sometimes eight-faceted. It might be placed at right angles to the spout, but was more usually opposite to it.

The lid of a Queen Anne tea-pot was generally raised in a high dome and fitted with a solid, silver knob; a scroll thumb-piece rose from the hinge. This right-angled hinge joining the lid to the upper handle-socket was not an invariable feature. Some lids were loose, and merely attached to the handle-sockets by slender silver chains.

In Queen Anne's day tea was always freshly made in the drawing-room or boudoir, the custom being for the boiling water to be brought in by a servant so that the hostess

Milk-jugs. (*Left*) silver-gilt helmet type on three lion-head and paw feet, its body ornamented with rococo chasing; by William Townsend, Dublin 1740. (*Right*) in the form of a cow; J. Schuppe, London 1765.

Three-piece tea-set decorated with embossed leaves and applied moulding on rims. Moulded base-ring with four short feet. By Charles Fox, London 1830.

Three-piece elliptical tea-set of classic design, consisting of tea-pot, sugar-bowl, and milk-jug; Edinburgh 1789.

Elaborately-embossed tea-set, consisting of tea-pot, coffee-pot, milk-jug, and sugar-bowl, on oval tray; by R. Emes and E. Barnard, London 1821.

herself could make the tea. At this period, therefore, the tea-pot might be equipped with a handled tripod stand mounted over a spirit lamp—as an alternative to the silver kettle and lamp, which were already becoming part of the tea-equipage (see Chapter 15).

George I tea-pots continued the established melon and pear outlines, the lower part of the latter sometimes decorated with chasing or repoussé work. An interesting change of style which began during this period was the increase of width—from spout-tip to handle—in proportion to height, the width frequently being the greater. The domed lid was less tall than formerly, moulded to harmonise with the body shape and hinged to the top socket of the handle, and spout and handle were invariably placed opposite each other.

The smoothly globular or bullet-shaped body, in which the lid was included in the spherical outline, appeared during this period. This stood upon a narrow moulded foot-rim of small diameter. Designs showing slight variations in spout, handle, and foot-rim were produced throughout the century. Paul de Lamerie chased the bodies of his later bullet tea-pots in high relief. The bullet-shaped tea-pot on a stemmed foot was of Scottish origin, the form apparently never being popular with Georgian tea-drinkers in England.

Soon after 1730 the lavish enrichment associated with the French *rocaille* phase appeared on some tea-pots. Their bodies might be elaborately chased with scrolls and flowers, their spouts moulded to represent dragons, and their lids surmounted with pineapples—symbol of hospitality—and the Chinamen who figured so largely in mid-century ornament and were considered particularly appropriate in association with the oriental drink. During this period a tea-pot might be designed to a customer's commission. Many a tea-pot with a hall-mark dating between 1730 and 1760 constitutes the sole example produced in that particular form and size.

A plain incurved body in the form of an inverted pear or a shallow ogee became fashionable late in the George II period. This might be on a wide moulded foot-rim. The spout retained the swan-neck form, although now frequently fluted and with a wrought orifice shaped like the head of a bird or occasionally a griffin, even when the rest of the pot was plain.

The design tended to be slightly ungainly until it was developed into the urn outline associated with the neo-classic vogue of the later years of the century. The lid and the top of the body were then slightly dished, the latter making a sharp angle with the sides which tapered smoothly to a short, narrow stem above a flattish round or elliptical foot. Spout and handle balanced in plain curves, the handle being given the sweeping arch typical of its period.

Until the reign of George III the body of the tea-pot was beaten out of the solid silver plate, continued hammering slowly reducing the thickness of the metal while forming the required shape. The expense involved in beating hollow ware was one reason for the small capacity of early silver tea-pots. In the 1780s, however, when silversmiths were under the spell of the neo-classic taste, they began to produce straight-sided oval tea-pots delicately engraved, and it was found that these straight-sided patterns could be made of rolled sheet silver. This reduced the cost and so made silver tea-pots available to a wider public. Tea-pots in the new style were made circular, oval or polygonal on plan, with flat bases and vertical sides, slightly domed lids, straight tapering spouts, and arched or scroll handles. Usually the sides of the oval bodies were delicately engraved with bands of foliage, knots of ribbons, festoons, medallions or diaper patterns.

In early work, such a tea-pot had neither foot-rim nor feet to lift the broad base, heated by the tea, above the polished table or tea tray, which was thus liable to be disfigured. In consequence a silver stand supported by four short ball or moulded feet was devised to place beneath the tea-pot. When found together the hall-marks of tea-pot and stand are seldom the same, the stand having been acquired somewhat later after the dangerous deficiencies of the tea-pot had been discovered. The stand was discarded before 1800, replaced by four feet on the tea-pot itself. These in turn were replaced on George IV examples by large flaring rim-feet moulded in elaborate outline.

Early in the reign of George II had appeared a cast silver

handle moulded in a re-curving scroll. Insulating discs of ivory were fitted between the handle and tea-pot body to prevent the metal becoming too hot to hold. Such handles became more popular from 1790 and many are found on early nineteenth century tea-, coffee-, and chocolate-pots. By 1750 ivory finials had appeared on tea-pot lids.

The severely straight-sided tea-pots were still in vogue in the last years of the century, but a hint of the more elaborate styles to come was expressed in the design with the whole body shaped in vertical fluting and reeding or some more elaborate combination of concave and convex curves, making the outline serpentine on plan. Before 1800 the enduringly popular half-height convex reeding was established. At first it was not uncommon for silversmiths to surround the lower half of the body with as many lobes as possible: these were soon numerically modified in the interests of economy.

By the end of the century the tendency was to round off the square corners, producing heavily capacious tea-pots, often lavishly ornamented and expressing the solid magnificence then expected of silver plate. Designs were so diverse that full description is impossible: the urn-shape, tapering to a narrow stem above a spreading foot, continued as ambitious alternative to the comfortable rounded-rectangular body, its lower part reeded. In some sets the coffee-pot assumed the urn outline, the tea-pot, sugar-basin, and cream-jug having matching bodies but resting squatly on narrow base rims instead of the stemmed foot.

When coffee was first introduced to England it found little favour. The abuse heaped upon it in the mid-seventeenth century gradually subsided, however, and, as it became fashionable, coffee-houses, which were really clubs, began to make their appearance. As early as 1651 the first was opened at Oxford, by a Syrian, Cirques Jobson; the next, in London, a year later. Within a few years there were more than two hundred in London, and so numerous did they become that in 1675 Charles II issued a proclamation ordering their suppression.

Coffee had become a fashionable drink in the home before the end of the century. It was customary to grind the beans at table when this refreshment was served. Pope in describing the famous game of ombre at Hampton Court Palace in "The Rape of the Lock" exclaims regarding coffee:

> For lo! the board with Cups and Spoons is Crown'd
> The Berries crackle and the Mill turns round.

The earliest known silver coffee-pot bears a London hall-mark for 1681 and is in the Victoria and Albert Museum. This resembles the earliest tea-pot of 1670 in almost every feature, except that the handle is set opposite the spout. The body is inscribed "A gift to Richard Sterne by the Honourable East India Company."

The early design followed the lantern shape of the tea-pot. The high cylindrical body tapered slightly to the top and was surmounted by a conical cover, the finial being a simple knob. The handle was leather-covered. The vessel differed from the early tea-pot in having the straight, tubular spout placed lower down the body. The handle might be placed at right angles to the spout (H.M. the King possesses such an example dated 1689) or opposite to it.

When coffee became a popular drink, coffee-pots with handles at right angles to their spouts were advertised as "right and left" and sold in pairs. This enabled the servant to hold one in each hand for pouring coffee and milk simultaneously, the idea being that by doing so the coffee acquired a finer flavour.

By the beginning of the eighteenth century silversmiths were adding more grace to the coffee-pot, first lifting the plain tapering body on to a shallow moulded foot and giving the hinged cover a high rounded dome with a moulded rim. To facilitate opening the lid a thumb-piece was fitted above the hinge.

The form of the early Georgian body might be cylindrical or polygonal with a domed lid to match. Both body and lid might be engraved with coats of arms. The tubular spout had by now been replaced by the graceful swan-neck type, such as was fitted on the contemporary tea-pot, and the foot-rim might be gadrooned. Although the prevailing vogue was for straight-sided vessels, both coffee- and chocolate-pots of bulbous form were made.

As in the case of the contemporary tea-pot, a plain incurved body in the form of an inverted pear on a spreading moulded foot-rim, deeper than formerly, appeared in about 1740. With this design the lid was a moulded dome with a cast finial, sometimes in the form of a pine cone. The spout retained the swan-neck form and might be moulded with acanthus foliage or other decoration; some were chased.

Fig. 64

From the beginning of the century designers lavished particular care on the junction of spout and body, masking it with cut-card work, or giving the base of the spout an escalloped outline. (Fig. 64 indicates the range of styles through the eighteenth century.)

Among the coffee-pots designed by Paul de Lamerie in the 1730s was one which became particularly fashionable with those able to afford the luxury of such a magnificent piece. Its pyriform body was exquisitely chased with cupids and scrolls, the conventional foot-rim being replaced by three feet, each in the form of a dolphin issuing from a mask. In this style of coffee-pot a short spout was modelled in the form of an eagle's head and placed near the body rim. Students of early Georgian furniture carvings recognize a close association in current trends of design.

With the establishment of the vogue for classical designs and decorations in silver, coffee-pots lost their air of solidity and deteriorated into fanciful urn-shaped vases, supported on moulded spreading feet, sometimes square, more usually circular. Lids were often designed to match and decorated with urn-shaped finials of cast silver. Bodies were decorated with repoussé foliage and scrolling motifs; later, convex spiral flutings ornamented the lower part of the body. The vase form was superseded by another version of the pyriform, the lower part of the body being larger in circumference than before and the decorated spout less graceful.

Throughout the Georgian period, until about 1800, the coaching coffee-pot had a considerable vogue. This was of a smooth-surfaced pyriform but, instead of being circular or elliptical in section, it had flat sides. The spout was a curved open cup applied to the lip-rim from which a piece was cut to allow the liquid to be poured. The handle was of light strap silver in the shape of a scroll and usually wicker-covered; earlier specimens had leather-covered handles. These pots were fitted into small travelling-cases with other coffee-making accessories.

Chocolate was instantly welcomed by the fashionable world when it became known in 1657 that the beverage could be bought "in Bishopsgate Street, in Queen's Head Alley, at a Frenchman's house and is an excellent West India Drink."

The silver chocolate-pot (*moulinet* it was sometimes called) was conspicuous in the dressing-room of the *élégante* who, if we may believe Swift, spent five hours in dressing before she made her appearance at the playhouse, at cards, at a rout or other social occasion.

The early chocolate-pot of silver usually resembled the plain cylindrical coffee-pot, but there were two differences: it was considerably smaller in size, and in the cover was a small hole for the insertion of a swizzle stick or rod for stirring the liquid chocolate immediately before pouring. This aperture was covered by a small lid, usually part of the finial.

Chocolate-pots with removable finials for the insertion of the swizzle-stick are rarely found hall-marked after 1740. Until then the forms resembled those of contemporary coffee-pots. Sometimes the lid finial was attached to the hinge with a silver chain. Later, the chocolate-pot might resemble a ewer or hot-water jug, a style copied in the earthenware pots made in Staffordshire by Thomas Whieldon.

Early examples of tea-, coffee-, and chocolate-pots have hall-marks punched in a line near the top of the body below the rim near the handle. After about 1760 the marks are found in a rectangular form on the bottom. In either case the lid may be hall-marked too.

15

TEA-KETTLES AND URNS

THE silver tea-equipage, radiant with careful polishing, set the tone of the whole elegant tea-time ritual practised by the eighteenth century hostess. Arranged upon a silver tea-board of handsome proportions were the tea-pot, a pair of tea-canisters, the sugar-bowl, and the cream-jug, dominated by the graceful tea-kettle on its tripod stand. Although the silver tea-kettle, in a heavy, dumpy design, was in use from the early 1680s, few examples are known bearing English hall-marks earlier than about 1705.

In that year the *London Gazette* noted "a gilt Tea Pot and a Tea Kettle." The early Queen Anne tea-kettle (Plate 31), had a bun-shaped body with an expansive flat base area, a grooved band encircling the shoulder, and the rim strengthened with narrow moulding. The minaret lid had a central knob of ebony or other wood stained black. The spout was in a moulded swan-neck design, its base sometimes faceted and its tip provided with a hinged cover. From the shoulder band swung a handle formed of a pair of recurving scrolls connected by a spindle fitted with a loose hand-grip of turned ebony or other dyed wood.

The kettle was mounted on a circular tripod stand. This consisted of a ring, plain or pierced, exactly fitting the kettle base, supported by three bifurcated scroll legs with circular feet resting on small buns or cushions of ebony or other hard wood. Horizontal branches curving from the legs connected to a smaller ring supporting a spirit-lamp,

Fig. 65

its wick covered by a hinged dome. A distinctive feature of the kettle-stand at this period was the inclusion of a pair of hinged D-handles hanging from the upper ring (Fig. 65). When lifted into a horizontal position these permitted the kettle, filled with already-boiling water and complete with stand and lamp, to be carried to the tea-table. A pair of lamp-snuffers might hang from the rim of the stand.

In accordance with the change of fashion in tea-pot design, the tea-kettle late in the reign of Queen Anne might have a pyriform or pear-shaped body. Some examples were eight- or twelve-sided on plan, with matching lamps (Plate 31). At the same time there was a vogue for kettles not merely matching in a general sense but as exactly as possible duplicating the tea-pots they accompanied, in size, shape, decoration, even position of handle and spout. In this design the arching swing handle of the kettle was replaced by a vertical wooden scroll-shaped tea-pot handle attached to the body with sockets. At this time the legs of the tripod stand were of inverted baluster form, each fitted with a horizontal lug to support the lamp-ring. The stand's hinged lifting-handles might be replaced by a single straight handle of turned ebony or ivory projecting from a socket soldered to one of the tripod legs or to the upper ring. By the early 1720s the lifting-handles were discarded from the stand design and the spirit-container was made more capacious, its depth being increased until it almost touched the table.

Very occasionally the tea-kettle was mounted on a silver tripod, some thirty inches high, which stood upon the floor at the side of the hostess (Fig. 66). Its baluster stem supported either a plate resembling a contemporary salver upon which kettle and lamp were placed, or the spirit-lamp itself with three scroll brackets to hold the kettle-ring.

The globular tea-kettle (Plates 31, 32), to match what

Tazzas. (*Left*) silver-gilt, on trumpet-shaped foot, with wide matt-surfaced border decorated in high relief with fabulous animals, flowers, and foliage, London 1668. (*Top right*) with flat rim decorated with hammered gadrooning encircling narrow slip-moulding. Domed foot gadrooned to match; by Edward Workman, Dublin 1700. (*Right*) raised plate encircled with plain moulding on stem with plain collet foot; by Isaac Dighton, London 1706.

Waiters. (*Left*) square with shaped corners and applied moulding, and mounted on four panel feet; by John Tuite, London 1726. (*Right*) with piecrust border and four moulded feet; by John Tuite, London 1738.

Waiters. (*Left*) square with indented corners and applied moulded rim, simple scroll feet and engraved border; by Paul de Lamerie, London 1727. (*Right*) sexfoil waiter with applied moulded rim; by Edward Cornock, London 1728.

(*Left*) with moulded piecrust rim. A floral and foliage border in flat chasing surrounds an elaborately-displayed crest; by Edward Feline, London 1730. (*Right*) with moulded piecrust rim enriched with moulded fan motifs; by Simon le Sage, London 1758.

is generally known as the bullet-shaped tea-pot, was established in fashion by 1730 and continued after the mid-century. The lid outline followed the curve of the body, its knob of ebony or ivory matching the turned grip of the arching handle. The rim of the body-opening was engraved with a narrow band of scrolls, flowers and foliage. The vessel was considerably lighter in weight than earlier designs, and its less expansive base was given additional stability with a narrow moulded foot-rim.

Fig. 66

By about 1735 the tea-kettle was beginning to reflect the general fashion for richly ornamented tableware, the plump, globular body being dignified with embossed ornament chased in high relief, including cherubs, sprays of flowers and foliage, while scrollwork enclosed a coat of arms cartouche (Plate 32). The cover was ornamented with an applied moulding terminating in an ivory or silver knob, and the elaborately-moulded spout enriched with handsome chasings. The sides of the swing handles were scrolled and the arched grip covered with leather or cane. The moulded legs of the tripod stand were elaborated with carved ornament and the lamp ring encircled with a deep band of ornate moulding. Frequently, now, the tea-kettle stood upon a footed tray, usually triangular. The flame of the spirit-lamp might be protected from draughts by enclosing two sides of the tripod in a two-panelled perforated wind-shield, also of silver. During the next fifteen years some extravagantly designed kettles were made, raised from silver sheet which had been flattened by means of the new spring rolling-machine. The plainer and less expensive globular body was, however, more frequent.

By 1740 the fashionable kettle had a more graceful ogee body with a flat lid, and the handle bows might be cast in the form of human figures. From the elaborated kettle-ring of the tripod stand a silver apron of festooned design hung between each leg. Retaining the ogee silhouette, the tea-kettle body of the mid-century was lavishly decorated with chased and embossed work. The lid had become highly domed with a cast knob of solid silver such as a flower or a pineapple. The ogee spout had become general, decorated with sprays of foliage and scrollwork, and sometimes terminating in an eagle's head with wide open beak (Fig. 67 shows typical spout ends between 1700 and 1770). The tripod stand from about 1735 might be equipped with a pair of silver pegs attached to guard chains. The pegs fitted into holes drilled through the foot-rim of the kettle and the kettle-rim of the stand, enabling a servant to carry the kettle, stand, and lamp by the kettle-handle.

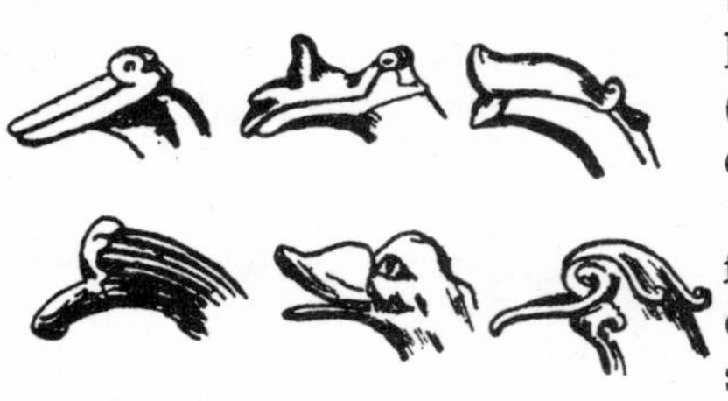

Fig. 67

By the late 1750s the kettle-opening had been raised into a gadrooned rim upon which fitted a flat domed lid (Plate 32). The earlier shapes continued until about 1775. By then tea-urns had largely superseded tea-kettles although these continued to be made well into the nineteenth century.

The silver tea-kettle was beginning to go out of favour shortly after 1760. The first indication of a general change in public requirements was the modification of the kettle design to include a ball-handled tap close to the vessel's broad base (Fig. 68). This saved the hostess the necessity of tilting the heavy kettle when water was required, and it quickly evolved into what Cowper called "the bubbling and loud-hissing urn". The tea-urn had a body capacious enough to contain two to three quarts of boiling water. The body rested upon four upright columns rising from a flat base holding a spirit-

Fig. 68

lamp. Urns in this style were made in silver until after 1830.

Fig. 69

The most typical tea-urn, vase-shaped and standing on a stemmed foot (Fig. 69), was lampless, the temperature of the water being maintained by means of a red-hot cylindrical box-iron. This was inserted into a close-fitting socket of solid silver within the body of the urn, around which the water circulated. After about 1800 the socket was fixed centrally in the body of the urn.

Some tea-urns were charcoal heated. In these the body could be removed from the base, above the stem, revealing a circular perforated container of silver or iron, in which was placed red-hot charcoal. Hot air from the burning charcoal passed through a copper tube rising through the body in gradually decreasing diameter to a loose finial on the lid. Removal of the finial created a draught which assisted combustion and drew hot air through the copper tube which in its turn kept the water hot.

Lamp-heated tea-urns appear to have been used for drawing off tea into cups; the iron- and charcoal-heated types contained reserves of hot water. For tea-time use the urn might accompany other articles of the tea-equipage upon the tea-tray, or stand separately upon a tripod table: at breakfast time the urn found a place upon the sideboard.

The early lampless tea-urn had a pear-shaped body, somewhat resembling the later tea-kettle, with an everted neck strengthened by applied gadrooning or other simple moulding. Many were embossed with plain and foliated scrolls, a cartouche being reserved for an engraved coat of arms. The bell-shaped lid terminated in a knob of classic design. A pair of scroll-shaped handles adorned the shoulders. The moulded silver spout to the tap was enriched with matching motifs, and the thumb-piece might be of ebony or green-stained ivory as were the insulating-discs in the handles. The tap projected horizontally from the base of the body which was supported on a high spool-shaped stem rimmed with gadrooning and embossed to harmonize with the body. This rested upon a square plinth having a finely-pierced frame raised on four feet.

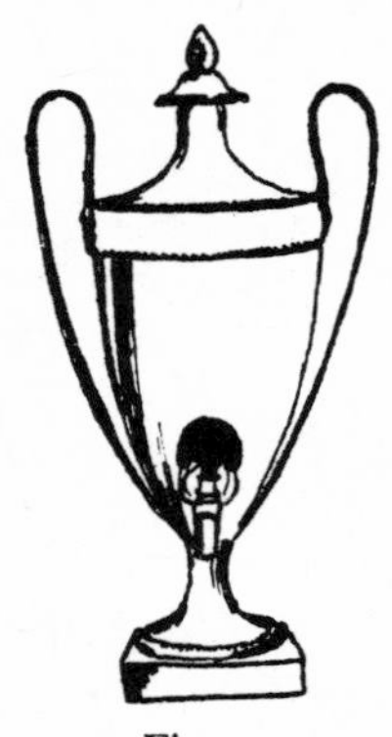

Fig. 70

The tea-urn shaped like a narrow-necked classical vase was fashionable between 1770 and 1790 (Plate 33 and Fig. 70). Narrow and tall but eminently graceful, this style was generally severely plain apart from an engraved heraldic symbol. Early in the period a pair of moulded handles was attached to the shoulders which were encircled with a band of sparsely-placed motifs such as classic medallions or acanthus leaves in low relief. Soon a pair of handles rising above the lid and recurving down to the base of the body became fashionable. Sometimes the decoration included fluting around the lower body, and in this case the foot and finial were fluted to match.

The narrow neck was widened from about 1790 and human or animal heads with solid pendant rings were used as handles (Plate 33). The tap end might be moulded in the shape of a dolphin, bird, or animal head. The body of a lamp-heated tea-urn was now supported by four flat columns rising from claw feet resting upon a flat plinth (Plate 33). The spirit-lamp was shaped as a miniature edition of the urn above it.

Fig. 71

At this time, too, the tea-urn with a ball-shaped body was popular (Fig. 71), usually with a plain surface, sometimes hollow fluted; but the demand for a wider body, less elongated than the classical urn, found happier expression towards 1805 when a design with a body resembling a wide vase became fashionable. Until about 1810 the body was purely hemispherical, with little applied decoration apart from fantastically-moulded handles. Below the body a stemmed foot stood upon a square

Oval tray with moulded rim showing thread decoration; by J. Crouch and T. Hannam, London 1798.

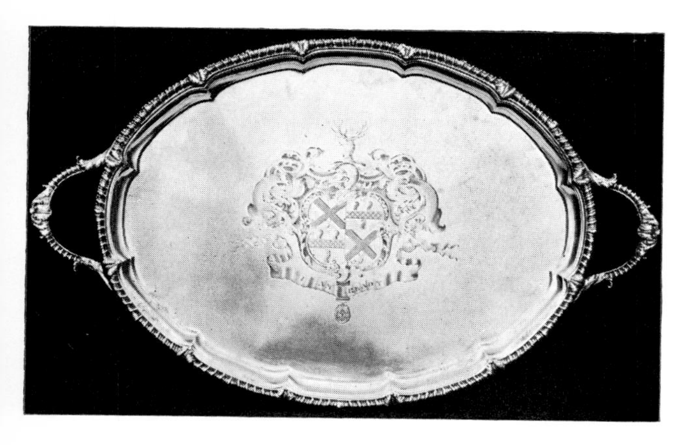

Oval tray with moulded gadrooned rim and handles; by William Stevenson, London 1810.

Rectangular tray with gadrooned rim and elaborately moulded D-shaped handles; Robert Garrard, London 1828.

Tankards. (*Left*) a Commonwealth example with deep, widely-spreading foot ring. London 1649. (*Right*) bulbous body, everted rim and openwork thumb-piece, and double-scroll handle; by Thomas Rowe, London 1770.

(*Left*) with double-step cover and volute scrolled thumb-piece; London 1677. (*Right*) embossed with a border of acanthus leaves; by John Sutton, 1678.

platform raised upon four heavy feet (Plate 33). From about 1810 the body rim was everted and the lower portion decorated with wide fluting. Many examples were so designed as to appear to have two lid rims, each bordered with matching gadrooning or other moulding. Florid mounts and ornate finials were applied in patterns apparently bearing no relation to each other or to the shape of the tea-urn. George IV tea-urns were made in almost every conceivable shape.

Tea and coffee machines advertised as "The Compleat Tea Equipage" were made from 1790, usually in Sheffield plate (Fig. 72). The design consisted of a centrally-placed hot-water-urn with double the capacity of a flanking pair of tea and coffee urns. The large urn swivelled on its base, enabling the smaller ones to be filled with hot water without being moved. Each urn was portable, however, and could be removed and used separately. With a matching waste-bowl placed in a recess between the vessels, the set was supported on a platform raised on four feet. Such a machine might be heated either by an iron or by a spirit-lamp.

Fig. 72

16

SUGAR-BOWLS AND TONGS

SUGAR has been used for sweetening food in England for at least six hundred and fifty years. Early sugar was imported in the form of refined sugar loaves weighing about 100 pounds each. The Durham Account Rolls for 1422 contain an entry, "1 sugrylaffe, 8/4". A cookery book published in 1430 advises cooks to use "whyte sugre to cast", and Heywood a century later noted that sugar was "as white and as fine as salt".

Not until the mid-Elizabethan period was sugar refining carried out in England. Judging by the inventories of the 1580s, retail grocers were then expected to stock sugar loaves, which were broken with a small chopper; brown and white sugar candy; "Barbary sugar", and fine white sugar at one shilling a pound. In 1630 members of the Pewterers' Company complained that "Vintners buy the sugar they sell to be drunk with wine vended in taverns at 18d or 19d the pound, which they make up into 19 or 20 several papers, selling each at 2d the paper, making of each pound 3/- and upwards, whereby the king is hindered in his customs, in respect that less sugar is spent with wine than would usually be if sold at a reasonable rate".

The amount of sugar imported during 1665 was less than 800 tons: by the end of the century the quantity had risen to 10,000 tons a year. In 1707 Lady Grisell Baillie paid £3. 7. 6. for a sugar loaf: this was a very white double refined sugar known as "sugar royal".

So far as is known, special containers for fine sugar were not made in silver plate until the sixteenth century, when a sugar-box and spoon might accompany the wine service.

Plate inventories of the seventeenth century contain frequent reference to sugar-boxes. In the Unton inventory of 1620 was entered "a sugar boxe, and one sugar boxe spoone". The "Twelfth Report of the Historical Manuscript Commission" noted a reference of 1639 to a "Scollup Sugar Boxe", and the Buccleugh MSS. for 1669 referred to "a silver sugar box". A number of early James I examples exist, struck with London hall-marks. These all conform to the same design, the hinged lid embossed into the shape of a scallop shell covering a shallow box of similar outline, raised upon four moulded shell feet (Plate 34).

Sugar-bowls with loose covers became fashionable during the last decade of the seventeenth century. Known as sugar-dishes, they were replicas of the covered bowls of Chinese porcelain then being imported from the East and for which the demand exceeded the supply. The silver sugar-bowl, hemispherical, and about six inches in diameter, stood upon an applied moulded foot ring, either spreading or vertical. The closely-fitting flanged cover, rising to a flattened dome, was lifted from its bowl by means of an applied moulded ring. This was about half-an-inch deep and one-third the diameter of the bowl rim, so that the whole lid was often just an inverted, shallower version of the bowl. Moulding of similar pattern might strengthen bowl and cover rims (Plate 34).

Some Queen Anne bowls were polygonal in form to match other members of the tea-equipage, and these were supported by spreading moulded ring bases. It is rare, however, to find a covered sugar-bowl surface-ornamented with more than a coat of arms on the side of the bowl and a pair of chased or engraved lines encircling the dome of the cover.

The most controversial feature of this popular design is the lid. The ring crowning the dome was obviously more serviceable as a base rim than as a handle, and the suggestion has been made that it was used as a stand under the bowl. A much more probable explanation, which does not appear to have been offered before, is that the lid was used on the tea-table as a tray in which the tea-spoons were placed. At a period when tea was often sipped from the saucer, a receptacle for the spoon was often required, and it is known that the need was met in various ways. For example the painting dating to about 1725 reproduced as the frontispiece of this book shows a flat tray, apparently the lid of an expansive silver waste-basin, put to this purpose. And in 1730, Lady Osbaldeston recorded the purchase, for sixteen shillings, of what was specifically called a silver teaspoon-dish (to be compared with four guineas paid for a tea-pot and two pounds seventeen shillings for a milk-pot). But the lid of the sugar-bowl must have been the obvious choice in many households. In some George I specimens the severely-flattened dome of the cover was topped by three small moulded lugs instead of a vertical rim (Fig. 73), even more obviously intended primarily as feet to support the lid when placed, inverted, on the table.

Fig. 73

By about 1725 the bowl was tending to lose its graceful hemispherical shape in favour of a heavier, more capacious line, and ten years later surface decoration was sometimes introduced, with low chasing or engraving in symmetrical designs, a cartouche enclosing the coat of arms. This appears to have been the standard pattern until about 1745, when the sugar-bowl became ogee-shaped with a deep, ringed cover to match. This was succeeded by the vase-shaped sugar-bowl elaborately embossed and with the cover ring replaced by a finial, most often a flower or pineapple (Plate 34).

The sugar-bowls so far described were designed as individual specimens in harmony with the rest of the tea-equipage but with no thought of forming part of a matching set. From early in the 1730s, however, a vogue had developed for keeping the precious canisters of tea in caskets or "tea-chests". At first only tea was kept in the chest, but by the mid-century a pair of canisters might be accompanied by a silver sugar-box. No survey of silver sugar-containers would be complete without reference to these boxes, but the details of their changes are merely reflections of those of the canisters themselves. The box matched its flanking canisters as closely as possible, but tended to be slightly squarer and more capacious. Whereas the canisters tended to have small lid-openings, the sugar-container's hinged lid covered the whole top of the box. By the 1770s, however, the use of silver for this purpose began to go out of favour, the box being replaced by a lidded flint-glass bowl.

Meanwhile, new trends in fashion were beginning to give the comfortable English tea-table the stately graces of Grecian ornament. Inevitably the sugar-bowl had to conform to the neo-classic craze and appear in the guise of a vase, wide at the shoulder where two short handles might support swag decoration, and tapering to a spool-shaped stem above a round foot (Fig. 74). The lid was highly domed with a vase-shaped finial. At the same time, technical developments of the 1760s had prompted the introduction of pierced decoration set off by a liner of blue glass.

Fig. 74

The upper portion of the vase body might now be both geometrically pierced and elaborately embossed with festoons, while the solid lower portion was embossed and chased, often with tall, thin leaves radiating upward from the foot stem. The cover was decorated to match the lower part of the body, and the stem, usually strengthened with gadrooning, was pierced to match the upper part. Pierced sugar-vases continued to be made with round and square feet until early in the nineteenth century. Others, from about 1775, were of unpierced silver. The classic design of vase or urn was developed to the full in the wide-brimmed bowl, often elliptical, with a pair of long narrow handles rising from the rim and recurving down to the base of the body. Such handles were sometimes strengthened with applied ribbon moulding.

Already by the 1760s some sugar-vases were being made without covers. This led to the development of an alternative arching handle design, for what was known as a sugar-bucket. This was often a more homely little vessel,

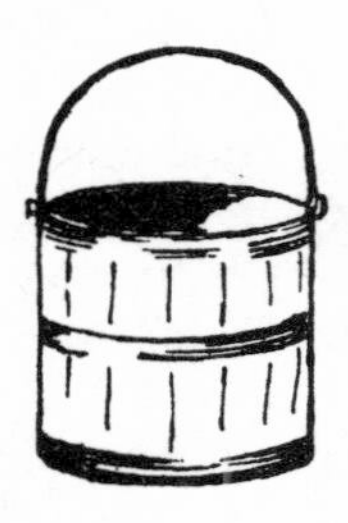
Fig. 75

Fig. 76

plainly bucket-shaped but often displaying the popular pierced decoration of the period over a blue glass liner (Figs. 75 and 76). Alternatively it might be of open wire work, in a neo-classical shape, on a high-spreading foot. The swing handle was also pierced. Although collectors generally assume that this bucket design was intended for sugar, it may be noted that Mrs. Delany, in June, 1752, referred to a "japan cream-pail and spoon" given to her with a china cup and saucer.

The boat-shaped sugar-basket was issued by the factory silversmiths in large numbers from the early 1780s. The body might be pierced and fitted with a blue glass liner, or solid and enriched with festoons and medallions in bright-cut engraving. The rim was strengthened with applied thread-work to support a hinged basket handle, and a short spool-shaped stem linked the bowl to a foot in a corresponding outline (Fig. 77).

Fig. 77

Just as the last decade of the century witnessed the re-establishment of a more stolid pitcher design for milk, so also it approved a low, flat-bottomed sugar bowl, sometimes the oval shape squared up so that on plan the vessel was a round-cornered rectangle. As in the jug, the sides bulged, but a balanced design was achieved with a flat-topped handle at each end, curving from rim to base. Such bowls were made *en suite* with tea-pot and cream-jug, and when designs were introduced raised on four ball feet, towards 1800, the sugar-bowl might conform, with fluting around the lower part of the body. Some early examples had narrow foot rings. With the reign of George IV, and a general return to rich versions of the rococo, came the widely-fluted melon-shaped sugar-bowl, often ornately embossed and with a pair of ornamental scroll handles. This had an applied base ring to which were soldered four ornamental cast feet.

Lumps of sugar, cracked from the loaf with steel sugar-nippers, were lifted from sugar-bowl to tea-cup with the aid of sugar-tongs. The earliest reference to this constituent of the silver tea-equipage appears in W. King's cookery book published in 1708. These early scissor-shaped sugar-tongs resembled candle douters with loop handles and scrolled stems terminating in wide, flat, shell-shaped claws for holding the sugar (Fig. 78).

Fig. 78

The scissor design long retained its popularity and, as with scissors themselves, included the stork design of the third quarter of the eighteenth century (Fig. 79). In this the tongs resembled a long-beaked stork, consisting of two long halves joined together by a rivet forming the bird's eyes and serving as a pivot. The body was shaped and chased to resemble wing feathers and the legs ended in circular loops for the fingers.

Fig. 79

It has been suggested that tongs of the scissor design were not joined by the simpler bow variety until about 1760. There is reason for believing that the latter were introduced considerably earlier, however. Although never exempt from hall-marking, a great number of sugar-tongs lack either the complete hall-mark or the date letter. Often eighteenth century examples have been repaired and the hall-marks mutilated beyond recognition. Asparagus-servers, giant, bow-spring tongs with wide blade-like terminals, are found with hall-marks as early as 1780, but extremely dainty little bow sugar-tongs are illustrated in the painting reproduced as the frontispiece to this book which is believed to date to 1725. Tongs of this less expensive design consisting of a pair of arms connected by a U-shaped arch of springy silver were made from five pieces of metal: the arch of silver plate hammered until springy; a pair of cast handles; two pressed claws, usually in shell or acorn shape. These were hard-soldered together. In the popular designs of the later eighteenth century the arms were pierced in attractive designs and the joints hidden by leaves or other motifs (Fig. 80). The outer surface of the arch might be chased with a border enclosing a flower or scroll ornament.

Fig. 80

Bow sugar-tongs continued in this style until the end of the century although few were pierced after 1790 when sugar-tongs were designed with flat tapering arms and finely-ribbed spoon ends. Arch and arms until about 1805 were slim and daintily decorated with bright-cut engraving. A set consisting of half a dozen tea-spoons and a matching pair of sugar-tongs engraved with initials was now included as a matter of course in many an unambitious dowry.

From 1805 sugar-tongs were plain with no more ornament than a threaded edge, the arms matching tea-spoons with fiddle ends, and culminating in plain spoon grips. By 1820 many were made of thicker metal and the length of the arms increased to suit the more massive sugar-bowls being made in bone china. Sugar-tongs *en suite* with the silver sugar-bowl, however, remained slenderly dainty, the final touch to that most lovely and well-loved collection of English domestic silver, the tea-equipage.

17

MILK- AND CREAM-JUGS

PEPYS and Evelyn both record their first cups of tea as being "clear and unspoiled" in the oriental fashion. Who first tempered the rough tang of early tea remains unchronicled. Collectors search in vain for a silver milk jug struck with hall-marks earlier than the first years of Queen Anne's reign, and then the vessel was generally referred to in contemporary records as a "milk-pot". This may be no more than an adaptation of the French term *pot au lait*, but the high prices originally paid for some early silver milk-pots suggests that they must have been considerably more weighty and elaborate than the tiny jugs generally accepted as part of the early tea-equipage. In the tea-drinking picture forming the frontispiece of this book, believed to date to about 1725, the tea-pot is accompanied by a tall, lidded jug, suggestive of a modern hot-water jug, and possibly containing hot milk. Nevertheless, the collector of an early tea-equipage looks for a small uncovered milk-jug.

Such a vessel, no more than three inches high, was built from four sections of cast silver: a body, which might be baluster-shaped, encircled at waist height by two rows of moulding, or pear-shaped in uninterrupted curves; an open spout; a narrow moulded foot-ring; and a plain scroll handle with a roundly projecting curve and a tiny thumb-piece on top. The handle and spout were at right angles to each other. From about 1710 the jug might be six- or eight-sided. These tiny Queen Anne milk-jugs are weighty for their size, with a capacity of about one-eighth of a pint.

The early Georgians were great tea-drinkers. Matthew

Prior in his verses *To a Young Gentleman in Love*, wrote, in about 1720: "He thanked her on his bended knee; Then drank a quart of milk and tea". In such circumstances the miniature milk-jug would be quite inadequate. By this time the body of the jug might be hand-raised from plate silver. Spout and handle were placed opposite to each other. Like the foot ring, they were still cast, but from 1725 the rim of the body, encircled with strengthening moulding, was sometimes shaped to form a small spout. By 1727 the jug might stand upon a spreading moulded foot (Plate 35), and some moulded ornament was introduced on the otherwise plain body immediately below the spout. The lower end of the scroll-shaped handle usually finished in a small reverse curve. This form of milk-jug continued until after 1760, eventually acquiring a deep, widely spreading foot-rim.

Until shortly before 1730, milk-jugs were almost invariably straight-rimmed. Then silversmiths devised a more graceful shape of jug in a form resembling an inverted helmet, and adapted from the design often used for the rose-water ewer. In this (Plate 35), the wide spout was an integral part of the body, which was raised from a single sheet of metal, so that there was no interruption in the flowing curves from rounded base to undulating rim. For the first time the design suggested the serving of cream rather than milk. The handle was still cast and soldered on, but the base presented a new problem, its deeply-rounded contour being unsuited to the usual rimmed foot and necessitating instead the introduction of three cast feet extending about one-third of the way up the body. In some instances the rounded base of the jug was lifted only slightly above the table. As a natural consequence of this design's popularity, milk-jugs in the older-established pear-shape were being mounted in the same three-footed style from about 1735, the tiny legs ending in scroll feet.

Throughout the period of their manufacture, helmet- and pear-shaped jugs were usually severely plain. Some specimens were gilded, however, and the comparatively few that were surface-decorated were given the highly ornate ornament associated with the French *rocaille*. During the 1730s the jug might be chased with scrolls and shells. Then came embossed and chased decorations including flowers and landscapes, and hunting and other sporting scenes.

Some rather florid examples, particularly those of the 1740s, reflected the Continental fashion for shaping the whole vessel to resemble a group of shells. In such a piece, each half of the vessel was cast separately, the handle included as part of the body. Three ornately-moulded feet completed the design. The undulating moulded rim might have a twisted shell on each side, and an applied scroll volute at the spout extremity. Beneath this scroll there might be an acanthus leaf or a shell, sometimes forming the basis for a mask.

Milk-jug handles became more ornamental as the mid-century was reached. (Fig. 81 shows a range of typical

Fig. 81

handles throughout the eighteenth century.) The early plain scrolls were succeeded by scrolls with reversed curves at top and bottom, these sometimes receiving added ornament in the form of beading, reeding or gadrooning. The upper curve of the handle was sometimes flattened to form a thumb-rest or was decorated with a finely chased acanthus leaf. Among the wide variety of ornate handles were the harp shape and the design twisted throughout its length, terminating at the top in a moulded and chased bust or the mask of a ram, fabulous bird, or other motif in full relief. In other specimens the lower curve ended in a volute tail, the upper section appearing to emerge from a monster's mouth before recurving to the rim of the jug.

Milk-jug legs usually terminated in scrolls, but in a small way they might be expressive of the same moods among designers that were demonstrated by early eighteenth century furniture, with the same representations of hooves, paws, and the simple Dutch pad. As with the knees of cabriole chair-legs, the junctions of legs and bowl in the milk-jug might be decorated with busts or animal masks.

More notable was the development of the particularly graceful boat-shaped jug—decidedly a vessel for cream rather than milk. This had the same general outlines as the helmet jug but with a considerably lower, wider body giving particular emphasis to the upsweeping lip and overcoming the tendency observed in the helmet-shape for the applied feet to dominate the design.

Milk-jugs shaped like cows and sometimes gilded were a vogue of the third quarter of the century. The cow milk-jug was built in sections, body, head, and so on being assembled by soldering. The tail was looped upward and over the haunches to serve as a handle. On top of the hollow body was fitted a curved hinged lid, like a saddle, either plain or bordered with engraved flowers and foliage, and having a moulded lifting-knob in the form of a large fly. The jug was filled through this opening, the milk being poured from the animal's mouth. The head and body might be tooled to represent hair, but others were left plainly smooth and the whole style of the modelling was fairly crude. The majority of specimens carry a maker's punch mark believed to be that of John Schuppe of Dean's Court, St. Martin's le Grand, who registered at Goldsmiths' Hall in 1753 and died twenty years later; but at least a dozen other silversmiths are known to have produced similar jugs.

These early Georgian milk-jug designs continued throughout the remainder of the century, but as the neo-classic mood developed in this country in the 1760s even milk-jugs had to conform to the new style of the whole tea-equipage. Thus the pear-shaped jug of earlier decades, with curved and everted spout, continued in favour but was freed of its old squat solidity, being raised on a noticeably high-moulded foot.

The silver plate used by the manufacturing silversmiths from this period was so thinly rolled that these milk-jugs tended to be flimsy. The rim might be strengthened with an encircling row of punched beads. The foot usually remained plain or was gadrooned, but on some examples its ornament matched that of the body. Many specimens lacked body-decoration, but others were embossed in swirling patterns of tapering convex flutes. Others again continued the mid-century rococo mood, being richly chased with floral sprays and irregularly shaped cartouches.

The helmet jug also underwent structural changes, a notable result of technical advances in the craft being the introduction of pierced patterns during the 1770s. These were fitted with blue glass liners held in position with clips. Such milk-jugs do not appear to have proved very successful, for few are known.

At the same time the general trend of fashion prompted the development of designs new to the English silversmith. Grecian vases, urns and ewers constituted stock motifs of the fashionable decorator, and by the 1770s cream jugs were being devised for the English tea-table in the unencumbered, flowing Grecian outlines. The body, often octagonal on plan, tapered smoothly from rim to base, a slender stem joining it to the circular or oval concave foot which might be mounted on a four-sided plinth. The handle had a similar simplicity of outline, rising sharply from the rim, recurving, and sweeping down to the base. Structurally, the jug body was generally stamped in two halves, the foot made separately as a single piece. Decoration usually consisted of body engraving, bright-cut engraving ornamenting later examples.

Until this period the silver milk-jug was seldom made *en suite* with the tea-equipage. The factories of Birmingham and Sheffield created a demand by the mass production of light-weight tea-services, consisting of tea-pot, sugar-basin and cream-jug at prices within the range of a much wider public. Such sets became more frequent after 1800, when a matching coffee-pot might be added. The terms "cream-ewer" and "cream-jug" date to the days when these factories issued milk-jugs in innumerable patterns. The ugly term "creamer"—a corruption of "cream-ewer"—is a late Victorian trade description.

A less easily overturned cream jug was introduced in about 1785, becoming generally popular some ten years later. This shapely little pitcher had the high everted spout of the classic design and the classic handle rising vertically from the rim, and then projecting horizontally for perhaps three-quarters of an inch before flowing smoothly down to the base. But instead of tapering to a stem foot, the whole body of the jug was wide and rested flatly on the table. The rim was strengthened with reeded moulding and the lower body might be ornamented with wide facets below a band of engraving, sometimes in patterns resembling the diamonds cut upon jugs of flint-glass at this period. By 1810 this style of cream-jug, its lines more graceful than formerly, was raised upon four ball feet. During the Regency the upper section of the body might be plain, the lower section reeded. An expansive, square-shouldered handle continued usual.

In conformity with the design of other table silver, the George IV cream-jug was generally an ornate little vessel, elaborately embossed, its rim strengthened with heavy applied moulding. It stood upon four short scroll feet moulded in a piece with a shallow base rim (Plate 36). By 1830 the melon-shaped body had become fashionable. The reign of William IV brought a return of the rococo designs of the previous mid-century, such as the pear-shaped jug, handsomely chased, the handle once more in a scrolling outline, and the rounded base of the body raised above the table on four short moulded feet.

18

TAZZAS, SALVERS, WAITERS, AND TRAYS

CEREMONIAL dining in the great halls of early Tudor days called for three hours of rigid etiquette. Among the responsible duties it involved for the butler was that of making the trial of the wine or other drink, usually beer, thus proving it free from poison. The gold or silver goblet was then placed at the host's right hand on a small plate of matching metal. This ceremony was known as the "try" or "assay".

By Elizabethan days it had become customary to use the elaborately wrought cover of the drinking-cup itself for testing, or trying, a little of the liquor offered to a guest. The host poured this from the cup into the cover, which thus acquired the name of "the try".

Not for more than a century did silversmiths make much use of the term "tray" in its current meaning, but an immediate link with the early ritual of assay was the stemmed form of tray then known as a salver. In name this piece was directly associated with the precautionary testing of food or drink, the article itself reaching England from the Continent upon the restoration of the Stuart régime.

Succeeding generations introduced other terms such as "tazza" and "waiter" for the trays required for various services, until to-day collectors make definite distinctions between their different styles. The development of each may thus be traced, telling in rim and foot and handle of the technical changes and fashion vagaries of these amenable pieces of silver plate. (Fig. 82 shows a range of designs in chronological order.)

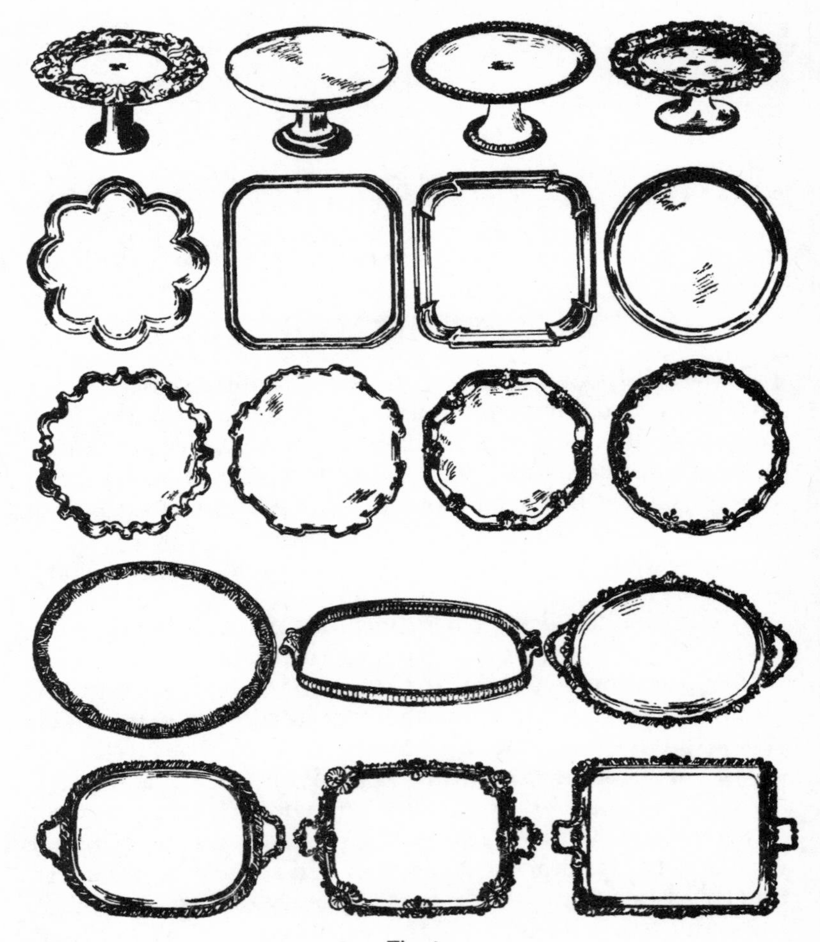

Fig. 82

First row: tazzas, Charles II to George II.
Second row: waiters or salvers, Queen Anne to early George II.
Third row: waiters or salvers, George II.
Fourth row: trays, George III.
Fifth row: trays, Regency and George IV.

Thomas Blount in 1661 defined the salver as a "new-fashioned peece of wrought silver plate, broad and flat with a foot underneath, and it is used in giving Beer, or other liquid things to save the carpet [table cloth] or cloathes from drops." This design consisted of a wide-rimmed plate on a short hollow stem and was carried by the goblet-boy. It is this footed design that collectors now refer to as a tazza.

The fashionable tazza of the Commonwealth and early Restoration periods was wide-rimmed with a plain, hand-beaten central depression occupying about half of the diameter. The wide, flat rim was embossed in high relief and chased. The stem might be in the form of a short hollow trumpet or a cylinder spreading into a domed and flanged foot of about one-third the plate diameter. Others, less expensively, possessed plain hand-raised plates, their rims decorated and strengthened with applied edgings of narrow cable moulding. A series of late Charles II tazzas were made from flat plates of silver, rectangular or octagonal, bordered with deep plain moulding applied in sections. In such a design the plate surface was a field for all-over engraving in the fashionable Chinese style.

The notable difference in manufacturing method was the fact that this rim was made separately and attached instead of being shaped or "raised" from the same piece of silver by hand-beating. As silversmiths achieved more perfect command of their material, the two styles of rim, raised and attached, went through alternate phases of popularity and obscurity, but it must be emphasised that always there would be some silversmiths leading the new trends and others keeping conservatively to earlier practices.

The surface of the late Stuart tazza might be enriched with an engraved border composed of amorini, birds, flowers, foliage, and other motifs of the period surrounding a central pictorial scene, or left severely plain unless engraved with the owner's coat of arms. Some examples were gilded. By the days of William and Mary, however, the first exuberance was over and the whole treatment more restrained. The hand-raised plate might be edged with an outer border of applied gadrooning encircling a narrow slip moulding, or with a band of gadrooning between two mouldings around the flat rim. The rim of the domed foot was gadrooned to match, and the stem might be attached to the lower surface of the plate with cut-card work.

The tazza, either square or round, continued to be made throughout the reigns of Queen Anne and George I. A new style of tray developed from about 1715, however, in which the central stem and domed foot were replaced by three or four moulded feet applied equidistantly. In shape these were usually simple scrolls, buns or spreading shells, attached to the plate by cut-card work. Such a tray stood more safely than the tazza upon the table, while yet being raised off it for easy lifting.

It was used by the servant when offering drinks, letters and other small articles, thus acquiring the name of waiter. Sets of two, four or six were usual. Early waiters, hall-marked from 1715, continued the style of hand-raised rim encircled with gadrooned strengthening moulding. At first they were square with rounded corners; by 1725 the rounded corners might be indented as on contemporary furniture panels. By then the waiter, with three or four small feet, was established as a lasting type of tray.

At the same time, for carrying drinks and prepared foods—for all the small services which the servant performed with the tray in his hand and not set down upon the table—an alternative was a simplified version of the earlier salver. This article, to which the name salver is still applied, lacked the pillar foot of the earlier tazza design. Daniel Defoe in his *English Tradesman*, 1745, refers to "six fine large silver salvers to serve sweetmeats", and in 1759 the author of *The Compleat Letter-Writer* recorded that "the company was treated with morning champaigne brought on salvers of silver."

Styles in waiters and salvers were always concurrent, and by the 1730s construction showed a return to the rim separately cast—in deeply moulded design—and applied to the flat plate of the tray. Technical improvements in the casting of silver at this period were responsible for that long series of finely finished trays of deeply indented outline with rims skilfully built from a number of curved moulded sections. The upper edge of such a rim was finished with narrow moulding, smooth or reeded, concealing the joins of the castings and enriching the whole effect. This pattern, resembling the tops of the mid-century mahogany tripod tables, is referred to as the piecrust or Chippendale border. The Chippendale title is misleading: examples are known bearing hall-marks earlier than 1730, whereas the furniture designs associated with Thomas Chippendale were not published until 1754. During the 1740s the upper surface of the piecrust-moulded rim might be elaborated by the addition of an applied edge enriched with volutes, shells, fans, and other rococo motifs. By 1750 such mounts had become heavier, with sections of curved reeding or gadrooning linking the motifs.

During the same period, 1730 to 1750, other waiters and salvers were produced with rims hand-raised in irregularly shaped outline. In early examples rim edges were strengthened with narrow moulding. But by 1740 even hand-raised rims might be enriched with wide applied borders built from innumerable small castings, the motifs including rosettes, shells, scrolls, dolphins, masks, oak and vine leaves and so on. Even when the hand-raised rim decoration was all worked on the single plate of silver, with no added castings, similar rich design was introduced by embossing and hand piercing. As might be expected, the decoration also crept back on to the face of the tray itself in the form of all-over flat chasing around a central reserve intended to display a coat of arms.

Shaped salvers and waiters continued uninterruptedly for another quarter-century, hand-raised and cast rims being equally popular. But even by the 1760s the neo-classical style was beginning to find expression in more restrained gadrooned edges applied to the rims. By about 1765 the gadrooning was accompanied by inner borders of delicate festooning—wheat-ears, ribbons, swags, and all the familiar neo-classic motifs—looped from mask heads and shells. As in the other expressions of the current fashion, the elliptical shape tended to replace the rectangle, and smooth outlines the earlier indentations. By 1775 many of these oval and round salvers and waiters were partially raised with a drop stamp by manufacturing silversmiths, and finished by minor master-silversmiths. Rims of this period seldom displayed the earlier lavishness, the usual decoration consisting of simple straight, diagonal, or shaped gadrooning, and beaded and reeded borders. Rosettes and festooning were applied to the rim, and the plate itself might carry a wide outer border of chased scroll work with foliage and flowers, sometimes on a matted ground.

The irregularly-shaped rim returned early in the nineteenth century, this time being raised from the plate by the drop hammer. Until about 1810 such rims were extended by elaborate shell and ropework ornament applied in sections. From 1810 the raised rim was made narrower, the applied mountings being heavy and elaborately florid.

As new styles of foot were evolved they merely supplemented the continued use of adaptations of earlier patterns, so that by the early nineteenth century waiters were being given any of a wide accumulation of foot designs, all spreading and heavily elaborated. The earliest waiter feet had been in conventional shapes, without surface ornament, but during the 1740s and 1750s naturalistic types were in vogue, such as the hoof, ball-and-claw, and mask-headed scroll. Volute feet in numerous patterns were used during the second half of the century (Fig. 83 shows a typical foot of the 1780s). Ball feet date from about 1790.

Fig. 83

The fashionable hostess of early Georgian days dispensed tea with the aid of a magnificent silver tea-equipage consisting of kettle and spirit-lamp, tea-pot, a pair of tea-canisters, and sugar-bowl, arranged on a circular silver tray some two feet in diameter and supported on four short feet. Rims followed the fashion set by salvers and waiters, the finer examples being ornamented with wide pierced and chased borders of masks, vine-leaves, and scrolls. Such trays were described in contemporary inventories as "solid silver tea tables". In the reign of George II such a tray might be associated with a polished wooden stand of similar diameter, containing sockets for the tray feet. The inventory of the Earl of Warrington's tea-room taken in 1752 refers to "2 Mahogany stands to set the silver Tea and Coffee Tables on." Another contemporary term was tea-board. Smollett in 1748 wrote of "the coming of a servant with a

Tankards. (*Left*) plain, with flat lid, London 1691. (*Right*) with convex gadrooned foot-ring and similar ornament encircling the rise of the cover; London 1698.

(*Left*) tankard cup by Petley Ley, London 1718. (*Right*) tankard with lion thumb-piece and double-domed lid; the body encircled by strengthening rib. By Ambrose Stevenson, London 1710.

Nefs. (*Top left*) three masted, pedestal, *c.* 1530; (*top right*) h wrought and fully rigged, with wh early eighteenth century; (*bottom* wheeled galleon, early nineteenth tury; (*bottom right*) single-masted, spout, mid-seventeenth centur

tea-board", and there is a reference in the Newgate Calendar for 1780 to "the silver tea-board".

The early tea-board was circular, but the emphasis upon elliptical shapes during the neo-classical Adam period prompted the introduction of this more convenient outline, which better accommodated the silver tea-urn. The rim was soldered to the flat oval plate, its edges strengthened with simple beading enclosing the usual range of applied husks, ribbons, and swags. The whole design was comparatively austere, the outline uninterrupted and the decoration in low relief. Other applied rims were pierced with vertical pales to which the current motifs were attached.

A series of trays appearing from about 1775 onwards had vertical rims, pierced and decorated with applied motifs and strengthened with simple thread edges. The notable feature of their design was the inclusion of hand-holds in the rim. Henry Clay of Birmingham bought such factory-made silver rims from Matthew Boulton and fitted them to bases made of his newly-patented heat-resisting paper-ware panels, glossily coated with japan. These rims bear hall-marks around 1780. During the 1790s the fashionable oval tea-tray had a moulded rim with thread edges, loop handles prolonging the line at the narrowest parts of the curve.

Early in the nineteenth century even the oval tray lost its regularity of outline, however. The thread edge was wider than formerly and enriched with occasional vine leaf and grape, shell, acanthus leaf, and other motifs applied to a deeply concave moulding. The loop handles were elaborated with matching motifs. By 1810 the rim had become wider, with coarse gadrooning added to the thread edge enclosing rococo embellishments. The handles, now D-shaped, became weighty with scroll-work and other ornaments. The outline tended to become an indented rectangle, and by the time of George IV the fashionable tea-tray was plainly rectangular with a wide rim of florid ornaments. Mounts were now cast in a bewildering array of patterns. The mask border was especially popular with large masks in the handle openings and small ones on the long sides. The entire surface of the silver tray might now be chased in complicated patterns.

The construction of silver trays presented comparatively few problems to the silversmith. The hand-raised rim, made in a piece with the flat plate, was shaped by placing a piece of silver upon a wooden sinking block—usually a two-foot section of a tree trunk into which a depression of the required size had been carved—and beating it with a large, flat-faced hammer. Starting from the centre the hammer worked outward towards the edge. By then the silver had become hard and springy and required annealing. These processes were repeated several times before the piece was ready for planishing.

The flat base for a salver or waiter with an indented outline was cut on a lathe fitted with a template governing the required shape. Any number of blanks precisely similar in shape and size could be produced speedily in this way with comparatively little effort. The flat plate was then planished—that is, the surface was smoothed and burnished by metal hammers with highly-polished faces. This left the surface true and bright and covered with innumerable brilliant facets. Such a plate had an applied rim, built from prepared castings and soldered on while held in position by iron cramps. The solder used was a hard silver-copper alloy fusable at a lower temperature than the silver plate itself, and much of the tray's final beauty depended upon the careful execution of this process.

19

TANKARDS

FROM at least as early as medieval days the tankard has been in everyday use in England, its design resembling that still favoured to-day, with arching handle, and bun-shaped lid equipped with hinge and thumb-piece. Fourteenth century records refer to such vessels as made of wooden staves, iron bound. Two-gallon examples were commonly used in breweries, but the name appears to have been applied first to still larger wooden vessels, lidded and of a similar tapering bucket shape, that were customary for conveying water from the street conduits. By the early sixteenth century "Leather Pottes and Tanckerts" were receiving occasional mention in inventories, but the earliest application of the word tankard so far noted in reference to silver is found in the will, dated 1576, of Sir George Heron of Harbottle who bequeathed three silver tankards to his daughter.

A "silver Cup and Cover worth from nine to ten pounds" specified in the will of Doctor Walter Wright, Archdeacon of Oxford, who died in 1561, is still in existence, the earliest known example of a silver tankard. It is struck with the London hall-mark for 1556, and a stag's head caboched. Handle and cover are engraved with the date 1556, the cover also bearing the initials W.W.

This one-pint tankard is silver-gilt with a short globular body merging into a contracted neck from which rises a slightly everted lip-band. Floral scroll work delicately engraved on this band is repeated on the flat bun cover and S-shaped handle. The whole design suggests adaptation from medieval pottery drinking-vessels. The vertical thumb-piece, cast in the form of two satyrs' masks, rises from a butt hinge, one leaf of which is soldered to the top of the handle. This handle is semi-circular in section and tapers towards the tail which curves upward almost at table level. The base-ring is moulded in convex form and encircled with stamped lozenge decoration. A similar tankard made by Robert Dance and struck with the London hall-mark for 1567 belongs to the Armourers' and Brasiers' Company. Its thumb-piece is designed as a classic bust.

Silver tankards of the Elizabethan period were usually cylindrical of body, tapering from base to lip in the style of Scandinavian horn drinking-vessels. Horn-bodied English tankards might be mounted with silver, the metal parts consisting of cover and handle, and bands around the body—neck band and foot ring and a central circle of rib-moulding. Similar mounts were applied to tankards of marble. An example from the Swathling collection, attributed to William Dyxson and struck with the London hall-mark for 1561, has a low domed cover embossed with satyrs' masks, bunches of fruit, and strapwork, and a neck-band engraved with scrolls of oak leaves and acorns, motifs repeated on the cast thumb-piece. The flat D-handle, engraved with foliated scrolls, extends to a coarsely gad-rooned rib-moulding encircling the body a little below half-height.

Elizabethan silversmiths made the majority of their lavishly ornamented and gilded tankards in this form. They vary from six to seven inches in height and hold one pint. Such a tankard was assembled from a number of units: lid and finial, strengthening moulding for the body rim, upper body section, lower body, made in a piece with the base, upper rib moulding, convex band, foot-ring, handle, hinge, and the vertical thumb-piece by which the lid was raised and held upright for drinking and which was known to silversmiths as the "purchase" or "lever". In some instances the body might be raised from a single sheet of silver plate; more frequently two body-sections were soldered together, the encircling hair-line of the join being concealed and strengthened beneath a decorative convex band.

Decoration on the bodies of tankards until the second decade of the seventeenth century included flat-chased strapwork enclosing birds, flowers, and fruit. The lip-band was strengthened with moulded reeding or beading. The hinged cover, domed and mounted with a cast finial resting on a raised collet, was embossed with designs matched on the convex foot-rim, the upper edge of which might be concealed beneath narrow moulding decorated with punch-applied geometrical patterns. One leaf of a butt hinge was soldered to the upper curve of the handle, and from the loose leaf, attached to the rim of the lid, rose a vertical rectangular thumb-piece. This thumb-piece was cast in solid silver with decoration in the form of masks and female figures.

The S-shape or swan-neck handle, hollow and semi-circular in section, was built from the hammered plate. It rose above the rim at an angle of about thirty degrees before curving downward, and was usually sliced obliquely across the upper end, this area being soldered direct to the body. The short tail of the handle might terminate in a graceful curve, or a heel-shaped slice, or might be modelled in the form of a monster's head. Then as now, inside the curve of each handle was a small hole, known to silversmiths as a blow-hole and made to permit the escape of hot air expanded by the heat of the soldering iron. This prevented the danger of a burst handle during manufacture.

Collectors refer to tankards in the style described above as Elizabethan, to distinguish them from the less frequent contemporary type in which the body was slightly concave, and from the purely cylindrical form. A typical example of the Elizabethan tankard, from the Swathling Collection, bears the London hall-mark for 1591. The domed cover and spreading convex foot are embossed and chased with bunches of fruit and strapwork panels. The S-shaped handle is engraved with arabesques and its lower curve attached to an applied convex body rib engraved with trellis work. The thumb-piece is moulded and chased with the figure of a satyr.

Purely cylindrical tankards appeared in silver by 1580, slightly taller and somewhat narrower than the tapering form. These are the dansk or Danish type so frequently specified in inventories of the period. The body might be chased on a matted ground and cable-moulding or reeding connected the body to the spreading foot-ring, which might be punched with egg and tongue or other simple decoration or embossed with ovate leaves and pellets matching similar motifs on the highly-domed cover topped with a vase-shaped finial. Thumb-piece and handle were similar to those on other tankards, the lower curve of the handle being soldered direct to the body.

The tankard design with a tapering silhouette was slightly accentuated during the early years of the seventeenth century and the embossed ornament elaborated on the domed cover and concave foot-ring. By 1610 the body might be slightly convex, and a few years later there was a fashionable reversion to the early Elizabethan globular body, now copiously ornamented with conventional designs including sea monsters chased on a matt ground. This model, with a low, single-step cover, continued until the mid-century, but less lavishly decorated.

Tankards made early in the reign of Charles I tended to be tall and flagon-like. The puritan influence and scarcity of silver brought simpler forms, and towards the end of the period ornament became less flamboyant. The high-domed styles of lid were succeeeded by a low, undecorated dome with a plain baluster finial. By 1640 the general fashion was for a flat lid, known to collectors as the single step cover, with a low, vertical-sided central lift, usually lacking a finial. Thumb-pieces were less ornate than on earlier work, the volute scroll being the most favoured, and the vessel's base-ring was reduced to a narrow moulding.

The bulbous tankard was also made, the central lift of the cover being decorated with chasing and matting to match that on the body.

Cromwellian silversmiths made severely plain tankards (Plate 41), slightly shorter in proportion to width, and decorated only with their owners' coats of arms in highly ornamental cartouches. Here again the lid was of the single step design, hinged to the top of the handle, and had a projecting rim three-eighths of an inch to half an inch wide which might be decorated with a single encircling line and extended to a point in front. The fashionable thumb-piece was of the twin-dome variety. Occasionally cover and body were ornamented with deep line chasing. The cylindrical body, with a slight upward taper, was supported by a widely-spreading foot-ring, plain and deeply concave. This skirt was hand-raised and joined to the base of the body with convex moulding which matched similar strengthening moulding encircling the rim. Deep skirts were discontinued after the Restoration. The lower curve of the S-handle, semi-circular in section, was soldered to the body immediately above the skirt and might terminate in an applied shield. Such handles continued throughout the eighteenth century.

It now became the practice for London hall-marks to be struck to the right of the handle immediately below the rim and upon the upper surface of the cover near to the thumb-piece. The maker's mark was also struck upon the handle.

The interior of a tankard from about 1650 was sometimes fitted with a vertical row of projecting pegs or studs, soldered in line with the handle. These were described by Doctor Pegge, the seventeenth century antiquary, as having:

> in the inside a row of eight pins one above the other from top to bottom, so there will be half a gill of ale between each pin. The first person who drank was to empty the tankard to the first peg or pin; the second was to empty to the next pin, etc. by which the pins were so many measures to the compotators, making them all drink alike the same quantity; and as the position of the pins was such as to contain a large draught of liquor, the company would be very liable by this method to get drunk, especially when, if they drank short of the pin or beyond it, they were obliged to drink again.

The restoration of the monarchy in 1660 caused the London silversmiths to produce more ornamental tankards. A style—now rare—from 1660 until about 1675 had a body raised from a single sheet of plate and supported by three pomegranate feet joined to the body by sprays of moulded foliage. Similar applied ornaments in the form of interlaced strapwork extended from the hinge down the flat surface of the handle. A double pomegranate thumb-piece was used; volute scrolls and double acorns are noted occasionally. The bun lid was raised in the form of a shallow cushion, rounded at the edge, to which strengthening moulding was added to match the rim moulding. The lower re-curve of the S-handle was soldered to the central leaf in the moulded foliage spray extending from one of the feet.

The most frequent style of silver tankard from 1660 until the close of the seventeenth century, however, had the customary slightly-tapering body mounted on a narrow, moulded foot ring that raised the base but slightly above the table, to replace the flaring skirt. The upper curves of this ring matched the strengthening moulding that encircled the rim. The broad rim of the single-stepped cover was engraved with three or more concentric circles and its front edge might be ornamentally waved. From about 1675 a double-step cover was usual and the rim, extended and serrated, might be ornamented with lightly-chased circles. The S-shaped handle, which curved down to the base-rim only slightly above table level, usually terminated in a shield. Thumb-pieces were now moulded in a variety of scroll designs including cork-screws, ram's horns, volute scrolls, and beaded work. The twin dome continued, together with upright thumb-pieces, in innumerable designs such as a pattern of interlacing straps. A weighty and finely modelled couchant lion with front paws extending towards the centre of the cover is sometimes found. The strength of the hinge was considerably increased by making it consist of five narrow lugs, two of which were in a piece with the thumb-piece. Three-lug hinges had formerly been the rule, a single lug extending from the thumb-piece.

From about 1675 embossed decoration might encircle the base of the body, usually in the form of a border of acanthus leaves (Plate 41) and other foliage. Alternatively, the principal decoration at this period might consist of body engraving with the chinoiserie scenes then immensely popular. From this time the foot-rings tended to become deeper: bead moulding might be added to conceal the body

Wine-taster with plain sides, highly-domed base, and moulded foot-ring. Maker's mark: S. R., London 1675.

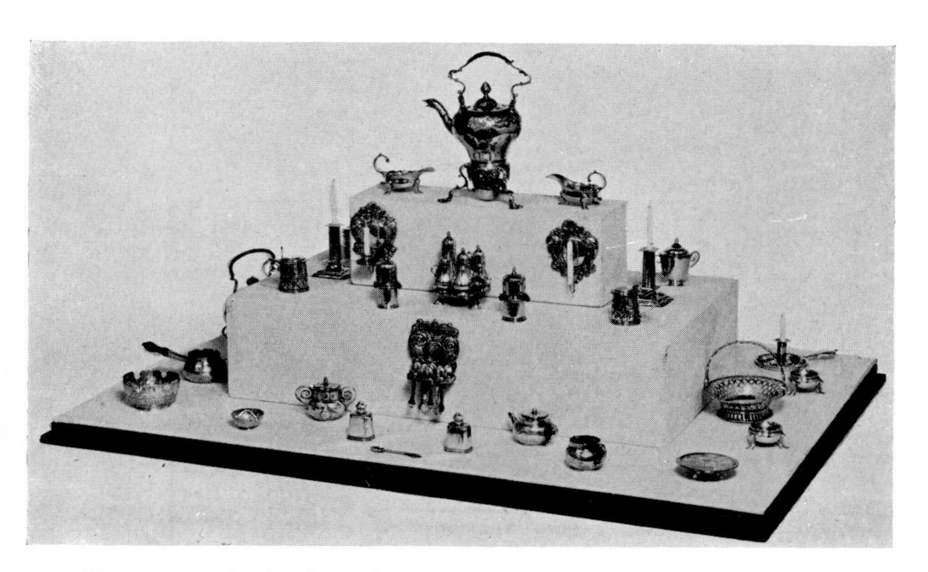

Silver toys: the kettle with stand and lamp by Edward Medleycott, London 1748; two tankards, spoon-rack with six trifid spoons, and pair of candlesticks, by George Middleton, London, from 1684 to 1691; cruet-stand and two casters by Augustin Courtauld, 1720. The base on which the pieces are arranged, twenty-six inches long, gives the scale.

Pierced épergne with eight baskets supported by branches curving out from scrolling legs; by Thomas Powell, London 1774.

(*Left*) two views of decanter-coaster with silver base and gallery hand-pierced in openwork design; by Peter Devese, London 1774. (*Right*) argyle with baluster-shaped body, the spout and handle at right angles; by W. Gundry, London 1776.

junction, and bold projecting moulding strengthened the lip. The single- or double-step cover might be embossed to match the body.

From about 1680 the silver plate for a tankard might be hammered more thinly than was usual. To prevent distortion when lifting a full tankard the handle of such an example was provided with a lug extending from the top attachment to about three-quarters down the body at the seam. Shallow moulding might strengthen the flat rim of the cover.

The cover strengthened by being raised in treble or quadruple steps was fashionable by 1690, and the lower body of the tankard was encircled with a plain or reeded strengthening rib. This might stand upon a boldly convex foot-ring with decoration matching that around the rise of the cover. Cut-card scalloping might encircle the base above the gadrooned foot-ring.

Other tankards of the period were ornamented around the base of the body with vertical concave flutes or spiral gadroons (Fig. 84), usually with a band of stamped motifs immediately above. The rise of the lid was then decorated with similar fluting and the flat top with a boss of matching decoration. A third type was produced by elaborating a plain tankard with simple cut-card work extending from the handle junctions and from the thumb-piece across the cover. A row of beads descending in diminishing size from the hinge decorated the flat surface of the handle.

Fig. 84

The whole body of a tankard, from about 1640 until the end of the century, was almost invariably raised from a single sheet of metal. It then became more usual to roll the body cylinder from a sheet of silver, join the vertical seam with solder, and insert a disc base.

The Queen Anne tankard had a low-domed cover but otherwise differed little from those of the 1690s. At this time the fashionable tankard was given a double-scroll handle extending from the rim to the widest diameter of the body. A further strengthener came into use in the form of a circular or shaped seal soldered between the body and the lower handle junction. Extended serrations on cover rims were discontinued from about 1715.

Early in the Queen Anne period appeared a new form of tankard with swelling or tulip-shaped body, tapering from base to rim and with a rounded base, supported by a concave moulded foot-ring with a diameter approximating that of the widest part of the body. The cover had a moulded edge surrounding a low, single dome. Back-curving volute thumb-pieces were general on such tankards which continued until about 1760, double domed lids being usual from about 1715. Such tankards almost always have the double-scroll handle. Until early in the reign of George II the body of such a tankard was almost invariably raised in a single piece. Then about 1740 it became customary to hand-raise the hemispherical lower part of the body and make the upper section separately, soldering the two together and concealing the join by a narrow rib of moulding.

During the second half of the eighteenth century and later, the silver tankard had a bulbous body of ogee outline supported by a foot-rim more boldly modelled than formerly and with an openwork thumb-piece. The body might have a narrow applied rib a little below the centre. Some late eighteenth century tankards had barrel-shaped bodies with wide encircling ribs representing the metal hoops.

Silver tankards of the early nineteenth century reproduced the earlier Georgian patterns with the addition of a type having a plain cylindrical body, slightly tapering, encircled with two bands of chased lines. The lid was usually of the low domed variety.

In some instances a tankard made between about 1675 and 1800 has a loose hinge-pin, attached to a chain extending from a loop on the lower curve of the handle. Removal of the lid enabled the tankard to be used as a mug (Plate 42). Such a vessel was known as a tankard cup.

In 1729 Dean Swift wrote in his *Directions to Servants*, "When anyone calls for ale, fill the largest tankard cup top full".

20

NEFS AND GALLEONS

SILVER galleons with all sails set and pennons flying have an irresistible appeal to our sea-faring race. For more than eight hundred years they have found a prominent place on the English dining-table, first as a symbol of power, then for the service of wine. Some of these ship models, known as nefs, were made with scrupulous accuracy. So great was their historic value in representing the lines and rigging of contemporary war vessels and merchantmen that the former Duke of Edinburgh, an Admiral of the Fleet, collected more than fifty examples which were always on view when he entertained naval officers. The collection later came into the possession of King George V. The finest and most valuable ship in this royal fleet dated to about 1550 and was made in Nuremburg.

Ships have been recorded in Court circles without intermission from the middle of the twelfth century, when Henry II brought from his French province of Anjou two richly-wrought golden nefs set with diamonds and pearls. Piers Gaveston at the court of Edward II in 1320 boasted a silver-gilt nef on four wheels, the earliest recorded example of an undercarriage. Edward III, ten years later, was proud of a magnificent pedestal nef, its hull enriched with gilt dragons and provided with lock and key.

In early days the possession of a nef was confined by a rigid code of etiquette to royalty, the higher clergy, and nobles from the rank of earl, and such vessels were set before them with princely ceremony as they took their places at the higher table. The nef was carried into the great hall by the butler, preceded by an usher carrying a flambeau and wand of office, and followed by the cup-bearer and other officials who ministered at the high table. Members of the household would pause to make obeisance when passing the nef. In lesser households the ceremonial salt might take the place of the nef.

The deck, supporting masts, rigging, poop, and so on, acted as a removable lid over the hollow hull in which lay the owner's personal salt cellar, his boxes of special condiments and oriental spices, a pair of knives and a spoon, a napkin, and the all-important essay with which the butler tested his master's wine to prove it free from poison. Before the lord's wife stood a less splendid nef for her spice-boxes and napkin.

These very early pieces of plate, masterpieces of the silversmith's art, were nearly all made at Nuremburg and Augsburg, where for nearly 250 years silversmiths specialized in their production. The Nuremburg examples, built to scale except for exaggeration in their ornamental forecastles, were perfectly rigged with sails squarish and fluted. They bear a great family resemblance to each other. None has been found bearing an English hall-mark, although it is known that examples made by Elizabethan goldsmiths were sent to Spain.

Early pedestal nefs were three-masted: the main mast with crow's-nest and pennon, two sails, shrouds and stays; the mizzen mast with crow's-nest and one sail; the fore mast with crow's-nest and a triangular sail. The standing and running rigging in silver wire of gossamer thinness were as accurately wrought as the guns, pulley blocks and other details. The swelling sails gave an effect of life and movement. The billowing foresail might be emblazoned in gold and enamels with the arms of its owner; more frequently the arms were engraved. The two-tiered poop and prow had gabled roofs and contained guns with pike-men. The extremely long forecastles of galleons at this period were intended to assist archers and spear-throwers in attacking smaller enemy from aloft; but by the 1580s the high stern was already being modified in English men-of-war to produce more battle-worthy vessels.

On the deck of the fashionable nef stood carefully-modelled miniature figures of the owner himself, his wife, family and immediate entourage, all sculptured in silver, sometimes gilded and enamelled, together with several musketeers. There was a navigator at the helm and figures of sailors were distributed about deck and rigging. The hull might be embossed and chased to represent the sides of an actual ship with guns projecting from port holes, but more frequently they were finely embossed with designs composed of sea horses and mermaids. At the stern was a working rudder.

This silver ship was supported by a finely moulded stem modelled as a mermaid, dolphin, triton, or fabulous sea-monster with water flowing from its mouth and rising from a domed foot, oval, rounded or lobed. This foot might be in the form of a mound embossed with sea monsters disporting among waves. Alternatively it might represent a stream flowing between reed-beds and rocky banks, or might be treated pictorially, showing members of a ship's crew at their various occupations. Sometimes the stem resembled those of contemporary ceremonial salts. In the British Museum is a nef of this type ascribed to the period *c.*1530 (Plate 43). Such vessels continued to be made as late as about 1700.

In the late sixteenth century appeared smaller, less magnificent nefs in the form of silver-gilt single or double-masted vessels with roofless poops and prows. These were mounted on moulded stems rising from substantial feet enriched with embossing in conventional designs. They were popular with men of lesser rank until about 1640; a powerful noble might place one such nef before each guest.

The sixteenth century saw also a series of silver-gilt nefs in which the elaborate style of finely-designed tiered fore-castle was continued, but the hull was flat-bottomed, enabling the piece to stand directly upon the table. During the seventeenth century an ivory nef enriched with diamond-set gold and other precious stones was a fashionable decoration in a lady's apartments.

Graceful hulls, hand-raised, embossed, and silver-gilt, without decks or rigging, were known as navettes. A pair of these might contain the napkins for those who sat at the high table. Others, suspended on chains, were used as perfuming pans. Records of their use in England for this purpose appear from about 1400; a frequent accompaniment was a silver spoon.

The ceremonial nef belongs to the days when the household dined together in the great hall. When the custom fell from favour with the introduction of private dining-rooms for members of the family and their guests, the use of the ceremonial nef declined, ending during the Cromwellian period. With the restoration of the monarchy the silver ship returned to the dining-table but was mounted on four wheels and employed in the service of wine.

Early examples of the service nef were less lavishly worked by the silversmiths than the earlier pedestal nefs. The wheeled nef continued in use for about two centuries, the hull of this silver vessel being designed to contain wine which was dispensed through the wide-open mouth of the dolphin or sea monster forming the figure-head. In the mid-seventeenth century parcel-gilt example illustrated (Plate 43), the hull is embossed with sea monsters, and the spout terminates in a monster's head. Wheels, sail, banner, and the eleven armed figures on deck are ungilded. This was the period before flint-glass serving-bottles and decanters appeared on the fashionable dinner-table.

By 1730 wheeled nefs had become more richly ornate than at any earlier period, embossing on the hull being in more intricate patterns and in higher relief, and the moulding more cleanly finished. The hull of a service nef during the eighteenth century was often in the form of a nautical monster with figure-head spout, scaled underbody, and embossed side-panels showing scenes in which Neptune figured prominently. The hull of such an early wine nef was raised by beating with the hammer from solid silver plate: consequently the surface is covered with a mass of tiny facets reflecting and breaking up the light. Some of the finest wheeled nefs made during the eighteenth century were models of actual ships, accurate to the finest detail and intended for decorative purposes only. Seldom were two made alike. In some of these the miniature figures on deck and rigging were carved from mother-of-pearl.

Early in the reign of George III Dutch silversmiths became aware that there existed in England an unsatisfied market for ornate table-ware among those wishing to display evidence of newly acquired wealth. By introducing factory methods into the production of silver plate they were able to undersell the finer products of English silversmiths. The Dutch service nef with wheeled undercarriage came within this category, the hull and most of the fittings being cast and then finished by hand. The hulls on such nefs were built from sections and were entirely smooth with a hard lustrous surface. By 1785 the Birmingham silversmiths were competing with less-costly ships in which the hull was shaped in two halves, stem to stern, by the use of a drop-hammer, each half finished with hand embossed decoration and the two invisibly soldered together.

Such silver ships were used as dining-table centre-pieces and contained sweetmeats, the deck and rigging being removed at the appropriate moment during the meal. Early in the nineteenth century the hull did duty as a wine-cooler or bottle-coaster. The majority of wheeled nefs struck with English hall-marks belong to this period. Pattern books in the Victoria and Albert Museum issued early in the nineteenth century by manufacturing silversmiths illustrate the basic parts of nefs which might be bought by master silversmiths to complete their own designs. Cast and drop-hammered hulls, rolled decks and sails, cast wheels, masts and other fittings, and coils of silver wire for the rigging enabled the enterprising silversmith to produce many outstanding models.

From such standard parts was made the "Naval Tureen in the form of a Man of War's Boat" advertised from early 1806 to about 1815 by J. Sanderson, a silversmith of St. James's Street, London. No doubt inspired by Nelson's victory at Trafalgar, such a ship model could be used on three occasions during dinner: as a soup-tureen, as a trifle-dish, and again as a wine-cooler or bottle-coaster. Three hulls, each handsomely embossed with a profusion of maritime emblems, accompanied one set of wheels and a single deck with all its appropriate rigging and sails. At the bow stood a figure of Britannia, her shield engraved with the British flag; at the stern, Neptune held a silver rudder to steer the vessel to victory, the success of which was expressed by the enemy's flagstaff being reversed and broken, the flag trailing beneath his feet.

21

WINE-TASTERS

THE profession of wine-tasting is as ancient as the cultivation of the vineyard, its symbol to-day the shallow, hand-beaten silver bowl known as a wine-taster. For six centuries men in this highly hereditary work have carried wine-tasters on their rounds among the vineyards of Europe, until these small bowls have become treasured as family heirlooms. To-day, wine-tasters are prized by the silver-collector whose particular delight is the formation of a chronological display restricted to a single type of small object. In size, shape, even in decoration, wine-tasters are designed specifically for use, and therefore have altered little enough down the centuries, but each passing era has been faithfully reflected in their smaller details.

The wine-taster consists of no more than a shallow circular bowl with a vertical loop handle at the side, and is small enough to slip into a coat pocket. It is of hand-beaten silver, often worked up from a single piece of metal without a joint. In size it may measure from two to three-and-a-half inches in diameter, and from half an inch to an inch-and-a-half in depth, containing from one-sixth to one-third of a pint. Some bowls are entirely plain and finished with equally plain ring handles, but most are enriched on base and lower sides with repoussé designs in low relief. The object of the decoration is two-fold: it tends to strengthen the sides of the bowl and it facilitates the work of the taster.

The patterns used are simple enough, consisting either of bosses or gadrooning or a combination of the two, or else of conventionalized grape and flower designs. Bosses in varying sizes form the simplest patterns, presenting a series of raised rounded knobs inside the bowl. Similarly, in gadrooned decoration the feather-shaped fluting around the sides presents the vintner with a series of raised hummocks inside the bowl to reveal the quality of the liquor. When the gadrooning only partly covers the bowl surface the remaining area may be decorated with large and small bosses. Floral design consists of little more than the obvious development of such bosses and gadrooning into leaf and petal shapes. The typical bowl has rounded sides in contrast to the base, which rises somewhat towards the centre in a manner accentuated by the repoussé decoration, so that the vintner is offered the maximum reflecting surface as he tilts and swirls the liquor, noting its colour, clarity, bouquet and all that contributes to his final verdict.

English vintners visiting the vineyards and wine-cellars of France, Portugal, and Spain for the purpose of replenishing stocks, are known to have carried such silver wine-tasters at least as early as 1477. In a statute of that year prohibiting the export of silver plate, exception was made in favour of "*un taster ou shewer par vine*", carried abroad by the vintner. With the aid of the little vessel he could observe and taste each liquor; generations of experience made him know at once what vineyard bore the grapes and the year the wine was sealed in its bottles.

For the vintner's purpose silver has always proved the ideal metal, but a few wine-tasters of gold and of pewter have been recorded, and even some of earthenware. The inventory of the Jewel House of the Tower taken in 1649, after the death of Charles I, records "A gold taster, 4 oz; a golden taster with a lion in the middle, 5 oz; one taster of gold, enamelled with a phoenix, 2 oz". These were valued at £36. 16. 8d. It is posssible, however, that these were cups of assay used by an official known as the taster on ceremonial occasions in royal and noble households. Gutch, writing in 1530, mentions "two litill Cuppes of assaye, silver gilt", and in the Earl of Northampton's inventory of 1614 is entered "a cuppe of Essaye". Cups of assay and wine-tasters were apparently similar in shape, the former being of gold, elaborately decorated, and sometimes covered, the latter almost invariably of silver. Nevertheless examples in gold and pewter have been recorded bearing marks which dated them to a period when assaying of food and drink had long gone out of fashion.

The earliest reference to a wine-taster's bowl is dated Michaelmas 1383 in the inventory of a Norwich taverner's goods where it is entered as a "taster argenter". The term again appears twenty years later in the will of a Bristol vintner. The testator of a will dated 1420 bequeathed "a tastour of silver with myn owne marke y made in ye bottom", and specific definition of the bowl's purpose is to be found as early as 1530 when Palsgrave described "a tastour" as "a lytell cuppe to tast wyne *tasse à gouster le vin.*" At this period tavern keepers were their own tasters and *Pilgrim Peregrinations*, written in 1526, records that it had long been the custom of the vintners at the great wine vaults of The Vintry, in the City of London, to "give freely to their customers or buyers a taste of their wine", silver cups being used. By the sixteenth century wine-tasting had become a specialized profession, but wills and inventories of the Elizabethan period indicate the wide-spread use of the little bowls from about 1570, only one specimen being found in the typical household plate list. Contemporary records are unhelpful regarding their appearance at this period. A typical will, dated 1545, specifies merely "a tastour of silver waing by estimacion vj ounces". The earliest known specimen now in existence carries the Norwich hall-mark for 1573-4. This piece, formerly in the collection of Sir John Noble, is distinctly larger than later specimens and possesses a low, spreading foot. The fluted body is punched with beaded ornament and the domed base is chased with honeycomb patterning. Nearly a century later, footed wine-tasters might still be made, an example being known with the hall-mark for 1646-7 and the inscription "Michael Robinson his taster Novem. 2nd 1670".

By the seventeenth century, however, the simpler design appears to have become more prevalent. Sir C. J. Jackson has recorded two examples of the James I period, one bearing the London hall-mark 1612-13, the other the maker's mark of Sem. Casson and the York hall-mark 1620-21. Of thinly beaten silver, these are merely shallow bowls clumsily embossed with punch-work patterns, and each is fitted with a pair of wire loop handles.

While the stiff conventional decoration on wine-taster bowls had a utilitarian purpose, handles were seldom given more than the simplest enrichment. The earliest known type of handle was made in a piece with the bowl, a narrow strip of silver being curled back and down to form a vertical ring (Fig. 85 shows this type of handle). The outer surface of such a handle might be chased with thin, shallow grooves. A late example of this style on a plain-bowled wine-taster bears the London hall-mark 1650-51.

Fig. 85

A wine-taster struck with the London hall-mark 1638-9, and formerly in the collection of Sir Thornley Stoker, has been illustrated by Jackson. The sides of the bowl are straight and spreading, encircled near the base with large ovals which appear as convex bosses on the interior. Further decoration takes the form of lines of closely placed punch dots on and around the ovals and circling the bowl. A Cromwellian example in the British Museum displaying the London hall-mark 1655-6 has a single vertical loop of silver wire. This would require less metal than a cast handle, and the metal of the bowl, too, is thinner than that used earlier. The centre of the base is embossed with a thistle and two leaves enriched with four roses and conventional foliage, separated by pairs of vertical lines.

As might be expected, the late seventeenth century, with its exuberant delight both in silver and in rich living, found uses in plenty for the silver wine-taster. This was a period when every taverner was said to drink from silver vessels, and considerable quantities of the favoured metal were hammered up into wine-tasters. Some followed the earlier style with similar punched decoration; others were of a plain design which proved popular with the Portuguese and was exported considerably (Plate 44). This pattern had no handle, and its plain, straight sides sloped outwards from a highly-domed base—sometimes as high at the centre as the bowl's rim. Such a bowl could be hammered into shape without any need for jointing.

More decorative, and more typical of the period's silver, was the design found, for instance, in a specimen with the London hall-mark for 1676-77, ornamented on its curved sides with alternative concave and convex flutes following the spiral lines then so widely favoured, and topped by a scalloped rim. There is a narrow base moulding, and the two handles have beaded edges, although still following the scroll design in round wire found earlier in the century.

E. Chamberlayne, writing in 1679, referred to "Mr. Henry Potkins, wine-taster", but many of the little vessels at this period were put to a more decorative purpose than the vintner's daily work. From about 1675 until early in the Georgian era it was fashionable for private owners of particularly fine wines to invite guests into their cellars and provide silver wine-tasters from which they might sip the rare liquor as it was taken direct from the barrels.

Yet another demand for the wine-taster had to be met at the auction sales of ales, wines and spirits, tasting being regarded as an essential preliminary to bidding. These wine-tasters were known as dram-cups during the seventeenth and eighteenth centuries, a term used by the *London Gazette* from 1674. The same journal referred to them in 1722 as "silver dram-dishes". Simmonds' *Dictionary of Trade*, 1858, defines dram-cups as wine-tasters.

There was considerable similarity between wine-tasters of the seventeenth and eighteenth centuries, and conspicuous differences in design between contemporary examples. The vessel might have either one or two vertical handles. The loop was sometimes topped by a flat thumb-plate (Fig. 86), or the thumb-plate alone might serve as handle. An example made by Thomas Peele, London, hall-marked 1703-4, with a pair of delicate scroll handles attached to its gadrooned bowl, may be contrasted with one hall-marked 1707-8 by another London maker, Christopher Atkinson, with a single thumb-plate as

Fig. 86

its only handle. Both styles had been made throughout the previous half-century. Eighteenth century handles sometimes appeared in more ambitious designs. From about 1715 one style was shaped to resemble a snake encircling the upper rim of the bowl and coiled once in the middle to form a ring grip. Some of the snakes were scaled, some were smooth, some modelled in the round, others cut in the flat.

A considerable number of eighteenth century wine-tasters carried embossed designs of grapes and vines, but others still showed the customary gadrooning low on the body. An undecorated bowl might be given individual interest by the addition of the owner's name engraved on the outside, or his coat of arms upon the base. This, too, was a style sometimes found on late seventeenth century specimens. An example in the Victoria and Albert Museum has its convex base engraved with the arms and crest of Richmond and the inscription "Andrew Richmond December the 3rd 1689". This is struck with the London hall-mark of the same year. The *London Gazette* of 1681 records "one Silver Brandy Taster, marked with R.H.A.". Yet another decoration consisted of a silver coin of the period inserted in the base.

Many wine-tasters for commercial purposes were ordered direct from the silversmith and not displayed for sale. These were not hall-marked although the maker's mark is usually present. Owing to the resemblance of form during the seventeenth and eighteenth centuries it is difficult to date such examples. A name or date engraved on the outside of the bowl near the rim may give a clue, but these inscriptions are no longer conclusive as they are sometimes of recent origin.

A dated coin inserted into the base of a wine-taster is of slight assistance for it may be considerably older than the cup, or it may have been inserted during the twentieth century to give the wine-taster an appearance of antiquity. Some cast silver wine-tasters decorated with fleur-de-lis and set with gilt coins of Louis XIII and Louis XIV are sometimes noted in shops. These were tourist souvenirs of Edwardian days and are to be avoided by the collector.

Large bowls of similar form with elaborate thumb-plates almost hiding the rings beneath are sometimes called wine-tasters, but more probably were made as porringers or as bleeding-bowls used by surgeons. If even half-filled such a vessel would prove an unsatisfactory and expensive means of tasting wines.

22

SILVER TOYS

SILVER toys, miniature replicas of furniture, table ware, and household accessories in general, have delighted children in noble families for at least five hundred years. The daughter of Henry II of France in 1576 ordered a set of silver toys including "buffet pots, bowls, plates and other articles such as they make in Paris" to be sent to the children of the Duchess of Bavaria. In the wealthy households of Holland and Germany such playthings were then usual. The plate inventory of the mother of Henry IV of France records "a doll's set of silver table plenishments sette with diamonds".

Not until after the accession of Charles II were children of wealthy English parents given silver toys with which to furnish their dolls'-houses—at a time when silver furniture was very much in vogue. The earliest of these came from Holland, but hall-marks prove their manufacture in London for at least a century from 1665; few examples have been found struck with provincial hall-marks.

Modern children would find little to admire in a pair of snuffers and a tray just large enough to snuff the tiny candles in their miniature silver wall-sconces, but in their day such toys were highly appreciated. A wide range of dolls'-house furnishings might be accumulated, and when the owner grew up the precious metal from which they were made caused them to be treasured and handed down from one generation to another.

The majority of the numerous silversmiths who made such toys were forced to keep costs low and therefore had to scamp accuracy of detail. At the same time an essential part of the charm of such tiny pieces was their close adherence to the fashions and customs of the moment. The range of objects included furniture, grates, fenders, firedogs, tea-kettles, tea-pots, tea-canisters, salvers, table baskets, milk-jugs, salt-cellars, candlesticks, tankards, monteiths, and many others. The evolution of industrial art during the period of their production may be observed to perfection in a chronological series of such pieces.

Some authorities consider miniature toys to have been travellers' models carefully made to display to prospective purchasers of full-size objects. There is no contemporary evidence to support this, however, and dimensioned perspective drawings would have been far more helpful. In the case of furniture and porcelain, special miniatures in wood and porcelain are known to have been prepared for travellers, but these were accurate to the smallest detail.

George Middleton (1660-1745), a descendant of Sir Hugh Middleton (1560-1631) the eminent goldsmith and jeweller to James I and Charles I, appears to have been the first London silversmith to set himself up as a specialist in silver toys. From his workshops in St. Martin's Lane came some of the most delicately-wrought toys produced before 1710. Middleton's toys were invariably struck with full London hall-marks and his personal emblem or initials. An early piece, one of the rarest types, is a rack of spoons with trifid ends, struck with the London hall-mark for 1684, the year that his personal mark—G.M. with three crescents, two above and one below—was entered at Goldsmiths' Hall. By 1691 this mark appears to have been altered to G.M. with two mullets above and one below. Possibly this may have been struck during a brief partnership with John Campbell at the St. Martin's Lane workshops. Their names are associated in the 1692 list of goldsmiths. In that year Campbell moved to the sign of the Three Crowns, near Hungerford Market, now the site of Charing Cross railway station. George Middleton joined him there in 1708.

The meticulous finish of Middleton's remaining silver toys shows his workmanship to be considerably finer than that of his many rivals in this medium. At the Three Crowns, however, Middleton and Campbell tended to neglect silversmithing in favour of the more lucrative business of banking. A profit of £1,000 was made in 1712, the year in which Campbell died. Middleton continued alone until 1727, when he took his late partner's son George into the business. Under Middleton's control the silversmithing prospered equally with the banking. In 1716 he was commanded by the Prince of Wales to design and execute a considerable amount of silver plate. Nevertheless, the banking activities became so extensive that by 1739 it was necessary to move to larger premises at No. 59, Strand. Ten years after the death of Middleton in 1745, Campbell took James Coutts into partnership. George Middleton, one-time worker of silver toys for dolls'-houses, may therefore be considered as the founder of Coutts, bankers to every English monarch from George III onwards.

Some excellent silver toys were made from 1699 to 1720 by Isaac Malyn, a plate-worker of Gutter Lane. So close is the resemblance between Malyn's toys and those of Middleton that the suggestion has been made that he served his apprenticeship at the St. Martin's Lane workshops.

Augustin Courtauld, of Church Street, St. Martin's Lane, who registered at Goldsmiths' Hall in 1708, became the most prolific maker of silver toys, all of exquisite workmanship. Examples struck with hall-marks dating from 1715 to 1740 include various articles of furniture, bed-warmers, candlesticks, tankards, tea-pots, and other table-ware including complete tea-equipages. Specimens not fully hall-marked date from 1739 when his toys were struck only with his personal mark—AC in small Gothic letters—repeated in two or three places. Courtauld's toys are remarkable for their careful detail, and he became pre-eminent as a specialist in this work.

A wide range of silver toys was made by Jonah Clifton, Foster Lane, London, whose existing hall-marks on such pieces date from 1708 to 1715. John Sotro, at the Acorn in St. Paul's Church Yard, styled himself "Goldsmith and Toyman", adding on his trade card of 1750 that he made "all sorts of children's toys". It must be emphasised that the term "Toyman" noted so frequently upon eighteenth century trade cards refers to makers of trinkets and fancy goods and has no association with the production of silver toys.

Hall-marks were struck in full on silver toys until 1739, and the personal emblems of London silversmiths have been found that may be dated as early as 1665. These include RD crowned, 1665; FC, 1669; G crowned, 1670; EM in monogram 1677; CK under a mitre, 1686; WP with mullet below, 1689; IC over a star, 1691. Later were Edward Jones, 1696; Matthew Madden, 1697; John Cole, 1697; Nat Green, 1698; Matthew Pickering, 1703; Joseph Smith, 1707; Jacob Margas, 1708; Jonah Clifton, 1708; James Godwin, 1710; George Smart, 1715; James Morson, 1720; Edward Conen, 1724; John le Sage, 1725, and many others. The smallness of silver toys and the thinness of their metal enabled silversmiths to claim exemption from hall-marking such pieces from 1739. Few were made so heavy as to necessitate a journey to the assay office. Makers continued, however, to strike their own personal marks upon their work. Fully hall-marked pieces have been noted with initials of Edward Medleycott, 1748, and Samuel Herbert and Company, 1750-1758. Craftsmanship in these flimsy light-weight productions did not equal that of the earlier pieces.

Collectors should take every precaution when acquiring miniature toys lacking a full series of hall-marks. Modern reproductions struck with makers' marks are far more numerous than originals.

23

ARGYLES : COASTERS AND WINE-WAGONS : DECANTER-LABELS : DISH-CROSSES : ÉPERGNES : MARROW-SPOONS: MONTEITHS : MUSTARD-POTS : NUTMEG-BOXES : PUNCH-BOWLS : PUNCH-LADLES : SKEWERS

SUCH, in outline, is the story of antique English domestic silver. From it the collector may acquire the fundamental information which can help him to recapture something of the spirit of the age that created his specimens, and of the homes into which they were introduced, not for ornament but for use.

Even while restricting the subjects in this book to useful articles, woven into the very fabric of gracious living, it has not proved possible, within the space available, to cover all collectable objects. As an appendix, a few are listed briefly in the succeeding pages, so that the reader who has studied the foregoing chapters may fit them into the complex and wholly fascinating story.

Argyles. The custom for the host himself to carve the joint at table was a mid-Georgian innovation. This made serving a lengthy ritual, during which the gravy grew cold in its silver boats. A few years before his death in 1776, John, 4th Duke of Argyle, introduced silver gravy containers to overcome this trouble. These, called argyles, continued in general use for about half a century.

The earliest resembled a small tea-pot with a capacity of two gills. Inside, rising vertically from the base, was a lidded socket into which fitted a cylinder of hot iron. This was capable of keeping the gravy hot for a considerable time. Opposite the scroll-shaped ebony handle rose a

Monteith bowl on circular foot, the body showing repoussé work and chased fluting, with mask and drop-ring handles; by Edward Richards, Exeter 1708.

Hemispherical punch-bowl with plain moulded rim. The collet foot has moulded ornament. By George Squire, London 1722.

Interior of a mid-eighteenth century silversmith's workshop: (a) pouring the molten silver into an ingot mould; (e) beating the ingot into plate; (b) raising a hollow vessel; (c) raising a circular tray.

A contemporary sketch showing the hand-operated machine by which specialist silversmiths could give regularly indented outlines to their salvers and waiters.

swan-neck spout, long and thin. This was set very low on the body where the gravy would be richest. The body shape followed that of contemporary tea-pots, the hinged lid being highly domed and decorated with a plain knopped finial. The body might be cylindrical or oval.

The argyle with a vase-shaped body, rising from a low spool stem on a round or square foot, might be plain-surfaced or the upper part might be encircled with classic ornament and festoons, and the lower part fluted.

Towards 1780 a more capacious argyle was evolved having a baluster-shaped body expanding into a spreading base. The interior was divided horizontally, only the upper portion containing gravy, while the lower one was filled with hot water through a projecting socket covered by a hinged lid. A narrow moulded foot-ring lifted the body above the table. Handle and spout in this type of argyle were placed at right-angles to each other.

During the 1780s appeared a more convenient modification of this design, in which the vertical-sided round or oval body was fitted with a double lining or outer jacket to contain hot water. The water was inserted through a socket placed at the rim near the handle and sealed with a screwed stopper. In later work a hinged cover was substituted for a screwed cap. The spout passed through the hot water jacket into the body of the argyle containing the gravy.

Coasters and Wine-Wagons. Known to Georgians variously as bottle-trays, wine-slides, and decanter-stands, coasters were fashionable adjuncts to flint-glass decanters from about 1760. Like the decanters themselves they were sold singly and in matching sets of two, four or six. At first both base and rim of the coaster were of silver, the upper surface of the base carrying an engraved coat of arms. By 1775, however, it was usual for the base to be made of boxwood cut with shallow concentric rings, and lined underneath with green baize to slide easily over the polished table when the cloth had been removed for dessert. Coasters became more widespread with the fashion for decanters deeply cut in diamond patterns that glittered in the candlelight.

The early coaster, with a silver base, was encircled with

a low vertical gallery, hand-pierced in open designs or built from fret-cut motifs. Its everted rim was bordered with narrow gadrooned moulding. This was soldered to the shallow, circular tray. Galleries became deeper and completely vertical during the 1770s, the join between gallery and wooden base being hidden beneath moulded reeding, more substantial than the gadrooned rim.

Coasters with press-pierced galleries were made from the late 1770s, a favourite pattern having vertical pales with applied swags and medallions, one medallion remaining smoothly solid for the reception of an engraved crest or monogram. Undulating and escalloped rims belong to the 1780s. Such an outline might be associated with a double row of horizontal piercing immediately below, while the remainder of the gallery was but sparsely pierced with geometric motifs.

In the 1790s the upper part of the gallery might be embossed or fluted, the lower part pierced. Early in the nineteenth century the positions of fluting and embossing were reversed. Succeeding galleries were decorated with all-over embossing. In the Regency the upper rim might be widely everted and ornamented with scroll and shell motifs, and from 1820 even this wide rim formed a field for heavy, florid decoration cast in relief. Ornament became lighter after about 1830.

The wine-wagon, now sometimes termed a double coaster, was made from the 1790s. This was in fact a small silver wagon, with four axle-mounted wheels supporting the flat platform that carried a pair of coasters, and drawn by a decorative handle or shaft. After about 1805 a less expensive design mounted each coaster separately on a pair of wheels, their upper rims being linked with two rigid couplings. A silver "jolly boat", with

Fig. 87

recesses for two decanters, was an alternative (Fig. 87).

Early in the nineteenth century a coaster might be accompanied by matching tumbler-holders. The little vertical gallery was decoratively pierced, and the base was of silver, mounted on three cast feet in a scrolling design.

Decanter-Labels. In what year silversmiths first turned their tools to such dainty articles is unknown, but hall-marks show that Sandilands Drinkwater and John Harvey, both of Gutter Lane, London, were producing what were then known as "bottle-tickets" during the late 1720s. These early tickets were in three shapes: the small, narrow oblong, the crescent (Fig. 88), and the shield. These were plain with merely the names of wines engraved upon them. Ornament appeared by 1740: at first the crescent was feather-edged and the shield engraved with tiny vine leaves on a matt ground. By 1770 the crescent horns were elongated and rounded more sharply to support an ornamental shield engraved with the owner's crest or cipher.

Fig. 88

These were superseded by rectangular designs with elaborate crestings, and other tickets were decorated with pierced motifs. Typical was the urn-shaped label supporting a laurel knot and with a laurel swag beneath (Fig. 89). More ornamental labels are associated not with murky bottles but with lavishly cut decanters from the end of the century. The simple hoop, fitting over the bottle neck and designed to replace ticket and chain, dates from about 1780.

Fig. 89

Until 1790 decanter-labels appear to have been wrought entirely by hand and lack the profusion of fine detail that marked the arrival of the die-made label. After about 1810 the die-stamping method was in its turn largely replaced by casting. The resultant labels were bigger and might be

Fig. 90

heavily ornamented with caryatides, masks, fauns, infant bacchanals, together with considerable elaborations of foliage encircling the inscribed names. These were joined in about 1820 by the boar's-head design; then came graceful trellis-work labels bearing masses of vine leaves and grapes (Fig. 90).

The decanter-label in the form of a vine- or acanthus-leaf upon which the name of the wine was given the clarity of perforation dates from 1824. Ten years later came the label formed of a single letter, cut in silhouette, the initial of the liquor concerned (Fig. 91). Single letters, less than an inch high, had been engraved as early as 1815, but in small square labels. The new letters, one to two inches high, were cast separately and either chased or engraved. From 1784 decanter-labels of any weight were subject to assay and hall-marking (see Chapter 2).

Fig. 91

Dish-Crosses. This purely utilitarian innovation of the 1750s was intended, like the argyle, to keep food hot upon table or sideboard (Fig. 92). The heat was supplied by a spirit-lamp, and the pivoted arms radiating from it were designed to hold any entrée dish within the current range of standard sizes. The lamp formed the central point in the X design, each pair of arms containing a central ring for which the lamp served as an axis. Each arm of the horizontal X terminated in a shapely little vertical scroll leg usually on a shell-shaped foot so that the lamp was raised slightly above the level of the table. To support the dish each arm was also fitted with an ornamental bracket rising an inch or more above it to keep the dish clear of the flame. In order to accommodate dishes in a wide range of sizes, the X of the arms could be narrowed or widened, and, in

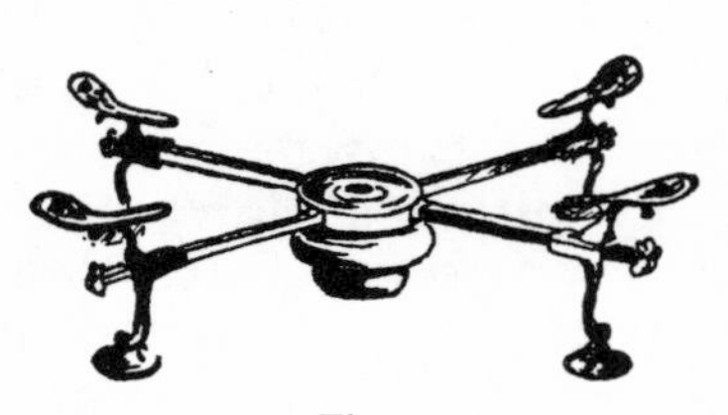
Fig. 92

addition, the leg and bracket unit on each arm was attached by a pierced silver socket so that it could be moved to any position along the arm. A small rosette on the end kept it from sliding too far. An attractive dish-cross design had a separate spirit-lamp, its flame warming the dish through a disc pierced in a scroll design that then formed the axis of the rings on which the arms revolved.

Épergnes. The épergne was a centre ornament for the dinner table usually in a branched form with each branch supporting a silver basket or dish (Plate 45). It was an early Georgian innovation, designed to hold a variety of sweetmeats or relishes, thus economising space on the heavily-laden table. The word itself is taken from the French *épargne*, meaning "economy". The various bowls, dishes and baskets contained relishes and condiments during the early courses of the meal. For dessert these were replaced with others containing a variety of sweetmeats. Ornamental finials were supplied to take the place of any branches not in use.

Mrs. Delany, in a letter written during 1752, sketches a dining-table lay-out which included two épergnes, dessert on that occasion consisting of "8 [silver] baskets of fruit". Pennant, in his *Bill of Fare*, 1761, refers to "a grande Epergnes filled with fine pickles", and on the occasion of Doctor Warton's retirement from the headmastership of Winchester in 1804 his pupils presented him with an épergne in the hope that it would remind him of "pickles" left behind.

The 1725 inventory of plate at the Jewel Office in Whitehall refers to a gilt "Aparn containing one Table Basket and Cover, one foote, four Salt Boxes, 4 small Salts, 4 Branches, 6 Casters, 4 Sauceboats". Their imposing dimensions and lavish ornament made such pieces costly. By the 1730s an épergne might consist of a heavy moulded stem on four feet, such as lion masks, supporting detachable branches fitted with small flat waiters or hanging baskets. Some had branches fitted with candle-sockets.

Other épergnes were made in the Chinese style, the central design consisting of pillars and bell-hung pagoda roofs of finely pierced work, with a pineapple finial, and fantastically scrolling branches to hold the little pierced baskets and finely chased plates.

From about 1760 épergnes of the lighter pierced styles were made in a greater diversity of form than any other article of silver plate. One fashionable type was crowned with a well-designed; expansive dish, its supporting column rising from a large circular or boat-shaped base mounted on four cast legs. Branches curving out from the scrolling legs supported the small dishes. Flint-glass dishes might be used from about 1770.

An épergne made after 1780 might be designed to revolve. In this case the base of the stem fitted into a pivot placed between tripod legs. Reeded drawn-wire branches might support five to eight dishes and an equal number of baskets might hang from hooks. Epergnes of the nineteenth century were loaded with heavy cut-glass dishes and baskets. The Regency épergne might stand on a matching plateau. For example, a central female figure might be posed on a circular platform to carry the main dish of cut glass, while, around her, four florid branches would rise from her feet holding matching dishes.

Marrow-Spoons. "For daintiness of diet they excell in the Mary bones of Beefe" wrote Morton in 1638, referring to one of England's table delicacies. In 1768 Tucker supped amply from "a pair of marrow-bones in a dish". A spoon for extracting marrow from cooked bones was a refinement of the late seventeenth century, popular throughout the following century. The earliest reference to such a spoon is found in the *London Gazette*, 1693, where it is referred to as a marrow spoon, a term used by the early nineteenth century silversmiths. Examples are known with Queen Anne hall-marks: these have wider scoops than later specimens.

The marrow-spoon has a narrow, elongated bowl, while the upper part of the handle consists of an even narrower scoop—no more than a deep, concave flute (Fig. 93). Either end could thus be used for extracting the marrow, depending on the size of the bones. There is little variation of style. Most of the flutes are parallel, but an occasional example narrows

Fig. 93

towards the rounded waist separating bowl from flute. Rarely, the stem is rectangular in section. The hall-mark is struck on the back of the stem. Marrow-scoops were also introduced as the handles of ordinary spoons.

Monteiths. Thought by many people to be punch bowls, these are in fact coolers for drinking-glasses (Plate 46). The Oxford diarist Anthony à Wood noted them in 1683:

"This year in the summer time came up a vessel or bason notched at the brims to let drinking vessels hang there by the foot, so that the body or drinking place might hang in the water to cool them. such a bason was called a 'Monteigh' from a fantastical Scot called Monsieur Monteigh who at that time or a little before wore the bottome of his cloake or coate so notched."

Fig. 94

Fig. 95

In 1773 Doctor Johnson defined a monteith as a "vessel in which glasses are washed". Monteiths were made in considerable numbers for almost a century and a half. In most instances the bowl is fitted with a loose rim moulded in the characteristic outlines. (Figs. 94 and 95 show examples of the late seventeenth and late eighteenth centuries.)

Mustard-Pots. Wynkyn de Worde in his *Boke of Curtasy*, 1460, recommended mustard sauce as a suitable accompaniment to brawn, beef, chine, bacon, and mutton. Mustard-and-sugar formed the gourmet's sauce for pheasant. A contemporary cookery book described mustard as "sharp biting sauce made of small seed bruised and mixed with vinegar". Even then, mustard-making was a recognised branch of the Grocers' Guild. In 1483 Caxton referred to "Nicholas the Mustard Maker", and Thomas More in 1583 noted "a musterde maker in Cambridge". In late Elizabethan times the mustard seeds were finely ground in a mill, mixed with flour and made into paste.

The earliest reference to a mustard-pot dates to 1380 when Wycliffe recorded that he kept a pot of ready-mixed mustard covered with parchment to exclude the air. The Halliwell Inventory of 1610 refers to "two silvar musterd pottes". Although references are frequent from 1670, the shape of these pots is a matter of conjecture, for no known examples are earlier than the reign of George I. Those hall-marked mostly date to later than 1765.

Fig. 96

Fig. 97

The typical design was plainly cylindrical (Fig. 96), oval, or octagonal (Fig. 97). The flat hinged lid was cut with a spoon aperture, and lifted by a vertical thumb-piece, often shell-shaped. The scroll handle was of flat silver ribbon. Rim and base were strengthened with narrow moulding. Fitted with a glass liner, this was the basic form for more than half a century during which the pot was known as a "mustard-tankard". The body was shaped from a flat strip of plate invisibly joined under the handle. Soon the manufacturing silversmiths were supplying hinged thumb-pieces which joined handle and lid. These were cast in attractive forms, the hinge itself being die-made. Spoons were standardised in the form of miniature ladles.

Fig. 98

Pierced mustard-pots with blue liners, catalogued as mustard-tankards, were made throughout the period. At first these were hand-pierced in attractive widely-spaced designs; the lids might be highly domed and the thumb-pieces pierced (Fig. 98). Mechanized piercing followed, consisting of the usual geometrical patterns in which vertical pales were a dominant feature until about 1800. Sometimes the pot was raised on three feet and had a low-domed lid. Vase-shaped mustard-pots,

Fig. 99

pierced and chased, were made from about 1780 until the end of the century. Some double-handled mustard-pots were made at this period and they might be fitted into cruets. Elliptical pots in neo-classic style might have flat or slightly-dished lids (Figs. 99 and 100.)

Fig. 100

The beginning of the nineteenth century saw a new delight in matching sets. Just as tea-pot matched with sugar and cream-containers, so salt and mustard-pot continued the same theme. The fluted pot was particularly popular with D-handles flattened at the top. This might have a footring or be raised on four feet. The oval mustard-pot was fashionable, the lower part decorated with vertical convex reeding, the upper part chased, and the domed cover embossed to match the reeding (Fig. 101).

Fig. 101

A series of mustard-pots was made between 1800 and 1835 combining silver and heavy cut glass. From a gilt dish, edged with gadrooning, rose four wire stems supporting a ring to fit the glass container. Some of this type had glass lids and spoons. From 1825 a rectangular mustard pot was made with the handle fixed to one of the long sides.

Nutmeg-Boxes. These were carried by both men and women. Travellers used grated nutmeg to flavour foods encountered in taverns, but its chief purpose was to add zest to punch or wine. The box was small enough to fit conveniently in the pocket, being designed to contain a single nutmeg. Some were egg-shaped, unscrewing to open into two sections, one holding the nutmeg and the other a rasp for grating it over the food or drink (Fig. 102). The majority, however,

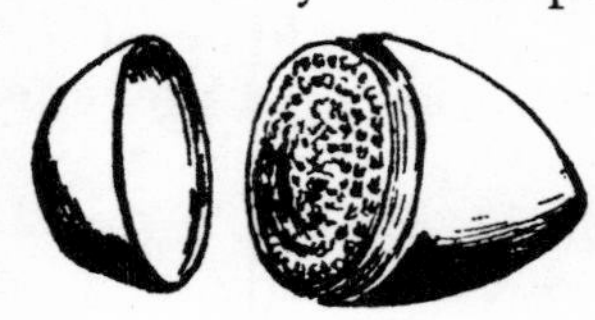
Fig. 102

more nearly resembled contemporary snuff-boxes, being rectangular, but only about two inches long and one inch wide. Both top and bottom of the box were hinged. Immediately beneath the upper lid was a perforated grid for grating the spice. The box space below the grid contained the nutmeg, inserted by opening the hinged base. Most nutmeg boxes found to-day bear Birmingham hall-marks for the period 1780 to 1820, but London examples are known with date letters of the 1760s.

Punch Bowls. Punch bowls of silver are to be noted in most important plate inventories from 1670 until 1820. They were costly to make, the wide-mouthed bowl, measuring 11 to 21 inches in diameter, being raised from a flat disc of silver plate. Three twelve-inch examples struck with the London hall-mark for 1666 are in the plate collection of the Skinners' Company.

Early punch bowls followed the pattern of oriental porcelain bowls, being very shallow and very open. Heavy plate was used and the body was more or less a section of a sphere with a plain smooth surface inside and out, not even the rim having any moulding to strengthen it, and was supported on a low, plainly moulded collet foot-ring. In the larger sizes, holding as much as four gallons, the design included two ring handles on the body. The only decoration until about 1715 was an engraved coat of arms or a crest enclosed in a wide border composed of scrolls, foliage, flowers and other fashionable motifs. By the end of the seventeenth century it was customary for the rim to be strengthened with a narrow, light rim-moulding, or with a gadrooned or rope pattern edge.

Queen Anne punch bowls introduced a slight elaboration in form: the bowl opening was less expansive than before, and below the rim might be embossed a wide border of vine leaves and fruit, or other ornament. The moulding of the foot-ring was slightly deeper than during the previous century.

Although a considerable number of Georgian punch bowls appear to have been plain-surfaced others were embossed with fluting, which might be wide or narrow, flat-faced or rounded. Melon-shaped flutes are also found, narrow at the base, rising with a right-hand twist and broadening at the rim. Alternate flutes might be heavily embossed with leaf and floral designs. From about 1730 a short spool-shaped stem was placed between foot-ring and bowl, thus lifting the bowl higher from the table. This stem became deeper as the century advanced and the lower ring might be gadrooned. The bowl rim from about 1730 was slightly incurved, still strengthened by decorative moulding and sometimes with a wide encircling border of chasing or engraving immediately below. This design, with embossed and chased ornament from the rococo to the classic style and back again to the nineteenth century, is characteristic of Georgian punch bowls until 1830. From about 1790 hot punch became fashionable and the punch bowl might be accompanied by a plain circular tray upon which it stood when in use.

Punch-Ladles. Punch drinking so captured the imagination and palate of Georgian society that puncheries were established in their homes, forerunners of the modern cocktail bar. The Georgian punchery was magnificent with its display of colourful punch-bowls, glittering flint-glass goblets, silver spice-dredgers and sugar-bowls, bottles hung with enamelled labels naming the numerous liquors from which modish punches were built, and long-handled punch-ladles.

To-day, punch-ladles in their changing styles, demonstrating the eye for design and pride in good craftsmanship of the English silversmith, offer interesting possibilities to the small collector.

The silver punch-bowl of the seventeenth century was accompanied by a sturdy ladle of solid silver, its stem engraved with the crest of its owner. The oval bowl and the long flat stem terminating in a finial matching those of contemporary spoons were hammered from a single strip of plate.

Silver scarcity late in the century, however, prompted silversmiths to design a less weighty ladle. The new style remained wholly of silver. Its deep cylindrical bowl, with a small angular lip expanded from its rim, was made in two parts, the flat base being soldered into a cylinder shaped from flat plate. Its smooth surface might be engraved with a coat of arms. A hollow handle, tapering and collared, and often terminating in a moulded baluster finial, was fitted to the body, often with a screw joint, at right angles to the lip. The silver handle, tapering to a socket, continued until the mid-century, elaborately chased and worked in repoussé.

Handles of turned ivory, ebony, whalebone or wood were fitted to the silver bowls of punch ladles, the ivory sometimes etched with a crest, from about 1710. Such a handle might be square or round in section near its junction with the bowl and twisted above to provide a better grip. Often it terminated in a flat silver finial engraved with the owner's crest.

The bowl, hand-raised from a single disc of silver, became hemispherical with a slightly everted rim. Decoration might include embossing and chasing with leaf motifs above narrow fluting rising from a smooth base engraved with a coat of arms. The handle was attached to the bowl by means of a tapering socket of silver terminating in an expanded circular or triangular flange curved to fit closely against the side of the bowl to which it was soldered. The surface of the flange might be left plain or be engraved to form part of the bowl decoration.

Punch-ladles of the eighteenth century were largely of London manufacture and the law required them to be submitted to the Assay Office and be fully hall-marked. Examples made before 1720 were of high-standard silver and struck with Britannia, lion's head erased, date letter and maker's mark (See Chapter 2). From 1784 a duty mark was also struck. Hall-marks are usually found within the bowl.

There was little variation in the bowls of punch ladles until two or three years after the return to the sterling standard for silver plate in 1720. Until 1730 the bowl was hemispherical, with or without an everted rim, and seldom lipped. Many were plain-surfaced, others embossed with flower and scroll designs, sometimes incorporating a cartouche for an engraved coat of arms. Two-piece cylindrical bowls with sides embossed and chased were also made during this period.

Punch-ladles from about 1730 were made in matching pairs and, in consequence of technical improvements in the production of silver plate, shapes became more ambitious. These included the goose-egg design, the more pointed end of the ovoid facilitating the pouring of punch into goblets less wide of rim than formerly. This ladle-bowl might be plain-surfaced or elaborately embossed. The handle was attached at right angles to its greatest length.

More frequent were circular and oval ladle-bowls beaten from discs of silver, the rim often expanded into a single pouring-lip at right angles to the handle. These might be smooth-surfaced or embossed and chased. Others, lobed and fluted, were double-lipped. By 1740 appeared the plain circular bowl with sides incurving towards an everted, spoutless rim. Such bowls later in the century might be enriched with embossing and chasing and by 1780 with thin vertical flutes. Bowls formed in the shape of nautilus shells were made around the mid-eighteenth century. At this period the handle socket might be fitted with a moulded V-shaped extension, each arm terminating in a flat flange by which it was soldered to the bowl.

Silversmiths soon found that crown pieces formed convenient discs of sterling silver from which to raise punch-ladle bowls, 2½ to 3 inches in diameter. By the middle of the century there was a vogue for hammering the coin in such a way that the marginal design or inscription encircled the bowl rim. A silver coin of an earlier period might be set in the base of a bowl, Queen Anne shillings being frequent in ladles bearing hall-marks of George III. Silver-gilt bowls might be inset with golden guineas or silver-gilt shillings or sixpences.

Bowl shapes of the George II period continued fashionable throughout the Georgian era. The handle attachment was altered, however. A strip of solid silver, usually square in section and slightly tapering, extended from the hollow socket, its end being shaped in the bowl outline to which it was soldered. Bone handles made their appearance during the 1770s.

The late Georgian bowl was generally hemispherical, with a wide lip extending upward above the rim, a favourite embossed and chased decoration consisting of vine leaves, grapes, and flowers.

Skewers. For centuries slender wooden skewers or skivers were used to fasten meat to the revolving spit and to preserve the shape of the joint while it was cooked. These giant pointed pins were cut from dogwood until about 1680, when lignum vitae began to be used. Handles were usually elaborately carved to facilitate removal from the meat. Swift, in his *Advice to Servants*, bade them "send up the meat well stuck with skewers to make it look round and plump."

A mid-eighteenth century refinement was the introduction of silver skewers for this purpose. Wooden skewers held the meat while it was on the spit or in the oven, but, before serving, these were replaced by silver ones. Silver skewers were made in sets of varying lengths. The smaller, six or seven inches long, were used for game and small joints of meat. Skewers eleven to fifteen inches long were for larger joints. Such a skewer, thrust through the meat on the dish, offered a projecting top which served as a handle to aid the carver.

The earliest silver skewers, dating from the 1730s, were cut from flat plate. In shape, this design resembled a bodkin, with the faces of the blade flat and terminating in an elongated oval eye, soldered on, which aided its withdrawal from the meat. Such skewers are very scarce. By 1760 the oval loop terminal soldered to the blade might be moulded with a shell decoration. After about 1765 the blade was chamfered or bevelled, and this and the circular loop were cast as a single entity. From 1770 the skewer might be die struck with a decorative end, such as the shell and thread design, matching forks and spoons of the period (Fig. 103).

A skewer was usually hall-marked close to the loop where the metal was about one-quarter of an inch thick. A crest might be engraved on the reverse. Counterfeiters have been known to transpose these marks to other articles of silver or to convert the silver into some more valuable article.

Fig. 103

INDEX

(*Figures in bold type indicate sketches*; *pl. indicates plate number*).